The North American Third Edition

# Cambridge Latin Course
## Unit 2

*Revision Editor*
**Ed Phinney**
Chair, Department of Classics, & Director, University Foreign Language Resource Center
University of Massachusetts at Amherst, U.S.A.

*Consulting Editor*
**Patricia E. Bell**
Teacher of Latin & Assistant Head of Languages
Centennial Collegiate and Vocational Institute, Guelph, Ontario, Canada

*Editorial Assistant*
**Barbara Romaine**
Amherst, Massachusetts, U.S.A.

CAMBRIDGE
UNIVERSITY PRESS

Published by the Press Syndicate of the University of Cambridge
40 West 20th Street, New York, NY 10011-4211, USA

The Cambridge Latin Course was funded and developed by the
University of Cambridge School Classics Project and SCDC Publications,
London, and is published with the sponsorship of the School Curriculum
Development Committee in London and the North American Cambridge
Classics Project.

This edition first published 1988
Reprinted 1990, 1991, 1992, 1993, 1994, 1995, 1997, 1998

Printed in the United States of America

*Library of Congress cataloguing in publication data*

Cambridge Latin Course. Unit 2.
Includes index.
1. Latin language – Grammar –

ISBN 0-521-34381-X hardback

Stories from Unit 2 which have been recorded on the cassette tapes accompanying
the course are so indicated by the cassette symbol .

Drawings by Peter Kesteven, Joy Mellor and Leslie Jones
Maps and diagrams by Reg Piggott and Jeff Edwards

## Acknowledgments

Thanks are due to the following for permission to reproduce photographs: Front cover, pp 56,
65 below, 73 Fishbourne Roman Palace/Sussex Archaeological Trust; pp iv,
25 Landesmuseum, Trier; p 5 by courtesy of the Yorkshire museum; p 6 Faculty of
Archaeology and Anthropology, Cambridge; p 9 courtesy of the Verulamium Museum,
St Albans; p 12 Stephen Hall, Cambridge; pp 13, 32, 36, 37, 101 above, 108, 133, 149, 153 the
Trustees of the British Museum; p 16 Cambridge University Collection, copyright reserved;
p 20 Corinium Museum, Cirencester; p 24 Royal Scottish Museum, Edinburgh; pp 41,
60 Colchester and Essex Museum; pp 53, 81, 128-29, 136 above, 144 © Scala, Firenze;
p 57 Aerofilms; p 65 above Robert Woodward, creator (with John Woodward) of this copy of
the Woodchester mosaic; p 67 Bernisches Historisches Museum; p 68 Ronald Sheridan's
Photo-Library; p 76 Sharon Pallent; p 80 Alinari; p 85 above Museum of London; pp 85
below, 92, 101 below Al Ahram, Cairo; p 93 above Barbara Romaine; p 93 below BBC Hulton
Picture Library; p 100 The Corning Museum of Glass; p 105 Musées Départementaux de la
Seine-Maritime, Rouen; p 113 Corning Glass Center; p 116 Ed Phinney; pp 125, 135, 141,
142 The Mansell Collection; p 136 below The Metropolitan Museum of Art, Gift of Edward S.
Harkness, 1917; p 156 from Cosmos.

**Cover picture: the central roundel of a second century floor mosaic in the palace
at Fishbourne showing a winged cupid riding a dolphin.**

# Contents

**Wall painting from eastern Gaul showing workers outside a villa.**

# Stage 13

# in Britanniā

hic vir est Gāius Salvius
Līberālis.
Salvius in vīllā
magnificā habitat.
vīlla est in Britanniā.
Salvius multōs servōs
habet.

uxor est Rūfilla.
Rūfilla multās ancillās
habet.
ancillae in vīllā
labōrant.

hic servus est Vārica.
Vārica est vīlicus.
vīllam et servōs cūrat.

hic servus est Philus.
Philus callidus est.
Philus numerāre potest.

hic servus est Volūbilis.
Volūbilis coquus
optimus est.
Volūbilis cēnam
optimam coquere potest.

hic servus est Bregāns.
Bregāns nōn callidus
est. Bregāns numerāre
nōn potest.
Bregāns fessus est.
Bregāns dormīre vult.

hic servus est Loquāx.
Loquāx vōcem suāvem
habet.
Loquāx suāviter cantāre
potest.

hic servus est Anti-
Loquāx.
Anti-Loquāx agilis est.
Anti-Loquāx optimē
saltāre potest.
Loquāx et Anti-Loquāx
sunt geminī.

Salvius multōs servōs
habet. servī labōrant.
servī ignāvī et fessī sunt.
servī labōrāre nōlunt.

# trēs servī

*trēs servī in vīllā labōrant. haec vīlla est in Britanniā. servī dīligenter labōrant,*
*quod dominum exspectant. servī vītam suam dēplōrant.*

Philus:     *(pecūniam numerat.)* iterum pluit! semper pluit! nōs sōlem
                numquam vidēmus. ego ad Ītaliam redīre volō. ego sōlem
                vidēre volō.                                             5

Volūbilis:  *(cēnam in culīnā parat.)* ubi est vīnum? nūllum vīnum videō.
                quis hausit? ego aquam bibere nōn possum! aqua est
                foeda!

Bregāns:   *(pavīmentum lavat.)* ego labōrāre nōlō! fessus sum. multum
                vīnum bibī. ego dormīre volō.                           10
                *(Vārica subitō vīllam intrat. Vārica est vīlicus.)*

Vārica:     servī! dominus noster īrātus advenit! apud Cantiacōs
                servī coniūrātiōnem fēcērunt. dominus est vulnerātus.

Bregāns:   nōs dē hāc coniūrātiōne audīre volumus. rem nārrā!

| | | | |
|---|---|---|---|
| dēplōrant: dēplōrāre | *complain about* | lavat: lavāre | *wash* |
| pluit | *it is raining* | labōrāre nōlō | *I do not want to work* |
| sōlem: sōl | *sun* | fessus | *tired* |
| redīre volō | *I want to return* | advenit: advenīre | *arrive* |
| aquam: aqua | *water* | apud Cantiacōs | *among the Cantiaci* |
| bibere nōn possum | *I cannot drink* | coniūrātiōnem: | |
| foeda | *foul, horrible* |   coniūrātiō | *plot* |
| pavīmentum | *floor* | vulnerātus | *wounded* |

Britanniā: Britannia   *Britain*
Ītaliam: Ītalia        *Italy*
Cantiacōs: Cantiacī   *the name of a tribe in southeastern Britain*

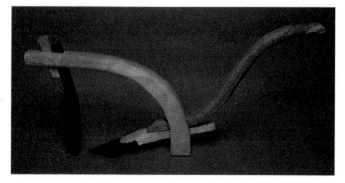

**Reconstruction of a Roman plow.**

# coniūrātiō

Vārica rem nārrāvit:

"nōs apud Cantiacōs erāmus, quod Salvius metallum novum vīsitābat. hospes erat Pompēius Optātus, vir benignus. in metallō labōrābant multī servī. quamquam servī multum ferrum ē terrā effodiēbant, Salvius nōn erat contentus. Salvius servōs ad sē vocāvit     5
et īnspexit. ūnus servus aeger erat. Salvius servum aegrum ē turbā trāxit et clāmāvit,

'servus aeger est inūtilis. ego servōs inūtilēs retinēre nōlō.'

**Slave chain which would have been attached to the necks of a line of slaves.**

postquam hoc dīxit, Salvius carnificibus servum trādidit. carnificēs
eum statim interfēcērunt.                                                      10

hic servus tamen fīlium habēbat; nōmen erat Alātor. Alātor
patrem suum vindicāre voluit. itaque, ubi cēterī dormiēbant, Alātor
pugiōnem cēpit. postquam custōdēs ēlūsit, cubiculum intrāvit. in
hōc cubiculō Salvius dormiēbat. tum Alātor dominum nostrum
petīvit et vulnerāvit. dominus noster erat perterritus; manūs ad    15
servum extendit et veniam petīvit. custōdēs tamen sonōs
audīvērunt. in cubiculum ruērunt et Alātōrem interfēcērunt. tum
Salvius saeviēbat. statim Pompēium excitāvit et īrātus clāmāvit,

'servus mē vulnerāvit! coniūrātiō est! omnēs servī sunt cōnsciī.
ego omnibus supplicium poscō!'                                              20

Pompēius, postquam hoc audīvit, erat attonitus.

'ego omnēs servōs interficere nōn possum. ūnus tē vulnerāvit.
ūnus igitur est nocēns, cēterī innocentēs.'

'custōdēs nōn sunt innocentēs,' inquit Salvius. 'cum Alātōre
coniūrābant.'                                                                      25

Pompēius invītus cōnsēnsit et carnificibus omnēs custōdēs
trādidit."

| metallum | *a mine* |
| hospes | *host* |
| quamquam | *although* |
| ferrum | *iron* |
| effodiēbant: effodere | *dig* |
| inūtilis | *useless* |
| carnificibus: carnifex | *executioner* |
| nōmen | *name* |
| vindicāre voluit | *wanted to avenge* |
| itaque | *and so* |
| ubi | *when* |
| cēterī | *the others* |
| pugiōnem: pugiō | *dagger* |
| custōdēs: custōs | *guard* |
| ēlūsit: ēlūdere | *slip past* |
| manūs . . . . . extendit | *stretched out his hands* |
| veniam petīvit | *begged for mercy* |
| saeviēbat: saevīre | *be in a rage* |
| cōnsciī: cōnscius | *accomplice* |
| supplicium | *death penalty* |
| poscō: poscere | *demand* |
| nocēns | *guilty* |
| innocentēs: innocēns | *innocent* |
| coniūrābant: coniūrāre | *plot* |
| invītus | *unwilling, reluctant* |

When you have read this story, answer the questions at the end.

# Bregāns

tum Vārica, postquam hanc rem nārrāvit, clāmāvit,

"Loquāx! Anti-Loquāx! dominus advenit. vocāte servōs in āream! ego eōs īnspicere volō."

servī ad āream celeriter cucurrērunt, quod Salvium timēbant. servī in ōrdinēs longōs sē īnstrūxērunt. vīlicus per ōrdinēs ambulābat; servōs īnspiciēbat et numerābat. subitō exclāmāvit,

"ubi sunt ancillae? nūllās ancillās videō."

"ancillae dominō nostrō cubiculum parant," respondit Loquāx.

"ubi est Volūbilis noster?" inquit Vārica. "ego Volūbilem vidēre nōn possum."

"Volūbilis venīre nōn potest, quod cēnam parat," respondit Anti-Loquāx.

Bregāns in mediīs servīs stābat; canem ingentem sēcum habēbat.

"rēx Cogidubnus dominō nostrō hunc canem mīsit," inquit Bregāns. "canis ferōcissimus est; bēstiās optimē agitāre potest."

subitō vīgintī equitēs āream intrāvērunt. prīmus erat Salvius. postquam ex equō dēscendit, Vāricam salūtāvit.

"servōs īnspicere volō," inquit Salvius. tum Salvius et Vārica per ōrdinēs ambulābant.

puerī puellaeque in prīmō ōrdine stābant et dominum suum salūtābant. cum puerīs stābant geminī.

"salvē, domine!" inquit Loquāx.

"salvē, domine!" inquit Anti-Loquāx.

Bregāns, simulac Salvium vīdit, "domine! domine!" clāmāvit. Salvius servō nihil respondit. Bregāns iterum clāmāvit,

"Salvī! Salvī! spectā canem!"

Salvius saeviēbat, quod servus erat īnsolēns.

"servus īnsolentissimus es," inquit Salvius. Bregantem ferōciter pulsāvit. Bregāns ad terram dēcidit. canis statim ex ōrdine ērūpit, et Salvium petīvit. nōnnūllī servī ex ōrdinibus ērūpērunt et canem retrāxērunt. Salvius, postquam sē recēpit, gladium dēstrīnxit.

"istum canem interficere volō," inquit Salvius.

"hoc difficile est," inquit Bregāns. "rēx Cogidubnus, amīcus tuus, tibi canem dedit."

5

10

15

20

25

30

"ita vērō, difficile est," respondit Salvius. "sed ego tē pūnīre 35
possum. hoc facile est, quod servus meus es."

| | | | |
|---|---|---|---|
| in āream | *into the courtyard* | geminī | *twins* |
| in ōrdinēs | *in rows* | simulac | *as soon as* |
| sē īnstrūxērunt: | | īnsolēns | *rude, insolent* |
|   sē īnstruere | *draw oneself up* | ērūpit: ērumpere | *break away* |
| sēcum | *with him* | nōnnūllī | *some, several* |
| rēx | *king* | retrāxērunt: retrahere | *drag back* |
| equitēs: eques | *horseman* | sē recēpit: sē recipere | *recover* |
| equō: equus | *horse* | pūnīre | *punish* |
| puerī puellaeque | *the boys and girls* | facile | *easy* |

Cogidubnus   *British ally of the Romans,*
                *appointed king under*
                *Emperor Claudius*

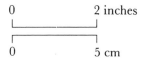

0            2 inches

0            5 cm

**British vase showing a hunting
dog chasing a hare.**

1 Who inspected the slaves before Salvius arrived?
2 Why were the slave-girls missing from the inspection?
3 What gift had been sent for Salvius? Who had sent it?
4 Why did Bregans want to attract Salvius' attention?
5 Why did Salvius draw his sword?
6 What impression of Bregans do you get from this story?

# About the Language

**1** Study the following pairs of sentences:

Bregāns dormit.
*Bregans is sleeping.*

Bregāns **dormīre** vult.
*Bregans wants to sleep.*

iuvenēs vīnum bibunt.
*The young men are
drinking wine.*

iuvenēs vīnum **bibere** volunt.
*The young men want to drink wine.*

servī currunt.
*The slaves are running.*

servī celeriter **currere** possunt.
*The slaves are able to run quickly.*

coquus cēnam parat.
*The cook is preparing dinner.*

coquus cēnam optimam **parāre** potest.
*The cook is able to prepare a very good dinner.*

The form of the verb in boldface is known as the *infinitive*.

**2** Further examples:

1 Anti-Loquāx currit.   Anti-Loquāx currere potest.
2 Bregāns labōrat.   Bregāns labōrāre nōn vult.
3 geminī fābulam audīre volunt.
4 puerī festīnāre nōn possunt.

**3** The verbs **volō** and **possum** are often used with an infinitive. They form their present tense as follows:

| | | | | | |
|---|---|---|---|---|---|
| (ego) | volō | *I want* | (ego) | possum | *I am able* |
| (tū) | vīs | *you* (singular) *want* | (tū) | potes | *you* (singular) *are able* |
| | vult | *s/he wants* | | potest | *s/he is able* |
| (nōs) | volumus | *we want* | (nōs) | possumus | *we are able* |
| (vōs) | vultis | *you* (plural) *want* | (vōs) | potestis | *you* (plural) *are able* |
| | volunt | *they want* | | possunt | *they are able* |

ego sōlem vidēre volō.
*I want to see the sun.*

tū pugnāre nōn potes.
*You are not able to fight.*

**4** **possum**, **potes**, etc. can also be translated as *I can, you can*, etc.:

nōs dormīre nōn possumus.   *We cannot sleep.*
ego leōnem interficere possum.   *I can kill the lion.*

**5** Further examples:

1 ego pugnāre possum.
2 nōs effugere nōn possumus.
3 nōs vīnum bibere volumus.
4 tū labōrāre nōn vīs.
5 vōs celeriter currere potestis.

# Salvius fundum īnspicit

postrīdiē Salvius fundum īnspicere voluit. Vārica igitur eum per fundum dūxit. vīlicus dominō agrōs et segetem ostendit.

"seges est optima, domine," inquit Vārica. "servī multum frūmentum in horreum iam intulērunt."

Salvius, postquam agrōs circumspectāvit, Vāricae dīxit,                     5

"ubi sunt arātōrēs et magister? nōnne Cervīx arātōribus praeest?"

"ita vērō, domine!" respondit Vārica. "sed arātōrēs hodiē nōn labōrant, quod Cervīx abest. aeger est."

Salvius eī respondit, "quid dīxistī? aeger est? ego servum aegrum        10
retinēre nōlō."

"sed Cervīx perītissimus est," exclāmāvit vīlicus. "Cervīx sōlus rem rūsticam cūrāre potest."

"tacē!" inquit Salvius. "eum vēndere volō."

simulatque hoc dīxit, duōs servōs vīdit. servī ad horreum      15
festīnābant.

"quid faciunt hī servī?" rogāvit Salvius.

"hī servī arātōribus cibum ferunt, domine. placetne tibi?" respondit Vārica.

| | | | |
|---|---|---|---|
| agrōs: ager | *field* | praeest: praeesse | *be in charge of* |
| segetem: seges | *crop, harvest* | eī | *to him* |
| frūmentum | *grain* | perītissimus: perītus | *skillful* |
| horreum | *barn, granary* | sōlus | *alone, only* |
| intulērunt: īnferre | *bring in* | rem rūsticam | *the farming* |
| arātōrēs: arātor | *plowman* | cūrāre | *look after, supervise* |
| magister | *foreman* | simulatque | *as soon as* |
| nōnne | *surely* | ferunt: ferre | *bring* |

"mihi nōn placet!" inquit Salvius. "ego servīs ignāvīs nūllum    20
cibum dō."

tum dominus et vīlicus ad horreum advēnērunt. prope horreum
Salvius aedificium vīdit. aedificium erat sēmirutum.

"quid est hoc aedificium?" inquit Salvius.

"horreum novum est, domine!" respondit vīlicus. "alterum    25
horreum iam plēnum est. ego igitur novum aedificāre voluī."

"sed cūr sēmirutum est?" inquit Salvius.

Vārica respondit, "ubi servī horreum aedificābant, domine, rēs
dīra accidit. taurus, animal ferōx, impetum in hoc aedificium fēcit.
mūrōs dēlēvit et servōs terruit."    30

"quis taurum dūcēbat?" inquit Salvius. "quis erat neglegēns?"

"Bregāns!"

"ēheu!" inquit Salvius. "ego Britannīs nōn crēdō. omnēs Britannī
sunt stultī, sed iste Bregāns est stultior quam cēterī!"

| | | | |
|---|---|---|---|
| ignāvīs: ignāvus | *lazy* | taurus | *bull* |
| aedificium | *building* | neglegēns | *careless* |
| dīra | *dreadful, awful* | | |

Britannīs: Britannī    *Britons*

**Soay sheep, a breed that has changed very little since the earliest domestication
of sheep. The Romans would have found them being farmed in Britain when
they arrived there.**

**Bronze statuette of
a plowman with a team
of oxen, from Roman Britain.**

# About the Language

**1** In this Stage, you have met a new way of saying *and* in Latin:

puerī puellae**que**        *boys and girls*
dominus servī**que**        *master and slaves*

Further examples:

1  servī ancillaeque
2  agricolae mercātōrēsque

**2** The next examples are slightly longer:

dominus ex equō dēscendit, vīllam**que** intrāvit.
*The master got off his horse and went into the house.*

Salvius mīlitēs centuriōnem**que** salūtāvit.
*Salvius greeted the soldiers and the centurion.*

Further examples:

1  Vārica servōs ancillāsque īnspexit.
2  Volūbilis ad culīnam revēnit, cibumque parāvit.

# Practicing the Language

1 Complete each sentence of this exercise with the most suitable word from the list below and then translate.

effugere, numerāre, dormīre, bibere, īnspicere, portāre

1 Volūbilis nōn est laetus. aquam in culīnā bibit. vīnum . . . . . vult.
2 Bregāns est rōbustus. amphoram ad culīnam portat.
   Bregāns trēs amphorās . . . . . potest.
3 Philus est callidus. pecūniam in tablīnō numerat.
   Philus pecūniam celerrimē . . . . . potest.
4 Salvius est dominus. Salvius servōs dīligenter īnspicit.
   Salvius fundum quoque . . . . . vult.
5 Loquāx et Anti-Loquāx sunt fessī. puerī in culīnā dormiunt.
   puerī saepe . . . . . volunt.
6 servī contentī nōn sunt. servī ā vīlicō effugiunt.
   servī ē vīllā . . . . . volunt.

| rōbustus | *strong* | celerrimē | *very quickly* |
| amphoram: amphora | *wine-jar* | ā vīlicō | *from the manager* |

2 Complete each sentence of this exercise with the most suitable word from the lists below, and then translate. Do not use any word more than once.

| cōnspexī | vituperāvī | obdormīvī | fūgī | verberāvī |
| cōnspexistī | vituperāvistī | obdormīvistī | fūgistī | verberāvistī |
| cōnspexit | vituperāvit | obdormīvit | fūgit | verberāvit |

1 servus in cubiculō labōrābat. servus, quod erat fessus, in cubiculō
   . . . . . .
2 Salvius, postquam cubiculum intrāvit, servum . . . . . ; statim fūstem cēpit et servum . . . . . .
3 Rūfilla Salviō clāmāvit, "tū es dominus dūrus! cūr tū servum . . . . . ?"
4 "ego servum . . . . . , quod in cubiculō dormiēbat," respondit Salvius.
5 "herī," inquit Rūfilla, "tū ancillam meam . . . . . , quod neglegēns erat. ancilla perterrita erat, et ē vīllā . . . . . ."
6 "in vīllā meā ego sum dominus," inquit Salvius. "ego ancillam . . . . . , quod ignāva erat."

dūrus *harsh, hard*

# Salvius

Gaius Salvius Liberalis was born in central Italy but, like many bright and ambitious young men, he soon moved to Rome, where he gained a reputation for speaking his mind. After becoming a successful lawyer, he was made a Roman senator, probably by the Emperor Vespasian. In A.D.78 he was chosen to be one of the Arval Brotherhood – a group of twelve distinguished men who met to perform religious ceremonies and in particular to pray for the emperor and his family. Salvius was also put in command of a legion; this was not only a great honor but could lead to further honors in the future. Not long afterwards, in about A.D.81, he was sent probably by the Emperor Domitian to help Agricola, the Roman governor of the province of Britain.

Salvius' main task was probably to supervise the law courts and look after the southern part of the province while Agricola was away fighting in the north. He would have traveled around the country acting as a judge; he may also have arranged for some of the money raised by farming and mining in Britain to be sent regularly to the emperor in Rome. The stories in Stages 13 and 14 imagine Salvius and his wife Rufilla living in an impressive villa not far from Noviomagus (Chichester) near the Sussex coast in southern Britain.

Our knowledge of Salvius comes mainly from the details on a gravestone discovered in central Italy and an inscription found in some woods near Rome. He is also mentioned by two Roman writers, Pliny and Suetonius. Another gravestone has been found dedicated to "Vitellia Rufilla, wife of Gaius Salvius Liberalis, priestess of the welfare of the emperor, best of mothers." It was set up by their son.

# Farming in Roman Britain

## The Villa

Most inhabitants of Roman Britain lived in the countryside. The native Britons were mainly peasants, living simply in round huts and farming small plots. But some Britons and a few Romans lived in villas and between six and seven hundred of these have been discovered by archaeologists.

**Aerial view of the remains of a Roman villa in Britain. Some aerial photographs also show outlines of cultivated fields from Roman times.**

Villas were well-built country houses with land for farming. The earliest villas had only three or four rooms, sometimes linked by a corridor; they were built mainly of timber and wattle-and-daub, with roofs of stone slabs, tiles, or thatch. Later villas were often more complicated in design and were built mostly of stone; the grandest ones might contain long colonnades, flushing latrines, glass windows, under-floor heating, mosaics, and a set of baths complete with **tepidārium** and **caldārium**. They also had workshops, barns, living-quarters for the farm laborers, and sheds for the animals. In choosing a place to build his villa, the owner would look not only for attractive surroundings but also for practical advantages, such as a nearby supply of running water and shelter from the cold north and east winds.

The main crops grown in Britain at this time were barley, oats, rye, and especially wheat. Archaeologists have found traces of all these crops, accidentally scorched or charred, and thus preserved in the earth. The outlines of some of the small fields where the crops were grown can still be seen today, particularly in photographs taken from the air. Wooden plows were used, often fitted with an iron plowshare to turn the soil more deeply. Grain was harvested with sickles; it was then dried, sometimes in hypocausts specially built for the purpose; then it was threshed, and winnowed by being thrown into the wind so that the chaff was blown from the grain. Farming tools were made of wood and iron; they included spades, pitchforks, and scythes, some of which have been found by archaeologists.

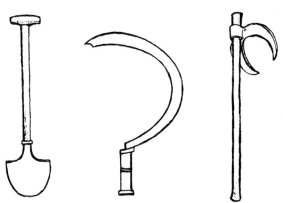

Most villas seem to have kept animals, such as cattle, sheep, goats, pigs, and horses, in addition to geese and hens. Bees were kept to produce honey, which was used to sweeten food (there was no sugar in the Roman world). Many fruits and vegetables were grown, including some (like cherries and peas) which had been brought to Britain by the Romans.

The villas could not produce everything they needed, but home-made products such as leather, meat, timber, and honey could be traded for shellfish, salt, wine, pottery, and ironware.

Many villas were supervised by a manager or overseer. He would probably, like Varica, be a slave or a freedman. The manager was responsible for buying any food or other goods that could not be produced on the villa's own land and looking after the buildings and slaves. In his book *On Agriculture,* the writer Columella says that the manager should be middle-aged and toughened from childhood by farm work.

## The Slaves

Farm slaves were described by one Roman landowner as just "farming equipment with voices." Most of Salvius' farm slaves would be British, whereas many of his house slaves would be imported from abroad. Slaves working on the land lived a much harsher life than domestic slaves, and slaves working in the mines had the harshest life of all. Some slaves were kept in chains; Columella says: "For chained slaves there should be an underground prison, as healthy as possible, letting in light through a number of narrow windows built above hand's reach." Slave-chains have been discovered in Britain, designed to fasten several slaves together by their necks. (See the photograph on page 6.)

In theory, the law gave slaves some protection: for example, any owner who killed a sick slave could be charged with murder. In practice, these laws were often ignored, as in the story of Salvius and the Cantiacan miners. However, in the first century A.D. slaves were becoming increasingly scarce and therefore expensive; this is why Columella wanted his prison to be healthy.

Many agricultural slaves were born as slaves. Columella recommends rewards for slave-women who produce many children. Such "home-grown" slaves were not cheap, since they took no part in the farming until they were old enough to work, but the son of a skilled slave would be able to learn his father's trade at a very early age. Some of these slaves are known to us by name. For example, a gravestone from Chester (in northwestern England, near the Welsh border) was set up by a master in memory of three of his slaves who died young: a slave-boy aged twelve and two ten-year-olds called Atilianus and Anti-Atilianus, probably twins.

# Words and Phrases Checklist

Verbs in the checklists for Unit 2 are usually listed as in the Unit 2 Language Information Section. See p.198 of that Section for details and practice examples. Nouns in the checklists for Stages 13-16 are usually listed as they were in the Unit 1 Language Information Section, pp. 214-21.

| | | | |
|---|---|---|---|
| adveniō, advenīre, advēnī | *arrive* | ita vērō | *yes* |
| aedificium | *building* | nōlō | *I do not want* |
| aeger | *sick, ill* | novus | *new* |
| alter: alterum | *the other, the second* | nūllus | *not any, no* |
| cantō, cantāre, cantāvī | *sing* | numerō, numerāre, | |
| cēterī | *the others, the rest* | numerāvī | *count* |
| coniūrātiō: coniūrātiōnem | *plot* | ōrdō: ōrdinem | *row* |
| custōs: custōdem | *guard* | possum | *I can, I am able* |
| dēcidō, dēcidere, dēcidī | *fall down* | retineō, retinēre, retinuī | *keep* |
| dīcō, dīcere, dīxī | *say* | ruō, ruere, ruī | *rush* |
| excitō, excitāre, excitāvī | *arouse, wake up* | sē | *himself, herself,* |
| fessus | *tired* | | *themselves* |
| geminī | *twins* | suāviter | *sweetly* |
| hauriō, haurīre, hausī | *drain, drink up* | trahō, trahere, trāxī | *drag* |
| horreum | *barn, granary* | volō | *I want* |
| interficiō, interficere, | | vulnerō, vulnerāre, | |
| interfēcī | *kill* | vulnerāvī | *wound* |

# Word Search

Match each definition with one of the words given below.

advent, conjure, deciduous, edifice, nullify, enumerate, vulnerable

1 . . . . .: to invoke by oath or magic spell
2 . . . . .: easily wounded
3 . . . . .: a structure or building
4 . . . . .: having leaves that fall at the end of the growing season
5 . . . . .: to list in detail
6 . . . . .: an arrival
7 . . . . .: to make ineffective or useless

**Reconstruction of a Romano-British triclinium.**

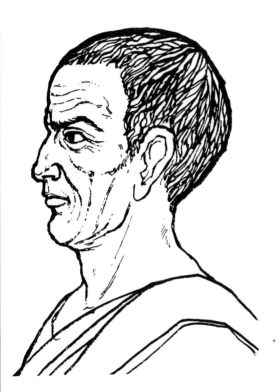

# apud Salvium

| Vārica: | Phile! portā hanc amphoram in vīllam! |
|---|---|
| Philus: | amphora magna est. difficile est mihi magnam amphoram portāre. |
| Vārica: | cūr? |
| Philus: | quod ego sum senex. |

| Vārica: | Loquāx! Anti-Loquāx! portāte hanc amphoram in vīllam! |
|---|---|
| Loquāx: | amphora gravis est. difficile est nōbīs amphoram gravem portāre. |
| Vārica: | cūr? |
| Loquāx: | quod nōs sumus puerī. |

| Vārica: | Bregāns! portā hās amphorās in vīllam! |
|---|---|
| Bregāns: | amphorae gravēs sunt. difficile est mihi |
| | amphorās gravēs portāre. |
| Vārica: | sed necesse est! |
| Bregāns: | cūr? |
| Vārica: | necesse est tibi amphorās portāre quod |
| | Philus est senex, quod Loquāx et frāter |
| | sunt puerī, et . . . |
| Bregāns: | quod tū es vīlicus! |

# Rūfilla

*Rūfilla in cubiculō sedet. duae ōrnātrīcēs prope eam stant et crīnēs compōnunt. Salvius intrat. Rūfilla, simulatque eum cōnspicit, ōrnātrīcēs ē cubiculō dīmittit.*

Rūfilla: Salvī! vir crūdēlis es. ego ad hanc vīllam venīre nōlēbam. in urbe Londiniō manēre volēbam. Londinium est urbs pulcherrima, ubi multās amīcās habeō. difficile est mihi 5
amīcās relinquere.

| | | | |
|---|---|---|---|
| ōrnātrīcēs: ōrnātrīx | *hairdresser* | amīcās: amīca | *friend* |
| dīmittit: dīmittere | *send away, dismiss* | relinquere | *leave* |
| crūdēlis | *cruel* | | |

Londiniō: Londinium  *London*

Salvius: Rūfilla! quam levis es! ubi in urbe Londiniō habitābāmus,
cotīdiē ad mē veniēbās. cotīdiē mihi ita dīcēbās,

"Semprōnia, amīca mea, est fortūnātior quam ego.
marītum optimum habet. marītus eī rēs pretiōsās semper   10
dat. vīllam eī prōmīsit. ego quoque vīllam habēre volō, sed
tū mihi nihil dās."

tandem vīllam tibi dedī, sed etiam nunc nōn es contenta.

Rūfilla: sed ego vīllam prope urbem habēre volēbam. haec vīlla ab
urbe longē abest.   15

Salvius: tū ipsa hanc vīllam ēlēgistī. ego, quamquam pretium
magnum erat, eam libenter ēmī. nōnne haec vīlla est
ēlegāns? nōnne etiam magnifica?

Rūfilla: sed hiems iam appropinquat. amīcae meae semper in urbe
hiemant. nōn commodum est mihi in vīllā hiemāre.   20
decōrum est mihi cum amīcīs hiemāre. mātrōna Rōmāna
sum. amīcās meās vīsitāre nōn possum. in hōc locō sōla
sum.

Salvius: quid dīxistī? sōla es? decem ancillās habēs, novem servōs,
duās ōrnātrīcēs, coquum Aegyptium . . .   25

Rūfilla: et marītum dūrum et crūdēlem. nihil intellegis! nihil cūrās!
(*exit lacrimāns.*)

| | |
|---|---|
| levis | *changeable, inconsistent* |
| fortūnātior: | |
|   fortūnātus | *lucky* |
| etiam | *even* |
| ab urbe | *from the city* |
| tū ipsa | *you yourself* |
| pretium | *price* |
| libenter | *gladly* |
| ēlegāns | *tasteful, elegant* |
| hiems | *winter* |
| appropinquat: | |
|   appropinquāre | *approach* |
| hiemant: hiemāre | *spend the winter* |
| commodum: | |
|   commodus | *convenient* |
| mātrōna | *lady* |
| decōrum: decōrus | *right, proper* |
| novem | *nine* |
| lacrimāns | *weeping, crying* |

**Portrait of a wealthy Roman woman.**

**Relief showing a Roman woman with her slave-girls.**

# Domitilla cubiculum parat

"Domitilla! Domitilla! ubi es?" clāmāvit Marcia. Marcia anus erat.

"in hortō sum, Marcia. quid vīs?" respondit Domitilla. "fessa sum, quod diū labōrāvī."

"necesse est nōbīs cubiculum parāre," inquit Marcia. "domina nōbīs hoc mandāvit, quod familiārem exspectat." 5

"ēheu! semper labōrō; numquam ōtiōsa sum," inquit Domitilla.

"puella ignāvissima es," inquit Marcia. "domina ipsa mē ad tē mīsit. necesse est tibi cubiculum verrere. necesse est mihi pavīmentum lavāre. curre ad culīnam! quaere scōpās!"

Domitilla ex hortō discessit et ad culīnam lentē ambulābat. īrāta 10 erat, quod cubiculum verrere nōlēbat.

"ego ōrnātrīx sum," inquit. "nōs ōrnātrīcēs nihil sordidum

| | | | |
|---|---|---|---|
| anus | *old woman* | domina ipsa | *the mistress herself* |
| quid vīs? | *what do you want?* | verrere | *sweep* |
| diū | *for a long time* | scōpās: scōpae | *broom* |
| necesse | *necessary* | lentē | *slowly* |
| hoc mandāvit | *has given this order* | nihil sordidum | *no dirty jobs* |
| familiārem: familiāris | *relative* | | |

facimus. nōn decōrum est ōrnātrīcibus cubiculum verrere."

subitō Domitilla cōnsilium cēpit et ad culīnam quam celerrimē
festīnāvit. simulac culīnam intrāvit, lacrimīs sē trādidit.                            15

Volūbilis attonitus, "mea columba," inquit, "cūr lacrimās?"

"lacrimō quod miserrima sum," ancilla coquō respondit."per
tōtum diem labōrāvī. quam fessa sum! nunc necesse est mihi
cubiculum parāre. nōn diūtius labōrāre possum."

"mea columba, nōlī lacrimāre!" inquit Volūbilis. "ego tibi       20
cubiculum parāre possum."

"Volūbilis! quam benignus es!" susurrāvit ancilla.

coquus cum ancillā ad cubiculum revēnit. dīligenter labōrāvit et
cubiculum fēcit pūrum. ancilla laeta dīxit,

"meum mel! meae dēliciae!" et coquō ōsculum dedit.              25

coquus ērubēscēns ad culīnam revēnit.

| | | | |
|---|---|---|---|
| lacrimīs sē trādidit | *burst into tears* | pūrum: pūrus | *clean, spotless* |
| miserrima | *very miserable, very sad* | mel | *honey* |
| diūtius | *any longer* | ōsculum | *kiss* |
| nōlī lacrimāre | *don't cry* | ērubēscēns | *blushing* |

# About the Language

**1** Study the following sentences:

| | |
|---|---|
| 1 **magnus** servus labōrābat. | *The **large** slave was working.* |
| 2 dominus servō **fessō** praemium dedit. | *The master gave a reward to the **tired** slave.* |
| 3 agricola servum **ignāvum** pūnīvit. | *The farmer punished the **lazy** slave.* |

The words in boldface are *adjectives*. They are used to describe nouns.
In each of these examples, the adjective is describing the slave.

**2** Adjectives change their endings to match the *case* of the nouns they
describe.

In sentence 1 above, **magnus** is nominative because it describes a
nominative noun (**servus**).

In sentence 2, **fessō** is dative, because it describes a dative noun
(**servō**).

In sentence 3, **ignāvum** is accusative, because it describes an
accusative noun (**servum**).

**3** Translate the following examples and pick out the adjective in each sentence:

1 ancilla perterrita ad culīnam contendit.
2 coquus ancillam perterritam salūtāvit.
3 cīvēs mercātōrem fortem laudāvērunt.
4 cīvēs mercātōrī fortī praemium dedērunt.
5 agricola parvum puerum cōnspexit.
6 agricola parvō puerō equum ostendit.

Find the noun described by each adjective, and say whether the noun and adjective are nominative, accusative, or dative.

**4** Adjectives also change their endings to match the *number* (i.e. singular or plural) of the nouns they describe. An adjective is singular if it describes a singular noun, and plural if it describes a plural noun. For example:

**parvus** servus dormiēbat.    *The small slave was sleeping.*
**multī** servī bibēbant.    *Many slaves were drinking.*

**5** Translate the following examples and pick out the adjective in each sentence:

1 fēminae laetae per viās ambulābant.
2 fēmina laeta per viās ambulābat.
3 gladiātor leōnem ferōcem necāvit.
4 gladiātor leōnēs ferōcēs necāvit.
5 pictūra pulchra erat in ātriō.
6 vīlicus multōs amīcōs in tabernā vīdit.

Find the noun described by each adjective, and say whether the noun and adjective are singular or plural.

**6** When an adjective changes its ending in this way it is said to *agree*, in case and number, with the noun it describes.

**7** Adjectives like **magnus** and **multī**, which indicate *size* or *quantity*, usually come before the noun they describe; other adjectives usually come after the noun.

# Rūfilla cubiculum ōrnat

tum Marcia cubiculum intrāvit. lentē prōcēdēbat, quod urnam portābat. Marcia urnam vix portāre poterat, quod anus erat. ubi Domitillam cōnspexit, clāmāvit,

"cūr nōn labōrās? puella ignāvissima es."

"quam stulta es!" respondit Domitilla. "dīligenter labōrāvī. 5 cubiculum fēcī pūrum. nunc necesse est tibi pavīmentum lavāre."

Marcia, quamquam erat attonita, Domitillae nihil dīxit. sōla pavīmentum lavābat. tandem rem cōnfēcit.

"euge!" inquit Domitilla. "optimē labōrāvistī. nitidum est pavīmentum!" 10

Rūfilla vōcēs audīvit et intrāvit. Domitilla, postquam eam cōnspexit, cubiculum dēmōnstrāvit.

"cubiculum tibi parāvimus, domina, et pavīmentum fēcimus nitidum."

"bene labōrāvistis," ancillīs respondit Rūfilla. "sed, quamquam 15 nitidum est pavīmentum, familiāris meus in hōc cubiculō dormīre nōn potest. nam cubiculum est inēlegāns. necesse est nōbīs id ōrnāre. familiāris meus est vir urbānus."

"tablīnum est ēlegāns," inquit Domitilla. "in tablīnō, ubi dominus labōrat, sunt multae rēs pretiōsae." 20

"ita vērō," inquit Rūfilla, "in tablīnō est armārium ēlegantissimum. in tablīnō sunt sella aēnea et candēlābrum aureum. age! Domitilla, necesse est nōbīs ad tablīnum īre."

| | | | |
|---|---|---|---|
| ōrnat: ōrnāre | *decorate* | inēlegāns | *unattractive* |
| urnam: urna | *bucket* | id | *it* |
| vix | *hardly, scarcely* | urbānus | *fashionable, sophisticated* |
| sōla | *alone, on her own* | armārium | *chest, cupboard* |
| nitidum: nitidus | *gleaming, brilliant* | aēnea | *made of bronze* |
| vōcēs: vōx | *voice* | candēlābrum | *lamp-stand, candelabrum* |
| dēmōnstrāvit: | | aureum: aureus | *golden, made of gold* |
|   dēmōnstrāre | *point out, show* | age! | *come on!* |
| bene | *well* | īre | *to go* |
| nam | *for* | | |

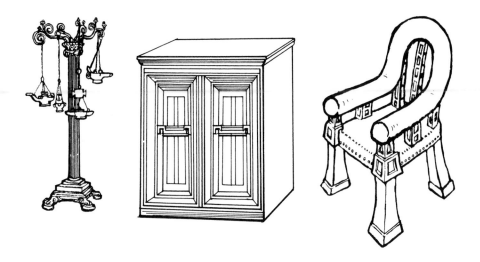

# About the Language

1  Study the following sentence:

cīvis servum **trīstem** salūtāvit.
*The citizen greeted the **sad** slave.*

The adjective **trīstem** is in the accusative case because it describes the accusative noun **servum**.

2  Although **trīstem** and **servum** are both accusative, they do not have the same ending. This is because they belong to different declensions, and have different ways of forming their cases. **trīstis** belongs to the third declension and **servus** belongs to the second declension.

3  Translate the following examples:

1  Quīntus fābulam mīrābilem nārrāvit.
2  in vīllā habitābat senex stultus.
3  gladiātor bēstiās ferōcēs agitābat.
4  dominus amīcō fidēlī dēnāriōs trādidit.
5  omnēs lībertī vīnum bibēbant.

Pick out the adjective in each sentence and say which noun it is describing.

---

# in tablīnō

*postrīdiē Salvius et Philus in tablīnō sunt. intrat Rūfilla.*

Rūfilla:  mī Salvī!

Salvius:  occupātus sum! necesse est mihi hās epistulās dictāre. ego
rem celeriter cōnficere volō. ubi est sella mea?
(*Salvius sellam frūstrā quaerit.*)                                                5
heus! ubi est ista sella?

Rūfilla:  mī cārissime! aliquid tibi dīcere volō.

Salvius:  tē nunc audīre nōn possum. epistulās dictāre volō. ecce!
Philus parātus adest. stilī et cērae adsunt – heus! ubi est
armārium meum? quis cēpit?                                                        10

Rūfilla:  Salvī! audī!
(*tandem Salvius uxōrī cēdit et Philum dīmittit.*)

Salvius:  ēheu! abī, Phile! nōn commodum est mihi epistulās
dictāre.

Rūfilla:  bene! nunc aliquid tibi dīcere possum. ubi in urbe Londiniō     15
nūper eram, familiārem convēnī.

Salvius:  tot familiārēs habēs! eōs numerāre nōn possum.

Rūfilla:  sed hic familiāris est Quīntus Caecilius Iūcundus. ubi
mōns Vesuvius urbem Pompēiōs dēlēvit, Quīntus ex urbe
effūgit. quam cōmis est! quam urbānus!                                           20

Salvius:  hercle! ego Pompēiānīs nōn crēdō. paucī probī sunt, cēterī
mendācēs. ubi in Campāniā mīlitābam, multōs
Pompēiānōs cognōscēbam. mercātōrēs Pompēiānī nōs
mīlitēs semper dēcipiēbant.

Rūfilla:  stultissimus es! familiāris meus nōn est mercātor. Quīntus     25
vir nōbilis est. eum ad vīllam nostram invītāvī.

Salvius:  quid dīxistī? Pompēiānum invītāvistī? ad vīllam nostram?

Rūfilla:  decōrum est mihi familiārem meum hūc invītāre. ancillae
familiārī meō cubiculum parāvērunt. ancillae, quod
cubiculum inēlegāns erat, sellam armāriumque tuum in eō     30
posuērunt.

Salvius:  īnsāna es, uxor! Pompēiānī mendāciōrēs sunt quam
Britannī. num tū sellam et armārium ē tablīnō extrāxistī?

Rūfilla:  et candēlābrum.

Salvius:  prō dī immortālēs! ō candēlābrum meum! ō mē miserum!     35

---

| mī Salvī! | my dear Salvius! |
|---|---|
| heus! | hey! |
| cārissime | dearest |
| aliquid | something |
| cēdit: cēdere | give in, give way |
| bene! | good! |
| nūper | recently |
| convēnī: convenīre | meet |
| tot | so many |
| cōmis | courteous, friendly |
| paucī | a few |
| mīlitābam: mīlitāre | be a soldier |
| cognōscēbam: cognōscere | get to know |
| mīlitēs: mīles | soldier |
| in eō | in it |
| num tū . . . . . extrāxistī? | surely you did not take? |
| prō dī immortālēs! | heavens above! |
| ō mē miserum! | Oh wretched me! Oh dear! |

1 Why has Rufilla come to see Salvius?
2 Why does she address him as "mī Salvī" and "mī cārissime"?
3 What mood is Salvius in? Why?
4 Why is Salvius not able to find his chair and cupboard? What else is missing from the study?
5 Why is Rufilla pleased about Quintus' visit? Why does Salvius not like the idea?

# Practicing the Language

1 Translate into English:

Salvius:   Vārica, quaere Bregantem!
Vārica:    ego Bregantem quaerere nōn possum. ē vīllā discēdere nōn possum. Rūfilla mē exspectat.
Salvius:   Loquāx, Anti-Loquāx, custōdīte vīllam!
Loquāx:    vīllam custōdīre nōn possumus. Rūfilla nōs exspectat.
Salvius:   Volūbilis, vocā servōs ad mē!
Volūbilis: servōs ad tē vocāre nōn possum. domina nostra eōs exspectat.
           (Rūfilla intrat.)
Salvius:   Rūfilla, manē!
Rūfilla:   manēre nōn possum. servī mē exspectant.

**2** Complete each sentence of these paragraphs with the right word from those given below, and then translate. You will have to use some words more than once.

1

|  | SINGULAR | PLURAL |
|---|---|---|
| NOMINATIVE | Salvius | servī |
| ACCUSATIVE | Salvium | servōs |

Salvius dominus est. Salvius multōs servōs habet. . . . . . in agrīs dīligenter labōrant. . . . . . est dominus dūrus. Salvius . . . . . verberat. servī . . . . . nōn amant. . . . . . ē vīllā effugere volunt.

2

|  | SINGULAR | PLURAL |
|---|---|---|
| NOMINATIVE | Rūfilla | ancillae |
| ACCUSATIVE | Rūfillam | ancillās |

Rūfilla domina est. Rūfilla multās ancillās habet. . . . . . in vīllā labōrant. . . . . . est domina benigna. Rūfilla . . . . . semper laudat. . . . . . . . . . . amant.

(The last sentence has *two* words missing.)

**Silver drinking cups found in Britain, probably made in Italy. They were found crushed flat, and have been restored to their original shapes.**

# Quīntus advenit

Quīntus ad vīllam advēnit. Salvius ē vīllā contendit et eum salūtāvit.
  "mī Quīnte!" inquit. "exspectātissimus es! cubiculum optimum
tibi parāvimus."
  Salvius Quīntum in tablīnum dūxit, ubi Rūfilla sedēbat. Rūfilla,
postquam familiārem suum salūtāvit, suāviter rīsit.                         5
  "cēnam modicam tibi parāvī," inquit. "tibi ostreās parāvī et
garum Pompēiānum. post cēnam cubiculum tibi ostendere volō."
  Salvius, postquam Quīntus cēnam cōnsūmpsit, dē urbe Pompēiīs
quaerēbat.
  "ubi in Campāniā mīlitābam, saepe urbem Pompēiōs vīsitābam.     10
nōnne illa clādēs terribilis erat?"
  Rūfilla interpellāvit,
  "cūr Quīntum nostrum vexās? nōn decōrum est. difficile est
Quīntō tantam clādem commemorāre."
  Rūfilla ad Quīntum sē convertit.                                          15
  "fortasse, mī Quīnte, fessus es. cubiculum tibi parāvī. cubiculum
nōn est ōrnātum. in eō sunt armārium modicum et candēlābrum
parvum."
  Salvius īrātus nihil dīxit.
  Quīntus, postquam cubiculum vīdit, exclāmāvit,                           20
  "quam ēlegāns est cubiculum! ego nihil ēlegantius vīdī."
  "cōnsentiō," inquit Salvius. "cubiculum tuum ēlegantius est
quam tablīnum meum."

| | |
|---|---|
| exspectātissimus: exspectātus | *welcome* |
| modicam | *ordinary, little* |
| ostreās: ostrea | *oyster* |
| garum | *sauce* |
| clādēs | *disaster* |
| terribilis | *terrible* |
| interpellāvit: interpellāre | *interrupt* |
| tantam | *so great, such a great* |
| commemorāre | *talk about* |
| sē convertit: sē convertere | *turn* |
| ōrnātum: ōrnātus | *elaborately furnished, decorated* |
| ēlegantius | *more elegant* |

# tripodes argenteī

servī in cubiculō Quīntum vestiēbant. ancilla eī togam tulit. Anti-Loquāx cubiculum intrāvit et Quīntō dīxit,

"necesse est dominō meō ad aulam īre. rēx Cogidubnus hodiē sacrificium facit. rēx omnēs nōbilēs ad aulam invītāvit."

"rēgem hodiē vīsitāmus?" rogāvit Quīntus. "ubi in urbe Londiniō    5
habitābam, saepe dē hōc rēge audiēbam. necesse est mihi dōnum ferre. fortasse est aliquid in arcā meā."

iuvenis ad arcam iit et duōs tripodas argenteōs extrāxit.

Anti-Loquāx attonitus ē cubiculō exiit et Salviō rem nārrāvit. Salvius, postquam dē tripodibus argenteīs audīvit, ad cellārium    10
contendit.

"necesse est mihi rēgem Cogidubnum vīsitāre," inquit. "dōnum eī ferre volō."

"nōn difficile est nōbīs dōnum invenīre, domine," Salviō respondit cellārius. "ecce! urna aēnea. antīquissima est. placetne    15
tibi?"

"mihi nōn placet," inquit Salvius. "dōnum aēneum Cogidubnō ferre nōlō."

cellārius Salviō amphoram dēmōnstrāvit.

"nōnne vīnum est dōnum optimum, domine?" inquit cellārius.    20

"minimē!" respondit Salvius. "Cogidubnus multās amphorās habet, multumque vīnum. rēx vīnum ex Ītaliā cotīdiē importat."

tum Salvius, ubi statuam parvam cōnspexit, clāmāvit,

"euge! hanc statuam rēgī ferre possum. aurāta est statua. Quīntus rēgī dōnum argenteum ferre vult; ego tamen aurātum    25
dōnum ferre possum!"

"domine! nōn dēbēs," inquit cellārius.

"cūr nōn dēbeō?" rogāvit Salvius.

"Cogidubnus ipse tibi hanc statuam dedit!" inquit cellārius.

"hercle!" clāmāvit Salvius. "necesse est mihi istam urnam ad    30
aulam portāre."

| | | | |
|---|---|---|---|
| tripodes | *tripods* | cellārium: cellārius | *steward* |
| argenteī: argenteus | *made of silver* | urna | *jar, jug* |
| vestiēbant: vestīre | *dress* | importat: importāre | *import* |
| tulit: ferre | *bring* | aurāta | *gilded, gold-plated* |
| aulam: aula | *palace* | nōn dēbēs | *you shouldn't, mustn't* |
| arcā: arca | *strong-box, chest* | | |

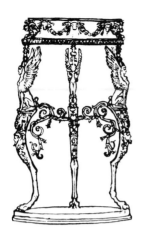
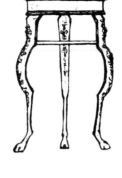

# About the Language

**1** In Stage 13, you met the present tense of **possum**, *I am able:*

Loquāx currere potest.          ego labōrāre nōn possum.
*Loquax is able to run.*          *I am not able to work.*

**2** You have now met **possum** in the imperfect tense:

Loquāx currere poterat.          ego labōrāre nōn poteram.
*Loquax was able to run.*          *I wasn't able to work.*
or                                      or
*Loquax could run.*                *I couldn't work.*

**3** The complete imperfect tense of **possum** is:

| | | |
|---|---|---|
| (ego) | poteram | *I was able (or I could)* |
| (tū) | poterās | *you* (singular) *were able* |
| | poterat | *s/he was able* |
| (nōs) | poterāmus | *we were able* |
| (vōs) | poterātis | *you* (plural) *were able* |
| | poterant | *they were able* |

**4** Further examples:

1 servī sōlem vidēre nōn poterant.
2 Bregāns amphoram portāre nōn poterat.
3 nōs labōrāre nōn poterāmus.
4 tū in urbe manēre nōn poterās.

# The Romans in Britain

The first Roman general to lead his soldiers into Britain was Julius Caesar, in 55 B.C. Britain was inhabited at the time by a number of different tribes each ruled by its own king or chieftain. Caesar wrote an account of his visit to Britain, in which he described the inhabitants as fierce warriors, living on good agricultural or pasture land, in a country rich in timber and minerals. Their skills included not only farming, but also making pottery and working with iron and bronze.

Caesar wanted to find out whether the wealth of Britain was worth the trouble of occupying it with Roman troops. But after another short visit in 54 B.C., he did not explore any further. His attention was needed for wars elsewhere, first in Gaul (modern France and Belgium) and then in a struggle against his own Roman government. Ten years later, he was assassinated.

Caesar's great-nephew Augustus became the first Roman emperor. He and his successors kept away from Britain for more than half a century. But in A.D. 43 the Emperor Claudius decided to invade. Perhaps he had received fresh information about British wealth; more probably he needed some military success for his own prestige. Claudius did not lead the invasion force himself, but he followed it, spending

**Gold denarius struck by the Emperor Claudius to commemorate his victory over the Britons. On one side is a portrait of Claudius; on the other he is shown on horseback between piles of trophies, above a triumphal arch.**

sixteen days in Britain, watching his army's assault on Colchester and giving official approval to the actions of his commander Aulus Plautius.

Eleven British kings surrendered after this campaign, and Britain was declared a Roman province, with Aulus Plautius as its first governor. This meant that the Romans were taking over the country as part of their empire. From then on, Roman officials would enforce Roman law and collect Roman taxes. Romans would be able to buy land in Britain and use it for agriculture or mining. And the Roman army would be present to keep the peace in the province, firmly and sometimes brutally.

Some British rulers, like King Cogidubnus in the south, chose to co-operate with the invaders and become allies and dependents of Rome. Others, such as Caratacus in the west, and Queen Boudica in the east, resisted the Romans bitterly but unsuccessfully. The Romans gradually pushed the frontier further north, to include the Midlands and Wales, then the northern kingdom of Brigantia.

**Bronze hand-mirror of Celtic craftsmanship, made in Roman Britain.**

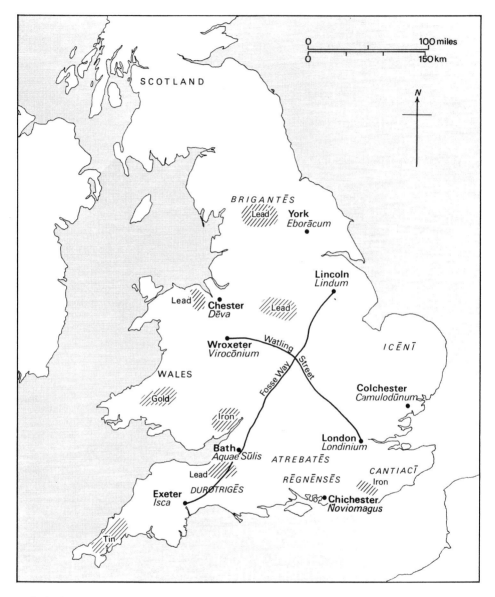

## Britain in the First Century A.D.

Showing main roads and towns, and the main tribal groupings. The map also shows the principal areas of mining at that time. Roman names are given in italics.

## Important Events and Dates

| Date | Emperor | Event |
|------|---------|-------|
| **B.C.** | | |
| 55, 54 | | Julius Caesar's expeditions to Britain |
| 44 | | *Assassination of Julius Caesar* |
| 27 | Augustus | |
| **A.D.** | | |
| 14 | Tiberius | |
| 37 | Gaius (Caligula) | |
| 41 | Claudius | |
| 43 | | Invasion of Britain under Aulus Plautius |
| | | Claudius enters Colchester in triumph |
| | | Vespasian's expedition against the Durotriges |
| | | Britain becomes a Roman province |
| 51 | | Defeat of Caratacus |
| 54 | Nero | |
| 61 | | Revolt of Boudica |
| 68–69 | Galba, Otho, Vitellius | Civil war in Rome: dispute over the succession of a new emperor |
| 69 | Vespasian | |
| 75 | | Fishbourne palace near Chichester is built |
| 78 | | Salvius becomes member of Arval Brotherhood |
| | | Agricola comes to Britain as governor |
| 79 | Titus | *Eruption of Vesuvius* |
| 81 | Domitian | Salvius goes to Britain |
| 83–84 | | Agricola's campaigns in Scotland |

The stories in Stages 13 and 14 are set in the time of Britain's most famous governor, Gnaeus Julius Agricola. Agricola stayed in the province for seven years (A.D. 78-84), longer than any other governor; he led his army into the Scottish highlands where he built a number of forts, some of which are still being discovered by aerial photography. But Agricola's purpose was not just military victory. His son-in-law, the historian Tacitus, says: "He wanted to accustom the Britons to a life of peace, by providing them with the comforts of civilization. He gave personal encouragement and official aid to the building of temples, forums, and houses . . . . He educated the sons of the chiefs . . . so that instead of hating the Latin language, they began to speak it well."

**Aerial view of a Roman road (Watling Street in England) still used by traffic today.**

Gradually, a network of roads spread across the province. One of the earliest, the Fosse Way, ran from Exeter to Lincoln (see the map on page 38) and may have marked the original "frontier" during the governorship of Aulus Plautius; it is still possible to walk or drive along stretches of it. Other roads (such as Watling Street, which is roughly followed by a modern highway) acted as links between the lowland areas of the southeast, where the Romans quickly gained control, and the hillier country in the north and west, where fighting continued on and off for many years and where the most important Roman forts were situated.

The roads were originally built for the use of Roman soldiers; but before long they were being extensively used by merchants as well. Trade between Britain and the European continent increased rapidly. Among the items exported from Britain in Roman times were three products mentioned in Stage 13: grain, hunting dogs, and iron from mines in the southeast. Gold, tin, and lead were also mined in Roman Britain. (Refer to the map on page 38 to locate the areas where these metals were mined.) In return, Britain imported many goods from Rome and the rest of the empire. Among them were olive oil and wine, carried in amphorae

**A model of the Temple of Claudius at Colchester in England.**

of the kind shown on pages 22–23. Romans who came to stay in Britain brought their own way of life with them; and many Britons, especially members of the leading families, wanted to imitate the manners of the invaders and to become as Roman as possible.

Some Britons became very wealthy from this trade and welcomed the Romans enthusiastically; others suffered severely from the arrival of the Romans; others again were hardly affected at all. Many of them no doubt had mixed feelings about becoming part of the Roman empire. It gave them a share in Roman prosperity and the Roman way of life; but it also meant Roman taxes and a Roman governor backed by Roman troops. However, whether welcome or unwelcome, the Romans were to remain in Britain for nearly four hundred years.

# Words and Phrases Checklist

| | |
|---|---|
| antīquus | *old, ancient* |
| apud | *among, at the house of* |
| argenteus | *made of silver* |
| attonitus | *astonished* |
| aula | *palace* |
| cotīdiē | *every day* |
| decōrus | *right, proper* |
| dēleō, dēlēre, dēlēvī | *destroy* |
| deus | *god* |
| dictō, dictāre, dictāvī | *dictate* |
| difficilis | *difficult* |
| dīligenter | *carefully* |
| domina | *lady (of the house), mistress* |
| dōnum | *present, gift* |
| familiāris: familiārem | *relative, relation* |
| fidēlis | *faithful, loyal* |
| ipse, ipsa | *himself, herself* |
| iste | *that* |
| lavō, lavāre, lāvī | *wash* |
| marītus | *husband* |
| necesse | *necessary* |
| nōbilis | *noble, of noble birth* |
| num? | *surely . . . not?* |
| pretiōsus | *expensive, precious* |
| quam | *how* |
| quamquam | *although* |
| -que | *and* |
| rēx: rēgem | *king* |
| sella | *chair* |
| ubi | *when* |

# Word Search

delete, diligence, fidelity, indecorous, lavatory, marital, regal

1 . . . . .: royal, kingly
2 . . . . .: to omit, cancel, or erase
3 . . . . .: loyalty
4 . . . . .: studious attention
5 . . . . .: pertaining to marriage
6 . . . . .: washroom
7 . . . . .: improper, inappropriate

# rēx
# Cogidubnus

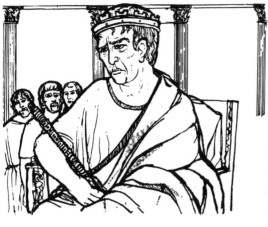

multī Britannī ad aulam
vēnērunt. senex, quī
scēptrum tenēbat, erat
rēx Cogidubnus.

fēmina prope
Cogidubnum sedēbat.
fēmina, quae diadēma
gerēbat, erat rēgīna.

multī Rōmānī Cogidubnō
rēs pretiōsās dabant.
dōnum, quod rēgem
maximē dēlectāvit, erat
equus.

duae ancillae ad rēgem
vēnērunt. vīnum, quod
ancillae ferēbant, erat in
paterā aureā. rēx vīnum
lībāvit.

servus agnum ad āram
dūxit. agnus, quem
servus dūcēbat, erat
victima.

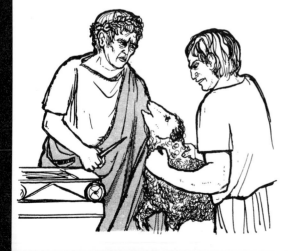

sacerdōs victimam
īnspexit. victima, quam
servus tenēbat, bālāvit.
sacerdōs victimam
interfēcit.

# ad aulam

Salvius et Quīntus ad aulam cum multīs servīs prōcēdēbant. agmen
erat splendidum. in prīmā parte decem servī ībant. hī servī erant
praecursōrēs; virgās longās tenēbant. in mediō agmine Salvius et
Quīntus equitābant. ancilla, quae post Salvium ambulābat, urnam
portābat. servus, quī post Quīntum ambulābat, tripodas portābat.      5
aliae ancillae flōrēs et unguentum ferēbant. vīgintī servī cum puellīs
ībant. agmen splendidum tōtam viam complēbat.

Britannī quoque multī ad aulam ībant. uxōrēs līberōsque sēcum
dūcēbant. magna turba erat in viā. tum Vārica, quī cum
praecursōribus equitābat, ad Salvium rediit.      10

"domine," inquit, "difficile est nōbīs prōcēdere, quod hī Britannī
viam complent. ē viā exīre nōlunt. quid facere dēbeō?"

Salvius īrātus eī dīxit,

"necesse est praecursōribus Britannōs ē viā ēmovēre. nōn
decōrum est Britannīs cīvēs Rōmānōs impedīre. ego quam      15
celerrimē īre volō, quod rēx nōs exspectat." 

Vārica, quī dominum īrātum timēbat, ad praecursōrēs rediit et
clāmāvit,

"asinī estis! virgās habētis. ēmovēte Britannōs!"

praecursōrēs statim virgās vibrābant. multī Britannī in fossās      20
dēsiluērunt, quod virgās timēbant. duo iuvenēs tamen impavidī in
viā cōnsistēbant. prope iuvenēs erat plaustrum, quod tōtam viam
claudēbat.

"cūr viam clauditis?" rogāvit Vārica. "necesse est dominō meō ad
aulam īre."      25

"nōs quoque ad aulam contendimus. rēgem vīsitāre volumus,"
respondērunt iuvenēs. "sed plaustrum movēre nōn possumus, quod
plaustrum rotam frāctam habet. amīcus noster, quem nōs
exspectāmus, aliam rotam quaerit. amīcum exspectāre dēbēmus."

Vārica anxius ad Salvium rediit, et eī rem nārrāvit.      30

"plaustrum, quod vidēs, domine, rotam frāctam habet. difficile
est nōbīs prōcēdere, quod hoc plaustrum tōtam viam claudit."

Salvius, quī nunc erat īrātior quam anteā, eum vituperāvit.

"num surdus es? caudex! nōn commodum est mihi in hōc locō
manēre. quam celerrimē prōcēdere volō."      35

Vārica, postquam ad plaustrum rediit, praecursōrēs vituperāvit.

"caudicēs!" clāmāvit. "ēmovēte hoc plaustrum! dēicite in fossam!"

praecursōrēs, postquam Vāricam audīvērunt, plaustrum in fossam dēiēcērunt. iuvenēs, quī erant attonitī, vehementer    40
resistēbant et cum praecursōribus pugnābant. tum praecursōrēs iuvenēs quoque in fossam dēiēcērunt. Salvius, quī rem spectābat, cachinnāns prōcessit.

"Britannī sunt molestissimī," inquit Salvius. "semper nōs
Rōmānōs vexant."    45

| agmen | procession |
| in prīmā parte | in the forefront |
| praecursōrēs: praecursor | forerunner (sent ahead of a procession to clear the way) |
| virgās: virga | rod, stick |
| equitābant: equitāre | ride |
| flōrēs: flōs | flower |
| unguentum | perfume |
| sēcum | with them |
| facere dēbeō | ought to do |
| ēmovēre | move, clear away |
| impedīre | delay, hinder |
| fossās: fossa | ditch |
| dēsiluērunt: dēsilīre | jump down |
| impavidī: impavidus | fearless |
| cōnsistēbant: cōnsistere | stand one's ground, stand firm |
| plaustrum | wagon, cart |
| claudēbat: claudere | block |
| movēre | move |
| rotam: rota | wheel |
| anteā | before |
| surdus | deaf |
| dēicite! | throw! |
| resistēbant: resistere | resist |
| cachinnāns | laughing, cackling |
| molestissimī: molestus | troublesome |

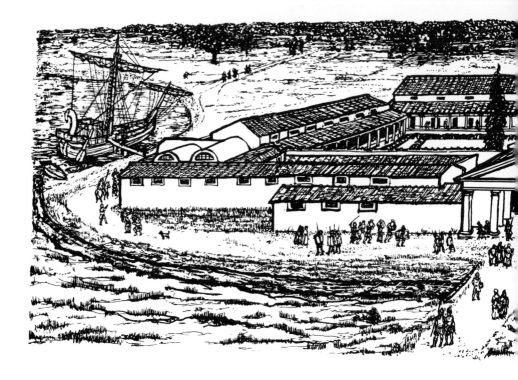

# caerimōnia

servus Salvium et Quīntum ad ātrium dūxit. illī, postquam ātrium
intrāvērunt, magnam turbam vīdērunt. multī prīncipēs Britannicī
in ātriō erant. sermōnēs inter sē habēbant. multae fēminae cum
prīncipibus sedēbant. aderant multī Rōmānī, quī prope prīncipēs
sedēbant. haec multitūdō, quae ātrium complēbat, magnum          5
clāmōrem faciēbat.

    Quīntus et Salvius ad medium ātrium contendērunt. ubi illūc
advēnērunt, lectum vīdērunt. in lectō erat effigiēs cērāta. Quīntus
effigiem agnōvit.

    "bona est effigiēs! imperātor Claudius est!" clāmāvit Quīntus.    10

    "ita vērō," respondit Salvius. "rēx Cogidubnus Claudium
quotannīs honōrat. fabrī, quī ex Ītaliā veniunt, effigiem quotannīs
faciunt. decōrum est Cogidubnō Claudium honōrāre. nam
Claudius erat imperātor, quī Cogidubnum rēgem fēcit."

    subitō turba, quae prope iānuam stābat, ad terram prōcubuit.    15
prīncipēs Britannicī, quī in mediō ātriō sedēbant, celeriter

surrēxērunt. etiam Rōmānī tacēbant.

"rēx adest," susurrāvit Salvius.

per iānuam intrāvit senex. parvus puer senem dūcēbat, quod claudicābat. rēx et puer lentē per turbam prōcēdēbant. rēx, 20 postquam ad effigiem advēnit, vīnum lībāvit. tum sacerdōtēs, quī prope effigiem stābant, victimās ad rēgem dūxērunt. Cogidubnus victimās dīligenter īnspexit. victima, quam rēx ēlēgit, erat agnus niveus. rēx eum sacrificāvit.

| | | | | |
|---|---|---|---|---|
| caerimōnia | *ceremony* | | honōrat: honōrāre | *honor* |
| illī | *they* | | fabrī: faber | *craftsman* |
| prīncipēs: prīnceps | *chief, chieftain* | | prōcubuit: prōcumbere | *fall* |
| sermōnēs: sermō | *conversation* | | claudicābat: claudicāre | *be lame, limp* |
| inter sē | *among themselves, with each other* | | vīnum lībāvit | *poured wine as an offering* |
| multitūdō | *crowd* | | sacerdōtēs: sacerdōs | *priest* |
| illūc | *there* | | victimās: victima | *victim* |
| effigiēs cērāta | *wax image* | | agnus | *lamb* |
| bona | *good* | | niveus | *snow-white* |
| imperātor | *emperor* | | sacrificāvit: sacrificāre | *sacrifice* |
| quotannīs | *every year* | | | |

Britannicī: Britannicus  *British*
Claudius  *Roman emperor, A.D. 41-54*

"decōrum est nōbīs Claudium honōrāre," inquit.          25

sacerdōtēs quoque victimās cēterās sacrificāvērunt. tum decem prīncipēs Britannicī lectum in umerōs sustulērunt. effigiem ex ātriō portāvērunt. post prīncipēs vēnērunt sacerdōtēs, quī sollemniter cantābant.

in āreā erat rogus. prīncipēs, quī effigiem portābant, ad rogum          30 cum magnā dignitāte prōcessērunt. effigiem in rogum posuērunt. servus rēgī facem trādidit. tum rēx facem in rogum posuit. mox flammae rogum cōnsūmēbant. flammae, quae effigiem iam tangēbant, cēram liquābant. omnēs effigiem intentē spectābant. subitō aquila ex effigiē ēvolāvit. omnēs spectātōrēs plausērunt.          35

"ecce!" clāmāvit rēx, "deī Claudium arcessunt. animus ad deōs ascendit."

| | | | | |
|---|---|---|---|---|
| umerōs: umerus | *shoulder* | liquābant: liquāre | *melt* |
| sustulērunt: tollere | *raise, lift up* | aquila | *eagle* |
| sollemniter cantābant | *were chanting solemnly* | ēvolāvit: ēvolāre | *fly out* |
| rogus | *pyre* | arcessunt: arcessere | *summon, send for* |
| cum magnā dignitāte | *with great dignity* | animus | *soul, spirit* |
| facem: fax | *torch* | ascendit: ascendere | *climb, rise* |
| tangēbant: tangere | *touch* | | |

# lūdī fūnebrēs

post caerimōniam rēx Cogidubnus pompam ad lītus dūxit. ibi
Britannī lūdōs fūnebrēs celebrāvērunt. aderant Rēgnēnsēs,
Cantiacī, et omnēs gentēs quae in amīcitiā cum Cogidubnō erant.

competītōrēs diū inter sē certābant. Cantiacī laetissimī erant,
quod semper vincēbant. vir Cantiacus celerius quam cēterī      5
cucurrit. pugil Cantiacus, quī rōbustissimus erat, cēterōs pugilēs
facile superāvit.

postrēmō erat certāmen nāvāle. nautae Cantiacī nāvem
caeruleam parābant, nautae Rēgnēnsēs nāvem croceam.
Dumnorix, prīnceps Rēgnēnsis, quī nāvī croceae praeerat,      10
gubernātor perītissimus erat. Belimicus, prīnceps Cantiacus, nāvī

| | | | |
|---|---|---|---|
| lūdī fūnebrēs | *funeral games* | vincēbant: vincere | *be victorious, win* |
| pompam: pompa | *procession* | celerius | *faster* |
| ad lītus | *to the seashore* | certāmen nāvāle | *boat-race* |
| gentēs: gēns | *tribe* | caeruleam | *blue* |
| amīcitiā: amīcitia | *friendship* | croceam | *yellow* |
| competītōrēs: competītor | *competitor* | gubernātor | *helmsman* |
| certābant: certāre | *compete* | | |

Rēgnēnsēs  *name of a tribe in southern Britain*

caeruleae praeerat. homō superbus et īnsolēns erat. nautae, postquam nāvēs parāvērunt, signum intentē exspectābant. subitō tuba sonuit. nāvēs statim prōsiluērunt; per undās ruēbant. rēmī undās vehementer pulsābant.                                                                15

spectātōrēs, quī in lītore stābant, magnōs clāmōrēs sustulērunt. Cantiacī clāmābant, "nōs Belimicō favēmus! Belimicus vincere potest! nautae nostrī sunt optimī!"

Rēgnēnsēs tamen Dumnorigī favēbant:

"nōs optimam nāvem habēmus! nōs optimum gubernātōrem   20
habēmus! gubernātor Cantiacus est stultior quam asinus!"

procul in marī erat saxum ingēns. hoc saxum erat mēta. nāvēs ad mētam ruēbant. nāvis Rēgnēnsis, quam Dumnorix dīrigēbat, iam prior erat. ā tergō Belimicus, gubernātor Cantiacus, nautās suōs vituperābat.                                                                              25

Dumnorix, ubi saxō appropinquāvit, nāvem subitō ad dextram vertit.

"ecce!" inquit Dumnorix. "perīculōsum est nōbīs prope saxum nāvigāre, quod scopulus sub undīs latet. necesse est nōbīs scopulum vītāre."                                                                          30

Belimicus tamen, quī scopulum ignōrābat, cursum rēctum tenēbat.

"comitēs," clāmāvit, "ecce! nōs vincere possumus, quod Dumnorix ad dextram abiit. hī Rēgnēnsēs sunt timidī; facile est nōbīs vincere, quod nōs sumus fortiōrēs."                                             35

nautae Cantiacī Belimicō crēdēbant. mox nāvem Rēgnēnsem superāvērunt et priōrēs ad mētam advēnērunt. Belimicus, quī scopulum nōn vīdit, Dumnorigem dērīdēbat. subitō nāvis Cantiaca in scopulum incurrit. nautae perterritī clāmāvērunt; aqua nāvem complēbat. Belimicus et Cantiacī nihil facere poterant; nāvis mox   40
summersa erat.

intereā Dumnorix, quī cum summā cūrā nāvigābat, circum mētam nāvem dīrēxit. nāvis ad lītus incolumis pervēnit. multī spectātōrēs Dumnorigem victōrem laudāvērunt. Rēgnēnsēs laetī, Cantiacī miserī erant. tum omnēs ad mare oculōs vertēbant. difficile   45
erat eīs nautās vidēre, quod in undīs natābant. omnēs tamen Belimicum vidēre poterant, quod in summō saxō sedēbat. madidus ad saxum haerēbat et auxilium postulābat.

| | | | |
|---|---|---|---|
| superbus | arrogant, proud | ignōrābat | did not know of |
| prōsiluērunt: prōsilīre | leap forward | cursum rēctum | a straight course |
| undās: unda | wave | comitēs: comes | comrade, companion |
| rēmī: rēmus | oar | timidī: timidus | fearful, frightened |
| in lītore | on the shore | dērīdēbat: dērīdēre | mock, make fun of |
| procul | far off | incurrit: incurrere | run onto, collide |
| in marī | in the sea | summersa | sunk |
| saxum | rock | intereā | meanwhile |
| mēta | turning point | cum summā cūrā | with the greatest care |
| dīrigēbat: dīrigere | steer | circum | around |
| prior | in front, first | incolumis | safe |
| ā tergō | behind, in the rear | oculōs: oculus | eye |
| ad dextram | to the right | eīs | for them |
| nāvigāre | sail | natābant: natāre | swim |
| scopulus | reef | in summō saxō | on the top of the rock |
| sub | under | madidus | soaked through |
| vītāre | avoid | haerēbat: haerēre | cling |

**Mosaic showing an underwater scene with sea-animals.**

# About the Language

1 Study the following pair of sentences:

ancilla urnam portābat.
*The slave-girl was carrying the jug.*

ancilla, **quae post Salvium ambulābat,** urnam portābat.
*The slave-girl, **who was walking behind Salvius,** was carrying the jug.*

The group of words in boldface is known as a *relative clause*.

2 A relative clause is used to describe a noun. For example:

Vārica, **quī cum praecursōribus equitābat,** ad Salvium rediit.
*Varica, **who was riding with the forerunners,** returned to Salvius.*

prope iuvenēs erat plaustrum, **quod tōtam viam claudēbat.**
*Near the young men was a wagon, **which was blocking the whole road.***

In the first example, the relative clause describes Varica; in the second, the relative clause describes the wagon.

3 Translate the following examples and pick out the relative clause in each sentence:

1 rēx, quī scēptrum tenēbat, in hortō sedēbat.
2 vīnum, quod Salvius bibēbat, erat optimum.
3 ancillae, quae dominum timēbant, ē vīllā festīnāvērunt.
4 Bregāns, quem Vārica quaerēbat, in horreō dormiēbat.
5 in viā erant multī Britannī, quī Rōmānōs impediēbant.
6 prope āram erat victima, quam rēx sacrificāvit.

In each example, find the noun which is being described by the relative clause.

# Practicing the Language

1 Complete each sentence with the right word or words from the list below and then translate. You will have to use some words more than once.

sum, es, est, sumus, estis, sunt

1 vīlicus . . . . . anxius; nam Salvius . . . . . īrātus.

---

2 vōs agnum sacrificātis quod vōs . . . . . sacerdōtēs.
3 prīncipēs in aulā . . . . . , ubi rēgem exspectant.
4 ego . . . . . dominus; decōrum . . . . . mihi celeriter prōcēdere.
5 nōs nōn . . . . . ignāvī; in fundō dīligenter labōrāmus.
6 tū servōs īnspicis quod tū . . . . . vīlicus.

**2** Complete each sentence with the right word and then translate.

1 parvus puer . . . . . ad effigiem dūxit. (Cogidubnum, Cogidubnō)
2 ubi sacerdōtēs erant parātī, servī vīnum . . . . . dedērunt. (rēgem, rēgī)
3 Cogidubnus, quī prope effigiem stābat, . . . . . ēlēgit. (victimam, victimae)
4 Dumnorix nāvem . . . . . ostendit. (amīcōs, amīcīs)
5 facile erat . . . . . Belimicum vidēre, quod ad saxum haerēbat. (spectātōrēs, spectātōribus)
6 post certāmen nāvāle, rēx . . . . . ad aulam invītāvit. (nautās, nautīs)

# About the Language

**1** In Unit 1, you met the question-word **num?** which is used to suggest that the answer to the question will be *no*. Notice again the different ways of translating it:

num tū servus es?      *Surely you're not a slave?*
                              *You're not a slave, are you?*

num fūr effūgit?      *Surely the thief didn't escape?*
                              *The thief didn't escape, did he?*

**2** From Stage 13 onwards, you have met the question-word **nōnne?** which is used to suggest that the answer will be *yes*. Notice the different ways of translating it:

nōnne vīnum est dōnum      *Surely wine is a very good present?*
optimum?                     *Wine is a very good present, isn't it?*

nōnne tū Rōmānus es?      *Surely you are a Roman?*
                              *You are a Roman, aren't you?*

nōnne Cogidubnus in aulā      *Surely Cogidubnus lives in a palace?*
habitat?                     *Cogidubnus lives in a palace, doesn't he?*

**3** Further examples:

1  nōnne haec pictūra est pulchra?
2  num perterritus es?
3  num Bregāns labōrat?
4  nōnne Bregāns in culīnā dormit?
5  nōnne rēx tibi illum canem dedit?

# Cogidubnus, King of the Regnenses

To Neptune and Minerva, for the welfare of the Divine House, by the authority of Tiberius Claudius Cogidubnus, great king of the Britons, the Association of Craftsmen, and those in it gave this temple from their own resources. . . . ens, son of Pudentinus, presented the forecourt.

A slab of stone inscribed with these Latin words was discovered in Chichester not far from the coast of southern Britain, in 1723. When found, the slab was broken, but as soon as the pieces had been fitted together, it was clear that this was the dedication stone of a temple built at the request of Cogidubnus in honor of Neptune, god of the sea, and Minerva, goddess of wisdom and craftsmanship. The elegant lettering, carved in the style of the first century A.D., suggested the work of Roman craftsmen. Roman dedication stones are rather like the foundation stones which are laid nowadays when an important public building, such as a church, library, or school, is being erected. They state the name of the person or group of people who gave the site and paid for the building.

This particular temple was paid for by the local **collēgium** or *association of craftsmen.*

The inscription also helps us to construct the life-story of Cogidubnus himself, although many details remain unknown. He was probably a member of the family that ruled the Atrebates, a tribe in southern Britain. After the Roman invasion in A.D. 43 the Romans appointed him king of this tribe and the tribe was renamed the Regnenses. Cogidubnus was a faithful supporter of the Romans, and the kingship may have been a reward from the Emperor Claudius for helping them at the time of the invasion.

Cogidubnus was granted the privilege of Roman citizenship and allowed to add the emperor's names to his own. He became a "client king," which meant that he ruled on behalf of the emperor and that he was responsible for collecting taxes and keeping the peace in his part of Britain. In this way he played an important part in keeping the southern region loyal to Rome, while the legions advanced to conquer the tribes in the north.

**Aerial view of Chichester (ancient Noviomagus) showing the traditional crossroads pattern of a Roman town.**

By dedicating the new temple to Neptune and Minerva rather than British gods, Cogidubnus publicly declared his loyalty to Rome. The temple was a sign and reminder of Roman power. Its priests may well have been selected from the local British chieftains, many of whom were quick to see the advantages of supporting the new government. And when the inscription goes on to say that the temple was intended "for the welfare of the Divine House," Cogidubnus is suggesting that the emperor himself is related to the gods and should be worshiped. The Romans encouraged the people of their empire to respect and worship the emperor in this way, because it helped to build up a sense of unity in a large empire that contained many tribes, languages and religions.

The Regnenses received not only a new king, but also a new capital town, Noviomagus. It was founded near the south coast, where Chichester now stands. Three miles (five kilometers) to the west is the modern village of Fishbourne, where the remains of a large Roman building were found in 1960 by a workman digging a trench for a new water main. During the eight years of excavation that followed, the archaeologists discovered that this was no ordinary country house. It was a palace as large and splendid as the fashionable houses in Rome itself, with one set of rooms after another, arranged around a huge courtyard. No inscription has been found to reveal the owner's name, but the palace was so large, so magnificent, and so near to Noviomagus that Cogidubnus seems the likeliest person.

The palace, however, was not the first building erected on the site. Underneath it the remains of earlier wooden buildings were found, and these go back to the time of the Roman invasion or very shortly afterwards. One of them was a granary. Pieces of metal and a helmet were also found nearby. These discoveries indicate the presence of soldiers; they may have been soldiers of the Second Legion, commanded by Vespasian, a brilliant young general who led the attack against the Durotriges in the southwest. There was a harbor nearby, where Roman supply ships tied up. It is therefore likely that the Romans first used Fishbourne as a military port and depot where Vespasian assembled his troops.

In A.D. 69, Vespasian himself became emperor. A few years later, work began on the building of the Fishbourne palace. Perhaps Vespasian was remembering the loyalty of Cogidubnus and was now presenting him with the palace in return for his long-standing support of the Romans.

# Words and Phrases Checklist

| | |
|---|---|
| agmen | *column (of people), procession* |
| alius | *other, another* |
| aqua | *water* |
| claudō, claudere, clausī | *shut, block* |
| commodus | *convenient* |
| dēbeō, dēbēre, dēbuī | *owe, ought* |
| effigiēs: effigiem | *image, statue* |
| equus | *horse* |
| etiam | *even* |
| fossa | *ditch* |
| frāctus | *broken* |
| honōrō, honōrāre, honōrāvī | *honor* |
| impediō, impedīre, impedīvī | *delay, hinder* |
| lectus | *couch* |
| lentē | *slowly* |
| lītus | *seashore* |
| miser | *miserable, wretched* |
| nauta | *sailor* |
| plaustrum | *wagon, cart* |
| praesum, praeesse, praefuī | *be in charge of* |
| prīnceps: prīncipem | *chief, chieftain* |
| prior | *first, in front* |
| quī | *who* |
| redeō, redīre, rediī | *return, go back* |
| sacerdōs: sacerdōtem | *priest* |
| saxum | *rock* |
| teneō, tenēre, tenuī | *hold* (also in other contexts: *own*) |
| unda | *wave* |
| victor: victōrem | *winner* |
| vincō, vincere, vīcī | *win* |

# Word Search

alien, debt, equine, fracture, impede, principal, undulate

1 . . . . .: foreign, strange, or unfamiliar
2 . . . . .: to obstruct
3 . . . . .: most important, first
4 . . . . .: something owed; an obligation
5 . . . . .: to billow
6 . . . . .: a break
7 . . . . .: pertaining to horses

**Reconstruction of a Roman dinner table with fruit, shellfish, wine, and nuts.**

# Stage 16

# in aulā

Cogidubnus Quīntum per aulam dūcēbat. in aulā erant multae pictūrae, quās pictor Graecus pīnxerat.

rēx iuvenem in hortum dūxit. in hortō erant multī flōrēs, quōs Cogidubnus ex Ītaliā importāverat.

tum ad ātrium vēnērunt. in mediō ātriō erat fōns marmoreus, quī aquam effundēbat.

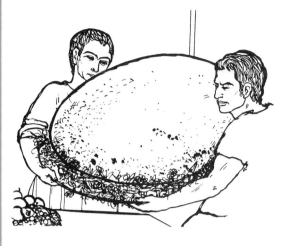

rēx et hospitēs in aulā
cēnābant. cēna, quam
coquī Graecī parāverant,
optima erat. servī
magnun ōvum in mēnsam
posuērunt.

ex ōvō, quod servī in
mēnsam posuerant,
appāruit saltātrīx.

tum pūmiliōnēs, quōs rēx
in Ītaliā ēmerat,
intrāvērunt. pūmiliōnēs
pīlās iactābant.

# Belimicus ultor

Belimicus, prīnceps Cantiacus, postquam Dumnorix in certāmine
nāvālī vīcit, rem graviter ferēbat. īrātissimus erat. omnēs hospitēs,
quōs rēx ad aulam invītāverat, eum dērīdēbant. Cantiacī quoque
eum dērīdēbant et vituperābant. etiam servī, quī dē naufragiō
cognōverant, clam rīdēbant.                                                    5
   "iste Dumnorix mē dēcēpit," Belimicus sibi dīxit. "mē in
scopulum impulit et praemium iniūstē cēpit. decōrum est mihi eum
pūnīre."
   Belimicus sēcum cōgitāvit et cōnsilium callidum cēpit. erant in
aulā multae bēstiae, quās rēx ē multīs terrīs importāverat. inter hās    10
bēstiās erat ursa ingēns, quam servus Germānicus custōdiēbat.
Belimicus ad hunc servum adiit.
   "hoc animal est magnificum," inquit. "mē valdē dēlectat. ursam
tractāre volō; eam nōn timeō."
   itaque prīnceps ad ursam cotīdiē veniēbat; ursae cibum et aquam     15
dabat. paulātim ursam mānsuētam fēcit. tandem sōlus ursam
tractāre potuit.
   mox Cogidubnus cēnam et spectāculum nūntiāvit. amīcōs ad
aulam invītāvit. Belimicus statim ad servum Germānicum
contendit, et eī dīxit,                                                    20
   "rēx hodiē spectāculum dat. hodiē hanc ursam in aulam dūcere
volō. nunc eam tractāre possum. hospitibus eam ostendere volō."
   servus invītus cōnsēnsit. Belimicus cachinnāns sibi dīxit,
   "parātus sum. nunc Dumnorigem pūnīre possum."

| | | | |
|---|---|---|---|
| ultor | *avenger* | iniūstē | *unfairly* |
| graviter ferēbat | *took badly* | sēcum | *to himself* |
| dē naufragiō | *about the shipwreck* | ursa | *bear* |
| cognōverant: cognōscere | *find out, get to know* | adiit: adīre | *approach, go up to* |
| clam | *secretly, in private* | tractāre | *handle* |
| impulit: impellere | *push, force* | paulātim | *gradually* |
| praemium | *prize* | mānsuētam | *tame* |

Germānicus *German*

**Opposite: Mosaic border from Fishbourne showing a bird, which probably
served as the mosaicist's signature, or "trademark."**

**Reconstruction of a mosaic from Woodchester (in the west of England), depicting Orpheus taming the wild animals.**

# rēx spectāculum dat

rēx cum multīs hospitibus in aulā cēnābat. Salvius et Quīntus prope rēgem recumbēbant. Britannī cibum laudābant, Rōmānī vīnum. omnēs hospitēs rēgī grātiās agēbant.

subitō Belimicus tardus intrāvit.

"ecce! naufragus noster intrat," clāmāvit Dumnorix. "num tū aliam nāvem āmīsistī?" 5

cēterī Belimicum dērīsērunt et Dumnorigī plausērunt. Belimicus tamen Dumnorigī nihil respondit, sed tacitus cōnsēdit.

rēx hospitibus suīs spectāculum nūntiāvit. statim pūmiliōnēs cum saltātrīcibus intrāvērunt et hospitēs dēlectāvērunt. deinde, ubi 10 rēx eīs signum dedit, omnēs exiērunt. Salvius, quem pūmiliōnēs nōn dēlectāverant, clāmāvit,

"haec cēna est bona. numquam cēnam meliōrem cōnsūmpsī. sed ursam, quae saltat, vidēre volō. illa ursa mē multō magis dēlectat quam pūmiliōnēs et saltātrīcēs." 15

rēx servīs signum dedit. servus Germānicus, quī hoc signum exspectābat, statim cum ursā intrāvit et hospitibus eam ostendit.

Belimicus, simulatque hoc vīdit, surrēxit, et ad medium triclīnium prōcessit.

"mī Dumnorix!" clāmāvit. "facile est tibi iocōs facere. sed ursam 20 tractāre nōn audēs! ego nōn timeō. ego, quem tū dērīdēs, ursam tractāre audeō."

omnēs Belimicum spectābant attonitī. Belimicus, quī servum iam dīmīserat, ursam ad Dumnorigem dūxit.

"nōnne tū quoque ursam tractāre vīs?" rogāvit īnsolēns. "nōnne 25 tū hospitibus spectāculum dare vīs?"

Dumnorix impavidus statim surrēxit et Belimicum dērīsit,

"facile est mihi hanc ursam superāre. tē quoque, homuncule, superāre possum."

tum cēterī, quī anteā timuerant, valdē cachinnāvērunt. 30 Belimicus, ubi cachinnōs audīvit, furēns ursam pulsāvit, et eam ad Dumnorigem impulit. subitō ursa saeva sē vertit, et Belimicum ferōciter percussit. tum prīncipēs perterritī clāmōrem magnum sustulērunt et ad iānuās quam celerrimē cucurrērunt. etiam inter sē pugnābant, quod exīre nōn poterant. ursa, quam hic clāmor 35 terruerat, ad lectum cucurrit, ubi rēx sedēbat.

rēx tamen, quod claudicābat, effugere nōn poterat. Dumnorix in ursam frūstrā sē coniēcit. Salvius immōtus stābat. sed Quīntus hastam, quam servus Germānicus tenēbat, rapuit. hastam celeriter ēmīsit et bēstiam saevam trānsfīxit. illa dēcidit mortua.

40

| | |
|---|---|
| tardus | *late* |
| naufragus | *shipwrecked sailor* |
| tacitus | *silent, in silence* |
| cōnsēdit: cōnsīdere | *sit down* |
| pūmiliōnēs: pūmiliō | *dwarf* |
| cum saltātrīcibus | *with dancing-girls* |
| saltat: saltāre | *dance* |
| multō magis | *much more* |
| iocōs: iocus | *joke* |
| audēs: audēre | *dare* |
| homuncule: homunculus | *little man* |
| cachinnāvērunt: cachinnāre | *roar with laughter* |
| cachinnōs: cachinnus | *laughter* |
| furēns | *furious, in a rage* |
| saeva | *savage* |
| sē vertit: sē vertere | *turn around* |
| coniēcit: conicere | *hurl, throw* |
| immōtus | *still, motionless* |
| hastam: hasta | *spear* |

**Small bronze figure of a bear.**

# Quīntus dē sē

postrīdiē Quīntus per hortum cum rēge ambulābat, flōrēsque variōs spectābat. deinde rēx eum rogāvit,

"quō modō ex urbe Pompēiīs effūgistī? paterne et māter superfuērunt?"

"periit pater," inquit Quīntus trīstis. "māter quoque in urbe 5 periit. ego et ūnus servus superfuimus. ad urbem Neāpolim vix effūgimus. ibi servum, quī tam fortis et tam fidēlis fuerat, līberāvī."

"quid deinde fēcistī?" inquit rēx. "pecūniam habēbās?"

"omnēs vīllās, quās pater in Campāniā possēderat, vēndidī. ita multam pecūniam comparāvī. tum ex Ītaliā discēdere voluī, quod 10 trīstissimus eram. ego igitur et lībertus meus nāvem cōnscendimus.

prīmō ad Graeciam vēnimus et in urbe Athēnīs paulīsper habitābāmus. haec urbs erat pulcherrima, sed cīvēs turbulentī. multī philosophī, quī forum cotīdiē frequentābant, contrōversiās inter sē habēbant. 15

post paucōs mēnsēs, aliās urbēs vidēre voluimus. ad Aegyptum igitur nāvigāvimus, et mox ad urbem Alexandrīam advēnimus."

**Roman marketplace in Athens, with the Tower of the Winds (depicting in relief the eight winds).**

| variōs: varius | *different* | comparāvī: comparāre | *obtain* |
| quō modō | *how* | cōnscendimus: cōnscendere | *embark on,* |
| superfuērunt: superesse | *survive* | | *go on board* |
| vix | *with difficulty* | prīmō | *first* |
| tam | *so* | frequentābant: frequentāre | *crowd, fill* |
| fuerat | *had been* | mēnsēs: mēnsis | *month* |
| possēderat: possidēre | *possess* | | |

| Neāpolim: Neāpolis | *Naples* |
| Campāniā: Campānia | *district on west coast of central Italy, surrounding Pompeii* |
| Athēnīs: Athēnae | *Athens* |
| Aegyptum: Aegyptus | *Egypt* |
| Alexandrīam: Alexandrīa | *Alexandria, a major port-city of Egypt and a commercial center of the Roman empire* |

1 Where did the king have this conversation with Quintus?
2 Who escaped with Quintus to Naples?
3 How did Quintus raise money after the eruption of Vesuvius?
4 Why did he want to leave Italy?
5 Where did he go first? What did he see in the forum there?
6 Where did he go next? How did he travel? Was the journey long or short?

# About the Language

1 In this Stage, you have met examples of the *pluperfect* tense. They looked like this:

in aulā erat ursa ingēns, quam rēx in Ītaliā **ēmerat**.
*In the palace was a huge bear, which the king had bought in Italy.*

hospitēs, quī ad caerimōniam **vēnerant**, plausērunt.
*The guests who had come to the ceremony applauded.*

2 The complete pluperfect tense is as follows:

| portāveram | *I had carried* |
| portāverās | *you* (singular) *had carried* |
| portāverat | *s/he had carried* |
| portāverāmus | *we had carried* |
| portāverātis | *you* (plural) *had carried* |
| portāverant | *they had carried* |

**3**  Further examples:

1 Rūfilla ancillās, quae cubiculum parāverant, laudāvit.
2 in ātriō sedēbant hospitēs, quōs rēx ad aulam invītāverat.
3 nōs fessī erāmus, quod per tōtum diem labōrāverāmus.
4 Belimicus, quī nāvem āmīserat, īrātissimus erat.
5 Salvius mē pūnīvit, quod ē vīllā fūgeram.

**4**  Study the differences between the present, perfect, and pluperfect tenses:

| PRESENT | PERFECT | PLUPERFECT |
|---|---|---|
| portat | portāvit | portāverat |
| *s/he carries* | *s/he carried* | *s/he had carried* |
| audiunt | audīvērunt | audīverant |
| *they hear* | *they heard* | *they had heard* |
| dīcit | dīxit | dīxerat |
| scrībit | scrīpsit | scrīpserat |
| ambulant | ambulāvērunt | ambulāverant |
| docent | docuērunt | docuerant |

# Practicing the Language

**1**  Complete each sentence with the right word from those given below, and then translate. You will have to use some words more than once.

| NOMINATIVE | Rōmānī | Britannī |
|---|---|---|
| DATIVE | Rōmānīs | Britannīs |

1 Rōmānī et Britannī ad aulam vēnerant. Cogidubnus Rōmānīs et . . . . . cēnam splendidam dabat.
2 rēx Rōmānīs favēbat. multī . . . . . prope rēgem sedēbant. rēx . . . . . vīnum optimum obtulit.
3 rēx . . . . . nōn favēbat. Cogidubnus Britannīs vīnum pessimum obtulit.
4 multī . . . . . erant īrātī. mox Britannī et . . . . . inter sē pugnābant.

obtulit: offerre *offer*

---

**2** Translate into English:

# Cogidubnus et Vespasiānus

Cogidubnus Quīntō dē vītā suā nārrābat:
    "ubi Rōmānī in Britanniam invāsērunt, Claudius legiōnem secundam contrā Durotrigēs mīsit. Vespasiānus, quī hanc legiōnem dūcēbat, ad mē vēnit et auxilium rogāvit. ego Vespasiānō auxilium dedī. Rōmānīs frūmentum comparāvī. Rōmānīs explōrātōrēs dedī.   5
hī explōrātōrēs Rōmānōs celeriter dūxērunt ad regiōnem, ubi Durotrigēs habitābant. Durotrigēs diū resistēbant sed Rōmānī tandem victōrēs erant. Vespasiānus ad mē ita scrīpsit:
    'Durotrigēs fortiter pugnāvērunt, sed nōs eōs tandem superāvimus. multōs Durotrigēs necāvimus; multās fēminās   10
līberōsque cēpimus; multōs vīcōs incendimus. nōs Rōmānī fortiōrēs erāmus quam barbarī. facile erat nōbīs eōs superāre.'
    post multōs annōs Rōmānī Vespasiānum imperātōrem fēcērunt. Vespasiānus, quī mihi amīcus fidēlissimus erat, mē honōrāvit. hanc epistulam ad mē mīsit:   15
    'tē honōrāre volō, quod mihi auxilium ōlim dedistī. decōrum est tibi in aulā habitāre. architectum igitur ex Graeciā arcessīvī, et fabrōs Ītalicōs comparāvī. eōs ad tē mīsī.'
    architectus et fabrī, quōs Vespasiānus mīsit, callidissimī erant. dīligenter labōrāvērunt et hanc aulam aedificāvērunt. ita   20
Vespasiānus mihi benignitātem summam ostendit."

| | |
|---|---|
| invāsērunt: invādere | *invade* |
| legiōnem: legiō | *legion* |
| contrā | *against* |
| explōrātōrēs: explōrātor | *scout, spy* |
| regiōnem: regiō | *region* |
| cēpimus: capere | *take, capture* |
| vīcōs: vīcus | *village* |
| incendimus: incendere | *burn, set fire to* |
| annōs: annus | *year* |
| benignitātem: benignitās | *kindness* |

| | |
|---|---|
| Vespasiānus | *Roman general in British campaigns, A.D. 43; later emperor (A.D. 69–79)* |
| Durotrigēs | *name of a tribe in southwestern Britain* |
| Ītalicōs : Ītalicus | *Italian* |

# About the Language

1 In Stage 13, you met several sentences containing the *infinitive* of the verb. For example:

Salvius fundum **inspicere** vult.   *Salvius wants to inspect the farm.*
geminī **labōrāre** nōn possunt.   *The twins aren't able to work.*
                              or   *The twins can't work.*

2 You have now met several other examples of sentences containing infinitives:

facile est nōbīs effigiem **portāre.**   *It is easy for us to carry the image.*
commodum est mihi hīc **manēre.**   *It is convenient for me to remain here.*
ad aulam **revenīre** dēbeō.   *I ought to return to the palace.*
                              or   *I must return to the palace.*

3 Further examples:

1 difficile est Cogidubnō festīnāre, quod senex est.
2 spectāculum vidēre nōlumus.
3 necesse est nōbīs fugere.
4 pecūniam reddere dēbēs.
5 Salvius est dominus; decōrum est Salviō servōs pūnīre.
6 perīculōsum est tibi in aulā manēre.
7 victimam sacrificāre vīs?
8 vōs pugnāre nōn audētis!

# The Palace at Fishbourne

When the Roman soldiers moved on from Fishbourne, they left behind them a few buildings, some roads, and a harbor. During the next thirty years many improvements were made. The roads were resurfaced, the drainage improved (it was a low-lying, rather marshy site) and the harbor developed. Merchant ships arrived regularly. A guest house was begun and a fine new villa with a set of baths was built in the late sixties. This could have been a residence built by Cogidubnus for himself on the outskirts of his new capital town.

But in about A.D. 75 everything changed. A vast area was cleared and leveled, and the villa and baths became part of the southeast corner of a huge new building. It was laid out in four long wings around a central garden. The entrance hall was situated in the middle of the east wing, and in the center of the west wing stood the audience chamber where the king received his subjects and interviewed officials.

Specialist craftsmen were brought in from Italy: makers of mosaics, marble-workers, plasterers to make stucco friezes, painters, carpenters, iron-smiths, hydraulic engineers to construct the fountains, and many others. Most of the floors were covered with mosaics, mainly geometric patterns in black and white (see the example on page 61). The walls were painted, like the walls of houses in Pompeii, with richly colored garden scenes and architectural designs. Some walls were even lined with marble. Many traces of the activity of the craftsmen have been found. The floor of the area used by the stonemasons was littered with fragments of marble and colored stone which had been imported from quarries in Italy, the Greek island of Scyros, Asia Minor, and elsewhere. In another area were signs of iron-working where the smiths had manufactured door-hinges, handles, and bolts. The craftsmen and the materials were brought in from outside, but all the construction and detailed manufacture was carried out on the site itself, where the builders lived and worked for many years.

The open area, which measured approximately 100 by 80 yards (90 by 70 meters), was laid out as a garden. A broad path, 40 feet (12 meters)

**A model of the palace at Fishbourne as it was in A.D. 75.**

wide and surfaced probably with gravel ran through the middle of it, leading from the reception hall to the audience chamber. On either side of the path were lawns, not rolled and mown like a modern lawn, but nevertheless with the grass kept short and neat. Paths ran around the outside of the lawns, and along the edges of the paths were beds for shrubs and flowers. The gardeners cut deep bedding trenches in the soil, and filled them with a mixture of loam and crushed chalk.

A line of holes across the eastern side of the garden shows where wooden poles stood to support a trellis for climbing plants. These may have been rambler roses: the Romans were fond of roses and good at growing them. The writer Pliny the Elder advised his readers to manure rosebushes with kitchen garbage and to see that the roots were embedded in it.

A system of underground pipes brought water to the fountains which stood at intervals along the paths. Small marble and bronze statues were placed here and there to provide further decoration.

So the garden, like the palace, was planned, laid out and decorated in the most fashionable Italian style. Whether the owner was Cogidubnus or somebody else, he wished his palace in Britain to be as Roman as possible.

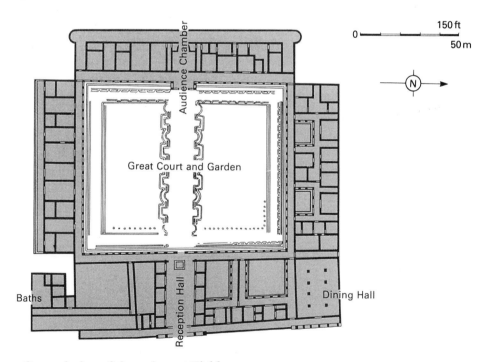

**Ground plan of the palace at Fishbourne.**

# Words and Phrases Checklist

| | |
|---|---|
| aedificō, aedificāre, aedificāvī | *build* |
| auxilium | *help* |
| bonus | *good* |
| cōnsentiō, cōnsentīre, cōnsēnsī | *agree* |
| cōnsilium | *plan, idea* |
| deinde | *then* |
| dēlectō, dēlectāre, dēlectāvī | *delight* |
| dērīdeō, dērīdēre, dērīsī | *mock, make fun of* |
| dīmittō, dīmittere, dīmīsī | *send away, dismiss* |
| effugiō, effugere, effūgī | *escape* |
| faber | *craftsman* |
| flōs: flōrem | *flower* |
| frūmentum | *grain* |
| imperātor: imperātōrem | *emperor* |
| inter | *among* |
| ita | *in this way* |
| melior | *better* |
| nāvigō, nāvigāre, nāvigāvī | *sail* |
| nōnne? | *surely?* |
| parātus | *ready, prepared* |
| pereō, perīre, periī | *die, perish* |
| pōnō, pōnere, posuī | *place, put* |
| postrīdiē | *(on) the next day* |
| pūniō, pūnīre, pūnīvī | *punish* |
| saltō, saltāre, saltāvī | *dance* |
| simulac, simulatque | *as soon as* |
| summus | *highest, greatest, top* |
| supersum, superesse, superfuī | *survive* |
| tollō, tollere, sustulī | *raise, lift up* |
| vertō, vertere, vertī | *turn* |

# Word Search

ameliorate, auxiliary, consensus, delectable, deride, impunity, summit

1 . . . . .: highest point
2 . . . . .: exemption from penalty
3 . . . . .: collective opinion, general agreement
4 . . . . .: to ridicule, scoff at
5 . . . . .: enjoyable, pleasing
6 . . . . .: supporting; additional
7 . . . . .: to improve, make better

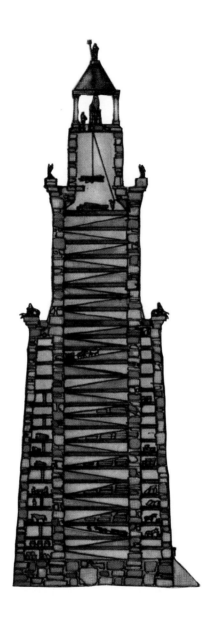

One possible reconstruction of the Pharos lighthouse at Alexandria. This cross section shows the spiral pathway by which animals were led up and down, carrying fuel for the fire at the top. A different reconstruction can be seen in the illustration opposite. The coin pictured on p. 133 shows an ancient depiction of the Pharos.

# Alexandrīa

# Quīntus dē Alexandrīā

Alexandrīa magnum portum habet. prope portum est īnsula. facile est nāvibus ad portum pervenīre, quod in hāc īnsulā est pharus ingēns. multae nāvēs in portū Alexandrīae stāre possunt.

īnsula *island*      pharus *lighthouse*      stāre *lie at anchor*

Alexandrīa est urbs turbulenta. ingēns turba semper urbem complet. multī mercātōrēs per viās ambulant. multī servī per urbem currunt. multī mīlitēs per viās urbis incēdunt. mīlitēs Rōmānī urbem custōdiunt.

incēdunt: incēdere *march*

ego et Clēmēns, postquam ad urbem pervēnimus, templum vīdimus. ad
hoc templum, quod Augustus Caesar aedificāverat, festīnāvimus. prō
templō Caesaris erat āra. ego vīnum in āram fūdī.

prō templō *in front of the temple*    Augustus Caesar *first Roman emperor,*
fūdī: fundere *pour*                    *27 B.C.-A.D. 14*

prope hanc urbem habitābat Barbillus, vir dīves. Barbillus negōtium
cum patre meō saepe agēbat. vīllam splendidam habēbat. ad vīllam
Barbillī mox pervēnī. facile erat mihi vīllam invenīre, quod Barbillus
erat vir nōtissimus.

Barbillus multōs servōs habēbat, ego nūllōs. "decōrum est tibi servum Aegyptium habēre," inquit Barbillus. inter servōs Barbillī erat puer Aegyptius. Barbillus, vir benignus, mihi hunc puerum dedit.

**Wall painting of a harbor scene.**

When you have read this story, answer the questions at the end.

# tumultus

in vīllā Barbillī diū habitābam. ad urbem cum servō quondam
contendī, quod Clēmentem vīsitāre volēbam. ille tabernam prope
portum Alexandrīae tenēbat. servus, quī mē dūcēbat, erat puer
Aegyptius.

in urbe erat ingēns multitūdō, quae viās complēbat. mercātōrēs    5

tumultus *riot*                  ille          *he*
quondam *one day, once*          tenēbat: tenēre *own*

per viās ambulābant et negōtium inter sē agēbant. fēminae et ancillae tabernās frequentābant; tabernāriī fēminīs et ancillīs stolās ostendēbant. plūrimī servī per viās urbis currēbant. difficile erat nōbīs per viās ambulāre, quod maxima erat multitūdō. tandem ad portum Alexandrīae pervēnimus, sed ibi nūllōs Graecōs vidēre   10
poterāmus. puer, postquam hoc sēnsit, anxius dīxit,

"melius est nōbīs ad vīllam Barbillī revenīre. ad tabernam Clēmentis īre nōn possumus. viae sunt perīculōsae, quod Aegyptiī īrātī sunt. omnēs Graecī ex hāc parte urbis fūgērunt."

"minimē!" puerō respondī. "quamquam Aegyptiī sunt īrātī, ad   15
vīllam redīre nōlō. longum iter iam fēcimus. paene ad tabernam Clēmentis pervēnimus. necesse est nōbīs cautē prōcēdere."

itaque ad tabernam Clēmentis contendimus, sed in triviīs magna multitūdō nōbīs obstābat. ego anxius hanc multitūdinem spectāvī. in multitūdine Aegyptiōrum erat senex, quī Graecōs Rōmānōsque   20
vituperābat. omnēs eum intentī audiēbant.

ubi hoc vīdī, sollicitus eram. puer Aegyptius, quī sollicitūdinem meam sēnserat, mē ad casam proximam dūxit.

"domine, in hāc casā habitat faber, quī Barbillum bene nōvit. necesse est nōbīs casam intrāre et perīculum vītāre."   25

faber per fenestram casae forte spectābat. ubi puerum agnōvit, nōs in casam suam libenter accēpit.

postquam casam intrāvimus, susurrāvī,

"quis est hic faber?"

"est Diogenēs, faber Graecus," respondit puer.   30

ubi hoc audīvī, magis timēbam, nam in casā virī Graecī eram; extrā iānuam casae Aegyptiī Graecōs vituperābant. subitō servus clāmāvit,

"ēheu! Aegyptiī īnfestī casam oppugnant."

Diogenēs statim ad armārium contendit. in armāriō erant   35
quīnque fūstēs, quōs Diogenēs extrāxit et nōbīs trādidit.

Aegyptiī iānuam effrēgērunt et in casam irrūpērunt. nōs Aegyptiīs fortiter resistēbāmus, sed illī erant multī, nōs paucī. septem Aegyptiī mē circumveniēbant. duōs graviter vulnerāvī, sed cēterī mē superāvērunt. prōcubuī exanimātus. ubi animum recēpī,   40
casam circumspectāvī. fenestrae erant frāctae, casa dīrepta. Diogenēs in mediā casā stābat lacrimāns. prope mē iacēbat puer meus.

"puer mortuus est," inquit Diogenēs. "Aegyptiī eum necāvērunt, quod ille tē dēfendēbat."   45

---

| | |
|---|---|
| tabernāriī: tabernārius | *storekeeper* |
| plūrimī | *very many* |
| sēnsit: sentīre | *notice* |
| melius est | *it would be better* |
| parte: pars | *part* |
| in triviīs | *at the crossroads* |
| nōbīs obstābat | *blocked our way, obstructed us* |
| sollicitūdinem: sollicitūdō | *anxiety* |
| casam: casa | *small house* |
| nōvit | *knows* |
| perīculum | *danger* |
| fenestram: fenestra | *window* |
| forte | *by chance* |
| accēpit: accipere | *take in, receive* |
| extrā iānuam | *outside the door* |
| īnfestī: īnfestus | *hostile* |
| oppugnant: oppugnāre | *attack* |
| effrēgērunt: effringere | *break down* |
| irrūpērunt: irrumpere | *burst in* |
| septem | *seven* |
| circumveniēbant: circumvenīre | *surround* |
| animum recēpī: animum recipere | *recover consciousness* |
| dīrepta | *torn apart, ransacked* |
| dēfendēbat: dēfendere | *defend* |

1 Why did Quintus visit the city? Who went with him?
2 Why did the slave-boy suggest turning back? Why did Quintus not agree?
3 What was happening at the crossroads?
4 When the craftsman looked out of the house, how did he guess that Quintus was a friend of Barbillus?
5 Why was Quintus frightened when the boy told him who the craftsman was?
6 What weapons did Diogenes have ready?
7 How did the Egyptians get into the house?
8 Who was killed? Why did the Egyptians kill him? Why do you think they did not kill anyone else?

# ad templum

per viās urbis quondam cum Barbillō ībam. in multitūdine, quae
viās complēbat, Aegyptiōs, Graecōs, Iūdaeōs, Syrōs vīdī. subitō vir
quīdam nōbīs appropinquāvit. Barbillus, simulatque eum
cōnspexit, magnum gemitum dedit.

"ēheu!" inquit. "quam miserī sumus! ecce Plancus, vir    5
doctissimus, quī numquam tacet! semper dē monumentīs et dē
portū Alexandrīae garrīre vult."

"salvē, mī dulcissime!" inquit Plancus. "quid hodiē agis? quō
contendis?"

"ad templum," respondit Barbillus invītus.    10

"ad templum Augustī?" rogāvit ille.

"minimē, ad templum Serāpidis īmus," inquit Barbillus. "nunc
festīnāre dēbēmus, quod iter longum est. nōnne tū negōtium cum
aliīs mercātōribus agere dēbēs? valē!"

ille tamen Barbillō respondit, "hodiē ōtiōsus sum. commodum est    15
mihi ad templum Serāpidis īre. dē Serāpide vōbīs nārrāre possum."

tum Plancus nōbīscum ībat garriēns. nōbīs dē omnibus
monumentīs nārrāre coepit. Barbillus, quī iam rem graviter ferēbat,
in aurem meam susurrāvit,

"comes noster loquācior est quam psittacus et obstinātior quam    20
asinus."

dēnique, ubi nōs miserī ad templum advēnimus, Plancus statim
dē Serāpide garrīre coepit,

"spectāte templum! quam magnificum! spectāte cellam! statuam
vīdistis, quae in cellā est? deus ibi cum magnā dignitāte sedet. in    25
capite deī est canistrum. Serāpis enim est deus quī segetēs cūrat.
opportūnē hūc vēnimus. hōra quārta est. nunc sacerdōtēs in ārā
sacrificium facere solent."

subitō tuba sonuit. sacerdōtēs ē cellā templī ad āram
prōcessērunt. sacerdōs clāmāvit,    30

"tacēte vōs omnēs, quī adestis! tacēte vōs, quī hoc sacrificium
vidēre vultis!"

omnēs virī fēminaeque statim tacuērunt. Barbillus, ubi hoc
sēnsit, rīsit et mihi susurrāvit,

"ehem! vidēsne Plancum? ubi sacerdōs silentium poposcit, etiam    35
ille dēnique tacuit. mīrāculum est. deus nōs servāvit."

| | |
|---|---|
| vir quīdam | *one man, a certain man* |
| gemitum: gemitus | *groan* |
| doctissimus: doctus | *educated, learned* |
| monumentīs: monumentum | *monument* |
| mī dulcissime! | *my good man!* |
| quid . . . agis? | *how are you?* |
| garriēns | *chattering* |
| coepit | *began* |
| aurem: auris | *ear* |
| loquācior: loquāx | *talkative* |
| psittacus | *parrot* |
| obstinātior: obstinātus | *obstinate* |
| dēnique | *at last, finally* |
| cellam: cella | *sanctuary* |
| in capite | *on the head* |
| canistrum | *basket* |
| enim | *for* |
| hōra | *hour* |
| quārta | *fourth* |
| facere solent | *are accustomed to make* |
| ehem! | *well, well!* |
| silentium | *silence* |
| mīrāculum | *miracle* |
| | |
| Iūdaeōs: Iūdaeī | *Jews* |
| Syrōs: Syrī | *Syrians* |
| Serāpidis: Serāpis | *the god Serapis* |

**Serapis**
**Egyptian deity associated with fertility and healing.**

**Sphinx and so-called Pompey's Pillar, which was part of the Temple of Serapis in Alexandria.**

# About the Language

1 Study the following sentences:

ad portum **Alexandrīae** mox pervēnimus.
*We soon arrived at the harbor of Alexandria.*

in vīllā **Barbillī** erant multī servī.
*In the house of Barbillus were many slaves.*

mīlitēs Rōmānī per viās **urbis** incēdēbant.
*Roman soldiers were marching through the streets of the city.*

in multitūdine **Aegyptiōrum** erat senex.
*In the crowd of Egyptians was an old man.*

The words in boldface are in the *genitive* case.

2 Compare the nominative singular with the genitive singular and genitive plural in each declension:

| | NOMINATIVE SINGULAR | GENITIVE SINGULAR | GENITIVE PLURAL |
|---|---|---|---|
| FIRST DECLENSION | puella | puellae | puellārum |
| SECOND DECLENSION | servus | servī | servōrum |
| THIRD DECLENSION | leō | leōnis | leōnum |

3 Further examples:

1 multī servī in viā clāmābant. Quīntus per multitūdinem servōrum contendit.
2 omnēs sacerdōtēs prō templō Augustī stābant.
3 agricola magnum fundum habēbat. Barbillus ad fundum agricolae saepe ambulābat.
4 nūllī Graecī in illā parte urbis habitābant.
5 multae ancillae viās complēbant. puer Quīntum per turbam ancillārum dūxit.
6 mercātor togās in tabernā vēndēbat. iuvenēs et puerī ad tabernam mercātōris contendērunt.

# mercātor Arabs

ego cum Barbillō cēnāre solēbam. Barbillus mihi gemmās suās quondam ostendit. gemmās attonitus spectāvī, quod maximae et splendidae erant. Barbillus hās gemmās ā mercātōre Arabī ēmerat. dē hōc mercātōre fābulam mīrābilem nārrāvit.

mercātor ōlim cum merce pretiōsā Arabiam trānsībat. in merce    5
erant stolae sēricae, dentēsque eburneī. multōs servōs quoque habēbat, quī mercem custōdiēbant. subitō latrōnēs, quī īnsidiās parāverant, impetum fēcērunt. mercātor servīque latrōnibus ācriter resistēbant, sed latrōnēs tandem servōs superāvērunt. tum latrōnēs cum servīs et cum merce mercātōris effūgērunt. mercātōrem    10
exanimātum relīquērunt.

ille tamen nōn erat mortuus. mox animum recēpit. sōlus erat in dēsertīs, sine aquā, sine servīs. dē vītā suā paene dēspērābat. subitō mōnstrum terribile in caelō appāruit; ālae longiōrēs erant quam rēmī, unguēs maiōrēs quam hastae. in capite mōnstrī erant oculī,    15
quī flammās ēmittēbant. mōnstrum mercātōrem rēctā petīvit. mercātor, postquam hoc mōnstrum dēscendēns vīdit, ad terram exanimātus prōcubuit. ubi animum recēpit, anxius circumspectāvit. iterum dē vītā dēspērābat, quod iam in nīdō ingentī iacēbat. nīdus in monte praeruptō haerēbat. in nīdō mōnstrī    20
erat cumulus. in hōc cumulō mercātor multōs lapidēs fulgentēs cōnspexit.

"nunc rem intellegere possum," mercātor sibi dīxit. "hoc

| | | | |
|---|---|---|---|
| gemmās: gemma | *jewel, gem* | mōnstrum | *monster* |
| merce: merx | *goods, merchandise* | ālae: āla | *wing* |
| trānsībat: trānsīre | *cross* | unguēs: unguis | *claw* |
| sēricae | *silk* | rēctā | *directly, straight* |
| dentēs . . . eburneī | *ivory tusks* | dēscendēns | *coming down* |
| latrōnēs: latrō | *robber* | nīdō: nīdus | *nest* |
| īnsidiās: īnsidiae | *trap, ambush* | praeruptō: praeruptus | *steep* |
| ācriter | *keenly, fiercely* | cumulus | *pile* |
| relīquērunt: relinquere | *leave* | lapidēs: lapis | *stone* |
| in dēsertīs | *in the desert* | fulgentēs: fulgēns | *shining, glittering* |

| | |
|---|---|
| Arabs | *Arabian* |
| Arabiam: Arabia | *Arabia* |

mōnstrum, sīcut pīca, rēs fulgentēs colligere solet. mōnstrum mē
petīvit, quod zōna mea fulgēbat." 25

postquam lapidēs īnspexit, laetus sibi dīxit, "hercle! fortūna
fortibus favet!"

in cumulō lapidum erant multae maximaeque gemmae. mercātor
nōnnūllās gemmās in saccō posuit. tum post cumulum gemmārum
sē cēlāvit. mōnstrum mox cum aliā gemmā revēnit, et in nīdō 30
cōnsēdit.

postquam nox vēnit, mercātor audāx in mōnstrum dormiēns
ascendit, et in tergō iacēbat. in tergō mōnstrī per tōtam noctem
haerēbat. māne hoc mōnstrum cum mercātōre, quī in tergō etiam
nunc iacēbat, ēvolāvit. quam fortūnātus erat mercātor! mōnstrum 35
ad mare tandem advēnit, ubi nāvis erat. mercātor, postquam
nāvem vīdit, dē tergō mōnstrī dēsiluit. in undās maris prope nāvem
cecidit. ita mercātōrem fortūna servāvit.

| | | | |
|---|---|---|---|
| sīcut pīca | *like a magpie* | saccō: saccus | *bag, purse* |
| colligere | *gather, collect* | audāx | *bold* |
| zōna | *belt* | dormiēns | *sleeping* |
| fulgēbat: fulgēre | *shine* | in tergō | *on its back* |
| fortūna | *fortune, luck* | cecidit: cadere | *fall* |

# Practicing the Language

**1** Complete each sentence with the right word and then translate.

1 ubi Diogenēs hoc dīxit, nōs casam . . . . . . (intrāvī, intrāvimus)

2 Aegyptiī tabernam nostram oppugnāvērunt, ubi vōs in Arabiā . . . . . . (aberās, aberātis)

3 ego, ubi in urbe eram, tēcum negōtium . . . . . . (agēbam, agēbāmus)

4 tū senem, quī Rōmānōs vituperābat, . . . . . . (audīvistī, audīvistis)

5 nōs . . . . ., quod sacerdōtēs ad āram prōcēdēbant. (tacēbāmus, tacēbam)

6 tū auxilium mihi semper . . . . . . (dabātis, dabās)

7 ego vīnum in āram, quae prō templō erat, . . . . . . (fūdimus, fūdī)

8 vōs mihi togās sordidās . . . . . . (vēndidistis, vēndidistī)

**2** Complete each sentence with the most suitable word from the lists below and then translate.

| volō | possum |
|------|--------|
| vīs | potes |
| vult | potest |

1 māne ad portum ambulāre soleō, quod nāvēs spectāre . . . . . .

2 mihi valdē placet puellam audīre, quae suāviter cantāre . . . . . .

3 longum iter iam fēcī; ad vīllam hodiē pervenīre nōn . . . . . .

4 amīce, festīnā! nōnne pompam vidēre . . . . . ?

5 mātrōna, quae fīliō dōnum dare . . . . ., togās in tabernā īnspicit.

6 Bregāns, quam rōbustus es! maximās amphorās portāre . . . . . .

# About the Language

**1** From Stages 4 and 6 of Unit 1 onwards, you have met the words **tamen** and **igitur**:

Quīntus **tamen** ad vīllam contendit.
*However, Quintus hurried to the house.*

rēx **igitur** multōs prīncipēs ad aulam invītāvit.
*Therefore the king invited many chieftains to the palace.*

Notice the position of **tamen** and **igitur** in the sentence.

**2** The word **enim** has a similar position in the sentence:

rēx Vespasiānum honōrāvit. Vespasiānus **enim** erat imperātor.
*The king honored Vespasian. For Vespasian was the emperor.*

**3** Further examples:

1 Diogenēs nōbīs fūstēs trādidit. Aegyptiī enim casam oppugnābant.
2 Quīntus sollicitus erat. senex enim Graecōs Rōmānōsque vituperābat.

# Alexandria

The site of this famous city was chosen by Alexander the Great when he came to Egypt in 331 B.C. Alexander needed a safe harbor for his large fleet of ships, and he chose a fishing village west of the mouth of the Nile, where there was good anchorage, a healthy climate and fresh water, and limestone quarries nearby to provide stone for building. He commanded his architect to plan and build a city which was to be a new center of trade and civilization.

Alexander died before the work had properly begun, but the city was named after him and his body was buried there in a magnificent tomb. He was succeeded as ruler by Ptolemy, one of his generals, whose descendents governed Alexandria and Egypt for the next three hundred years.

By the first century A.D., when Egypt had become part of the Roman empire, Alexandria was probably as large and splendid as Rome itself; it was certainly the greatest city in the eastern part of the empire, with perhaps a million inhabitants. Much of its wealth and importance was due to its position. It stood at a meeting-place of great trade routes, and was therefore excellently placed for trading on a large scale. Merchants and businessmen were attracted to the city because it offered them safe harbors for their ships, huge warehouses for storage, a vast number of dock-workers to carry their goods, and a busy market for buying and selling.

Into Alexandria came luxury goods such as bronze statues from Greece or fine Italian wines, and raw materials such as wood and marble to be used by craftsmen in the local workshops. Out to other countries

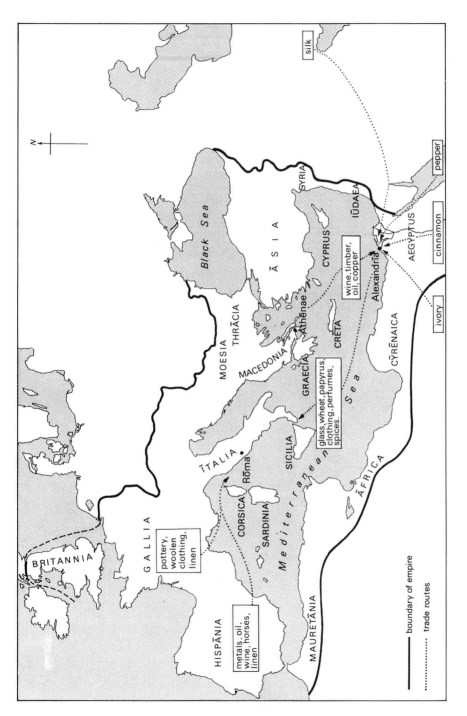

**The Roman empire at the end of the first century A.D.**

went wheat, papyrus, and much else. A list in the *Red Sea Guide Book*, written by an Alexandrian merchant in the first century A.D., gives some idea of the vast range of goods bought and sold in the city: "clothes, cotton, skins, muslins, silks, brass, copper, iron, gold, silver, silver plate, tin, axes, adzes, glass, ivory, tortoise shell, rhinoceros horn, wine, olive oil, sesame oil, rice, butter, honey, wheat, myrrh, frankincense, cinnamon, fragrant gums, papyrus."

Travelers from Greece or Italy would approach Alexandria by sea. The first thing they would see, rising above the horizon, would be the huge lighthouse that stood on a little island called Pharos just outside the harbor. This lighthouse, which was itself called Pharos, was one of the seven wonders of the ancient world. It was over 400 feet (122 meters) high, with a fire constantly lit at the top, and it acted as a marker day and night for the thousands of ships that used the port each year.

Alexandria had three harbors. The Great Harbor and the Western Harbor lay on either side of a breakwater three quarters of a mile (1,200 meters) long which joined Pharos island to the mainland. The third harbor was a large lake which lay behind the city and was connected by canals to the river Nile and then by a further canal to the Red Sea; this was the route that led to India.

**Modern Alexandria: Fort of Kait Bey, site of the Pharos.**

Cleopatra's Needle, Central Park, New York City.

Aerial view of the Great Harbor (top left) and the Western Harbor (right) at Alexandria.

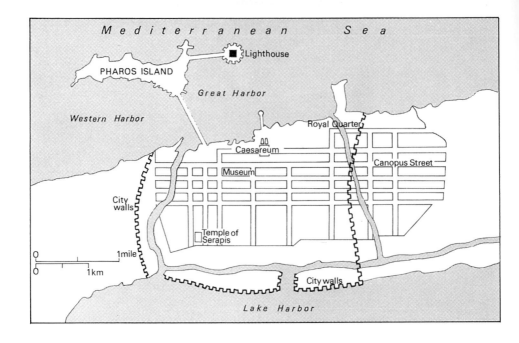

**Plan of Alexandria.**

Alexander's architect had planned the city carefully, with its streets set out in a grid system, crossing each other at right angles as in many modern American cities. The main street, Canopus Street, was more than 100 feet (30 meters) wide, wider than any street in Rome and four times the size of any street that Quintus would have known in Pompeii. Some of the houses were several stories high, and many of the public buildings were built of marble. By the Great Harbor was the Royal Quarter, an area of more than one square mile (260 hectares) containing palaces, temples, gardens, and government offices. West of the Royal Quarter was the Caesareum, where Quintus, in the paragraph on page 79, made his offering of wine. The Caesareum was a temple begun by Queen Cleopatra in honor of the Roman general Marcus Antonius and completed by the Emperor Augustus as a shrine dedicated to himself. In the words of the Jewish writer Philo, it was "wonderfully high and large, full of precious paintings and statues, and beautiful all over with gold and silver; it contains colonnades, libraries, courtyards, and sacred groves, all made as skillfully as possible with no expense spared."

Nearby stood two obelisks, tall narrow pillars of granite, pointed at the top. They were brought from an ancient Egyptian temple at Heliopolis and placed in front of the Caesareum by a Roman engineer in 13 B.C. In the nineteenth century one was removed to London and placed on the embankment of the river Thames, and the other was taken to Central Park, New York. They are known as Cleopatra's Needles.

But Alexandria was more than a city of fine streets, glittering marble, and busy trading; it was a center of education and study. The university, known as the Museum, had the largest library in the ancient world with more than half a million volumes on its shelves. Professional scholars were employed to do research in a wide range of subjects—mathematics, astronomy, anatomy, geography, literature, and languages. Here improved maps of the world were drawn, based on travelers' reports; here Euclid wrote his famous geometry textbook and Aristarchus put forward his theory that the Earth goes around the Sun.

Alexandria was a city of many different races, including Egyptians, Jews, Romans, Africans, and Indians. But on the whole, the people with most power and influence were the Greeks. They had planned the city and built it; they had ruled it before the Romans came and continued to play a part in running it under the Romans; theirs was the official language; they owned great wealth in Alexandria and enjoyed many privileges. This caused jealousy among the other peoples, and was one of the reasons why fights and riots frequently broke out. The Roman governor, or even the emperor himself, often had to step in and try to settle such disputes as fairly and peacefully as possible. After one violent riot involving the Jews, the Emperor Claudius included the following stern warning in a letter to the Alexandrians:

"Although I am very angry with those who stirred up the trouble, I am not going to inquire fully into who was responsible for the riot—I might have said, the war—with the Jews. But I tell you this once and for all: unless you stop quarreling with each other, I shall be forced to show you what even a kind emperor can do when he has good reason to be angry."

# Words and Phrases Checklist

Nouns in the checklists for Stages 17–20 are usually listed in the form of their nominative and genitive singular. Verbs are listed as before. ⟶

| | |
|---|---|
| ā, ab | *from* (also in other contexts: *by*) |
| animus, animī | *spirit, soul* |
| appropinquō, appropinquāre, appropinquāvī | *approach, come near to* |
| āra, ārae | *altar* |
| bene | *well* |
| benignus | *kind* |
| dēsiliō, dēsilīre, dēsiluī | *jump down* |
| dēspērō, dēspērāre, dēspērāvī | *despair* |
| diū | *for a long time* |
| exanimātus | *unconscious* |
| facilis | *easy* |
| fulgeō, fulgēre, fulsī | *shine* |
| gemma, gemmae | *jewel, gem* |
| graviter | *seriously* |
| haereō, haerēre, haesī | *stick, cling* |
| hasta, hastae | *spear* |
| hūc | *here, to this place* |
| impetus, impetūs | *attack* |
| īnsula, īnsulae | *island* |
| itaque | *and so* |
| latrō, latrōnis | *robber* |
| mare, maris | *sea* |
| maximus | *very big, very large, very great* |
| multitūdō, multitūdinis | *crowd* |
| negōtium, negōtiī | *business* |
| numquam | *never* |
| paucī | *few, a few* |
| perveniō, pervenīre, pervēnī | *reach, arrive at* |
| quondam | *one day, once* |
| recipiō, recipere, recēpī | *recover, take back* |
| sine | *without* |
| soleō, solēre | *be accustomed* |
| sordidus | *dirty* |
| tergum, tergī | *back* |
| vīta, vītae | *life* |

# Word Search

effulgence, facilitate, impetuous, paucity, marine, recipient, vitality

1 . . . . .: a brilliant radiance
2 . . . . .: vigor, liveliness
3 . . . . .: impulsive, abruptly spontaneous
4 . . . . .: of or pertaining to the sea
5 . . . . .: one who receives
6 . . . . .: scarcity, dearth
7 . . . . .: to make easier, assist

# Stage 18

# Eutychus et Clēmēns

# pugna

quattuor servī senem in viā pulsābant.
tabernārius et uxor et ancilla pugnam spectābant.
omnēs perterritī erant.

tabernārius perterritus erat, quod senex vehementer clāmābat.
ancilla perterrita erat, quod multus sanguis fluēbat.
uxor perterrita erat, quod servī fūstēs ingentēs vibrābant.

# taberna

postquam ad urbem advēnimus, ego Clēmentī diū tabernam quaerēbam. tandem Barbillus, quī trīgintā tabernās possidēbat, mihi tabernam optimam obtulit. haec taberna prope templum Īsidis erat. in hāc parte urbis via est, in quā omnēs tabernāriī vitrum vēndunt. facile est illīs tabernāriīs mercem vēndere, quod vitrum 5 Alexandrīnum nōtissimum est. taberna, quam Barbillus mihi offerēbat, optimum situm habēbat, optimum lucrum. Barbillus tamen dubitābat.

"sunt multae operae," inquit, "in illā parte urbis. tabernāriī operās timent, quod pecūniam extorquent et vim īnferunt. operae 10 lībertum meum interfēcērunt, quī nūper illam tabernam tenēbat. eum in viā invēnimus mortuum. lībertus, quī senex obstinātus erat, operīs pecūniam dare nōluit. operae eum necāvērunt tabernamque dīripuērunt."

"Clēmēns vir fortis, nōn senex īnfirmus est," ego Barbillō 15 respondī. "fortūna semper eī favet. hanc tabernam Clēmentī emere volō. tibi centum aureōs offerō. placetne?"

"mihi placet," respondit Barbillus. "centum aureī sufficiunt."

Barbillō igitur centum aureōs trādidī.

| | |
|---|---|
| vitrum | *glass* |
| situm: situs | *position, site* |
| lucrum | *profit* |
| dubitābat: dubitāre | *be doubtful* |
| operae | *hired thugs* |
| extorquent: extorquēre | *extort* |
| vim īnferunt: vim īnferre | *use force, violence* |
| dīripuērunt: dīripere | *ransack* |
| īnfirmus | *weak* |
| centum aureōs | *a hundred gold pieces* |
| sufficiunt: sufficere | *be enough* |

Alexandrīnum: Alexandrīnus  *Alexandrian*

Egyptian glass of the thirteenth century B.C. and Roman glass of the first century B.C. and first century A.D., from the Corning Museum of Glass, Corning, New York.

Core-formed palm-column flask from Egypt (left).

Millefiori bowl (top right) and ribbon-glass bowl (bottom right).

Cover in the form of a fish. The serving dish that matched this cover was probably used to serve a fish dinner: when the fish-shaped cover was removed, an actual cooked fish would be found underneath.

**Blown glass pitcher with trailed decoration (left).**

**The Roman theater at Alexandria (below).**

# in officīnā Eutychī

postquam tabernam Clēmentī dedī, ille mihi grātiās maximās ēgit.
statim ad viam, in quā taberna erat, festīnāvit: adeō cupiēbat
tabernam tenēre.

in viā vitreāriōrum erat ingēns turba. ibi Clēmēns tabernam
suam prope templum Īsidis cōnspexit. valvās ēvulsās vīdit,      5
tabernam dīreptam. īrātus igitur Clēmēns tabernārium vīcīnum
rogāvit,

"quis hoc fēcit?"

"rogā Eutychum!" inquit tabernārius, quī perterritus erat.

Clēmēns statim Eutychum quaesīvit. facile erat Clēmentī eum      10
invenīre, quod officīnam maximam possidēbat. prō officīnā Eutychī
stābant quattuor servī Aegyptiī. Clēmēns numquam hominēs
ingentiōrēs quam illōs Aegyptiōs vīderat. eōs tamen nōn timēbat.
ūnum servum ex ōrdine trāxit.

"heus! Atlās!" inquit Clēmēns. "num dormīs? Eutychum,      15
dominum tuum, interrogāre volō. cūr mihi obstās? nōn decōrum est
tibi lībertō obstāre."

tum Clēmēns servōs attonitōs praeteriit, et officīnam Eutychī
intrāvit.

Eutychus in lectō recumbēbat; cibum ē canistrō gustābat. valdē      20
sūdābat, et manūs in capillīs servī tergēbat. postquam Clēmentem
vīdit, clāmāvit,

"quis es, homuncule? quis tē hūc admīsit? quid vīs?"

"Quīntus Caecilius Clēmēns sum," respondit Clēmēns. "dē
tabernā, quae dīrepta est, cognōscere volō. nam illa taberna nunc      25
mea est."

Eutychus, postquam hoc audīvit, Clēmentem amīcissimē
salūtāvit, et eum per officīnam dūxit. ipse Clēmentī fabrōs suōs
dēmōnstrāvit. in officīnā erant trīgintā vitreāriī Aegyptiī, quī ōllās
ōrnātās faciēbant. dīligenter labōrābant, quod aderat vīlicus, quī      30
virgam vibrābat.

Eutychus, postquam Clēmentī officīnam ostendit, negōtium
agere coepit.

"perīculōsum est, mī amīce, in viā vitreāriōrum," inquit. "multī
fūrēs ad hanc viam veniunt, multī latrōnēs. omnēs igitur tabernāriī      35
auxilium ā mē petunt. tabernāriī mihi pecūniam dant, ego eīs

praesidium. tabernam tuam servāre possum. omnēs tabernāriī mihi decem aureōs quotannīs dare solent. paulum est. num tū praesidium meum recūsāre vīs?"

Clēmēns tamen Eutychō nōn crēdēbat. auxilium igitur recūsāvit.    40

"ego ipse tabernam, in quā habitō, servāre possum," inquit Clēmēns. "praesidium tuum operāsque tuās floccī nōn faciō."

tum lībertus sēcūrus exiit.

| | |
|---|---|
| officīnā: officīna | *workshop* |
| adeō | *so much, so greatly* |
| in viā vitreāriōrum | *in the street of the glassmakers* |
| valvās: valvae | *doors* |
| ēvulsās: ēvulsus | *wrenched off* |
| vīcīnum: vīcīnus | *neighboring, nearby* |
| quattuor | *four* |
| interrogāre | *question* |
| praeteriit: praeterīre | *go past* |
| sūdābat: sūdāre | *sweat* |
| manūs . . . tergēbat | *was wiping his hands* |
| capillīs: capillī | *hair* |
| admīsit: admittere | *let in* |
| amīcissimē: amīcē | *in a friendly way* |
| ōllās: ōlla | *vase* |
| ōrnātās: ōrnātus | *decorated* |
| praesidium | *protection* |
| paulum | *little* |
| floccī nōn faciō | *I don't give a hoot about* |
| sēcūrus | *without a care* |

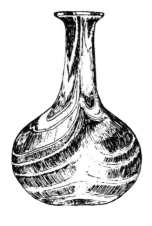

When you have read this story, answer the questions at the end.

# Clēmēns tabernārius

Clēmēns mox tabernam suam renovāvit. fabrōs condūxit, quī
valvās mūrōsque refēcērunt. multās ōllās cum aliīs ōrnāmentīs
vitreīs ēmit. cēterī tabernāriī, quamquam Eutychum valdē
timēbant, Clēmentem libenter adiuvābant. nam Clēmēns cōmis
erat et eīs invicem auxilium dabat. facile erat eī lucrum facere, quod     5
pretium aequum semper postulābat.

haec taberna, ut dīxī, prope templum deae Īsidis erat. ad hoc
templum Clēmēns, quī pius erat, cotīdiē adībat. ibi deam Īsidem
adōrābat et eī ōrnāmentum vitreum saepe cōnsecrābat.

sacerdōtēs, quī templum administrābant, mox Clēmentem     10
cognōvērunt. deinde Clēmēns Īsiacīs sē coniūnxit. sacerdōtēs igitur
eum in cellam dūxērunt, in quā fēlēs sacra habitābat. sacerdōtēs eī
librum sacrum dedērunt, in quō dē mystēriīs deae legere poterat.
postquam Īsiacīs sē coniūnxit, saepe in templō cēnābat, fēlemque
sacram vidēbat. eam semper mulcēbat, et eī semper aliquid ex     15
paterā suā dabat.

mox plūrimōs amīcōs Clēmēns habēbat. nam tabernāriī, quī
Eutychō pecūniam invītī dabant, paulātim Clēmentī cōnfīdēbant.
tabernāriī Eutychum inimīcum putābant, Clēmentem vindicem.
tandem omnēs Eutychō pecūniam trādere nōluērunt. 20

itaque Eutychus operās Aegyptiās collēgit et eīs fūstēs dedit.

"nunc," inquit Eutychus, "occāsiōnem capere dēbēmus. necesse
est istī Clēmentī poenās dare."

operae, postquam fūstēs cēpērunt, ad tabernam Clēmentis
contendērunt. 25

| | |
|---|---|
| renovāvit: renovāre | *restore* |
| condūxit: condūcere | *hire* |
| refēcērunt: reficere | *repair* |
| ōrnāmentīs: | |
|   ōrnāmentum | *ornament* |
| vitreīs: vitreus | *glass, made of glass* |
| invicem | *in turn* |
| aequum: aequus | *fair* |
| ut | *as* |
| pius | *respectful to the gods* |
| adōrābat: adōrāre | *worship* |
| cōnsecrābat: cōnsecrāre | *dedicate* |
| sē coniūnxit: | |
|   sē coniungere | *join* |
| sacra: sacer | *sacred* |
| mystēriīs: mystēria | *mysteries, secret worship* |
| mulcēbat: mulcēre | *stroke* |
| cōnfīdēbant: cōnfīdere | *trust* |
| putābant: putāre | *think* |
| vindicem: vindex | *champion, defender* |
| occāsiōnem: occāsiō | *opportunity* |
| poenās dare | *pay the penalty, be punished* |
| | |
| Īsiacīs: Īsiacī | *followers of Isis* |

1  How did Clemens get his store repaired and restocked?
2  Why did the other storekeepers help Clemens?
3  Whose temple did Clemens visit? What offerings did he make there?
4  How did Clemens learn more about the worship of the goddess?
5  What animal lived in the temple? In what ways did Clemens show
   kindness to it?
6  Why did the storekeepers stop paying Eutychus?
7  What did Eutychus do? What was his plan?

# About the Language

1 You have already seen how an adjective changes its ending to agree, in *case* and *number*, with the noun it describes. For example:

ACCUSATIVE SINGULAR:     rēx nūntium **fēlīcem** salūtāvit.
*The king greeted the lucky messenger.*

NOMINATIVE PLURAL:     mercātōrēs **fessī** dormiēbant.
*The tired merchants were sleeping.*

2 An adjective agrees with the noun it describes not only in case and number but also in a third way, *gender*. All nouns in Latin belong to one of three genders: *masculine, feminine,* and *neuter*. Compare the following sentences:

Clēmēns amīcōs **callidōs** laudāvit.
*Clemens praised the smart friends.*

Clēmēns ancillās **callidās** laudāvit.
*Clemens praised the smart slave-girls.*

In both sentences, the word for *smart* is accusative plural. But in the first sentence, the masculine form **callidōs** is used, because it describes **amīcōs**, which is masculine; in the second sentence, the feminine form **callidās** is used, because it describes **ancillās**, which is feminine.

3 The forms of adjective which you have met most often are listed on p.167 of the Review Grammar.

4 Translate the following examples and pick out the adjective in each sentence:

1 "ubi est coquus novus?" rogāvit Salvius.
2 "ubi est horreum novum?" rogāvit Salvius.
3 magnae nāvēs in portū Alexandrīae stābant.
4 tabernāriī ignāvī per fenestrās spectābant.
5 nūntius dominō longam epistulam trādidit.
6 mīlitēs custōdem stultum mox invēnērunt.

Find the noun described by each adjective, and refer to the "Complete Vocabulary" in the Language Information Section to find the gender of each noun-and-adjective pair.

**5** The Latin word for *who* or *which* at the beginning of a relative clause changes like an adjective to match the gender of the word it describes. Notice how the forms **quī** (masculine), **quae** (feminine), and **quod** (neuter) are used in the following examples:

rēx, **quī** in aulā habitābat, caerimōniam nūntiāvit.
*The king, **who** lived in the palace, announced a ceremony.*

puella, **quae** per forum contendēbat, operās vīdit.
*The girl, **who** was hurrying through the forum, saw the thugs.*

dōnum, **quod** āthlētam maximē dēlectāvit, erat statua.
*The gift, **which** pleased the athlete very much, was a statue.*

**6** Nouns referring to males, e.g. **pater, fīlius, centuriō,** are usually masculine; nouns referring to females, e.g. **māter, fīlia, uxor,** are usually feminine. Other nouns can be masculine (e.g. **hortus**), feminine (e.g. **nāvis**), or neuter (e.g. **nōmen**).

# prō tabernā Clēmentis

Clēmēns in templō deae Īsidis cum cēterīs Īsiacīs saepe cēnābat. quondam, ubi ā templō, in quō cēnāverat, domum redībat, amīcum cōnspexit accurrentem.

"taberna ardet! taberna tua ardet!" clāmāvit amīcus. "tabernam tuam dīripiunt Eutychus et operae. eōs vīdī valvās ēvellentēs, 5 vitrum frangentēs, tabernam incendentēs. fuge! fuge ex urbe! Eutychus tē interficere vult. nēmō eī operīsque resistere potest."

Clēmēns tamen nōn fūgit, sed ad tabernam quam celerrimē contendit. postquam illūc advēnit, prō tabernā stābat immōtus. valvās ēvulsās, tabernam dīreptam vīdit. Eutychus extrā tabernam 10 cum operīs Aegyptiīs stābat, rīdēbatque.

**Bronze cat from
Roman Egypt.**

"mī dulcissime!" inquit Eutychus cachinnāns. "nōnne tē dē hāc viā monuī? nōnne amīcōs habēs quōs vocāre potes? cūr absunt? fortasse sapientiōrēs sunt quam tū."

Clēmēns cum summā tranquillitāte eī respondit,                          15

"deī tamen nōn absunt. deī mē servāre possunt; deī postrēmō hominēs scelestōs pūnīre solent."

"quid dīcis?" inquit Eutychus īrātissimus. "tūne mihi ita dīcere audēs?"

tum Eutychus operīs signum dedit. statim quattuor Aegyptiī cum        20
īnfestīs fūstibus Clēmentī appropinquābant. Clēmēns cōnstitit. via, in quā stābat, erat dēserta. tabernāriī perterritī per valvās tabernārum spectābant. omnēs invītī Clēmentem dēseruerant, simulatque Eutychus et operae advēnērunt.

subitō fēlēs sacra, quam Clēmēns mulcēre solēbat, ē templō exiit.     25
Clēmentem rēctā petīvit. in manūs Clēmentis īnsiluit. omnēs Aegyptiī statim fūstēs abiēcērunt et ad pedēs Clēmentis prōcubuērunt. operae Clēmentem, quem fēlēs sacra servābat, laedere nōn audēbant.

saeviēbat Eutychus, sīcut taurus īrātus. tum fēlēs in caput          30
Eutychī īnsiluit, quod vehementer rāsit.

"melius est tibi fugere," inquit Clēmēns.

Eutychus cum operīs suīs perterritus fūgit. posteā neque Clēmentem neque tabernāriōs laedere temptābat. mox etiam ex urbe discessit. nunc Clēmēns est prīnceps tabernāriōrum.        35

| | |
|---|---|
| domum: domus | *home* |
| accurrentem: accurrēns | *running up* |
| ēvellentēs: ēvellēns | *wrenching off* |
| frangentēs: frangēns | *breaking* |
| incendentēs: incendēns | *burning, setting on fire* |
| monuī: monēre | *warn* |
| sapientiōrēs: sapiēns | *wise* |
| tranquillitāte: | |
|   tranquillitās | *calmness* |
| scelestōs: scelestus | *wicked* |
| dēseruerant: dēserere | *desert* |
| īnsiluit: īnsilīre | *jump onto, jump into* |
| abiēcērunt: abicere | *throw away* |
| laedere | *harm* |
| sīcut | *like* |
| rāsit: rādere | *scratch* |
| neque . . . neque | *neither . . . nor* |
| temptābat: temptāre | *try* |

# Practicing the Language

1 Complete each sentence with the right word or phrase and then translate.

1 . . . . ., quam Clēmēns tenēbat, in viā vitreāriōrum erat. (taberna, tabernae)

2 . . . . . ad tabernam Clēmentis veniēbant, quod ille pretium aequum postulābat. (fēmina Rōmāna, multae fēminae)

3 in tabernā Clēmentis erant . . . . ., quās vitreāriī Aegyptiī fēcerant. (ōlla pretiōsa, multae ōllae)

4 ubi Eutychus et operae advēnērunt, . . . . . valdē timēbant. (tabernārius Graecus, cēterī tabernāriī)

5 . . . . . ad templum Īsidis festīnāvit et Clēmentī dē tabernā nārrāvit. (amīcus fidēlis, amīcī Graecī)

6 . . . . . ē templō Īsidis celeriter discessērunt et ad tabernam cucurrērunt. (amīcus fidēlis, duo amīcī)

2 Complete each sentence with the right word and then translate.

1 Clēmēns Quīntō, quī tabernam . . . . ., grātiās maximās ēgit. (ēmerat, ēmerant)

2 taberna, in quā operae lībertum Barbillī . . . . ., dīrepta erat. (interfēcerat, interfēcerant)

3 Clēmēns igitur ad Eutychum, quī operās . . . . ., festīnāvit. (mīserat, mīserant)

4 Eutychus Clēmentem, quī quattuor servōs ingentēs . . . . ., amīcissimē salūtāvit. (praeterierat, praeterierant)

5 Eutychus dē tabernāriīs, quī praesidium . . . . ., Clēmentī nārrāvit. (petīverat, petīverant)

6 Clēmēns tamen operās, quae tabernam . . . . ., floccī nōn faciēbat. (dīripuerat, dīripuerant)

3 Complete the sentences of the story with the right word from the following list, and then translate. Do not use any word more than once.

| mīsī | frēgī | vituperāvī |
|------|-------|------------|
| mīsistī | frēgistī | vituperāvistī |

Eutychus in officīnā stābat. vīlicum ad sē vocāvit.

"ego amīcō meō ducentās ōllās herī prōmīsī," inquit Eutychus. "quot ōllās ad tabernam amīcī meī mīsistī?"

"ego centum ōllās ad eum . . . . .," respondit vīlicus.

"centum ōllās!" exclāmāvit Eutychus. "cūr tū centum sōlum ōllās ad amīcum meum . . . . .?" 5

"servus canistrum, in quō ōllae erant, stultissimē omīsit. multae ōllae sunt frāctae," respondit vīlicus.

"ubi est iste servus, quī ōllās frēgit?" rogāvit Eutychus.

vīlicus statim servum ad Eutychum trāxit. 10

"cūr tū tot ōllās . . . . .?" rogāvit Eutychus.

"ego ōllās . . . . ., quod vīlicus mē terruit," inquit servus. "vīlicus virgam vibrāvit et mē vituperāvit."

"cūr tū virgam vibrāvistī et hunc servum . . . . .?" rogāvit Eutychus. 15

"ego servum . . . . ., quod ignāvus erat," respondit vīlicus.

"servus ignāvus erat, tū neglegēns," inquit Eutychus. "necesse est vōbīs per tōtam noctem labōrāre."

| | | | | |
|---|---|---|---|---|
| ducentās: ducentī | *two hundred* | stultissimē: stultē | *foolishly* |
| quot? | *how many?* | omīsit: omittere | *drop* |
| sōlum | *only* | frēgit: frangere | *break* |

# About the Language

1 In Unit 1, you met a number of verbs, such as **faveō, crēdō,** etc., which are often used with a noun in the dative case. For example:

mercātōrēs **Holcōniō** favēbant.
*The merchants gave their support **to Holconius.***
or *The merchants supported Holconius.*

2 You have now met some other verbs which are used in the same way:

turba **nōbīs** obstat.
*The crowd is an obstacle **to us.***
or *The crowd is obstructing us.*

Quīntus **operīs** resistēbat.
*Quintus put up a resistance **to the thugs.***
or *Quintus resisted the thugs.*

3 Further examples:

1 quattuor servī Aegyptiī mihi obstābant.
2 omnēs tabernāriī Quīntō cōnfīdēbant.
3 Eutychō resistere nōn possum.
4 sacerdōtēs lentē templō appropinquāvērunt.

# Glassmaking

In the stories in this Stage, Quintus sets Clemens up in what is thought to have been one of Alexandria's most successful industries—glassmaking. The earliest Egyptian glass vessels, discovered in tombs, date from about 1500 B.C., and glass continued to be made in Egypt throughout the period of the Pharaohs.

When Alexandria was founded in 331 B.C., craftsmen of many kinds were attracted to the new city from older cities of the eastern Mediterranean and Egypt. Among these craftsmen were glassmakers, who introduced some new glassmaking techniques and produced new shapes of vessels. These glassmakers, along with glassmakers in other eastern Mediterranean cities, thrived in the centuries which followed. During the reign of the Emperor Augustus (27 B.C.–A.D. 14), glassmakers from Syro-Palestinian cities like Sidon and Tyre brought the latest techniques of glassmaking to Rome, and soon the industry grew to meet the increasing demand for glass throughout the Roman world, not only in Greece, Syria, Palestine, and Egypt where it had long been in demand, but also in newer, northern areas of the empire such as Gaul, the Rhineland in Germany, and Britain.

Glass is made from sand, plant ash or natron, and lime. Its earliest use was as a colored, opaque, or transparent glaze applied to ceramics before they were fired (as is still done today). As time went on, craftsmen discovered that if glass is heated until it becomes semi-liquid, it can be shaped and left to cool into a new, solid, independently standing shape. At first this shaping was carried out by wrapping a coil of molten glass around a core (clay, mud, sand, and an organic binder like dung) which had been molded around a rod into the shape of a vase or any other object which was required. When the glass had cooled, the rod was pulled out from the core and the remaining parts of the core scraped out. This method, however, was only suitable for making small vessels, such as perfume containers.

The colors used for glass in Egypt of the late Bronze Age were still favored by glassmakers of the Roman period: pale shades of blue, bluish green, green, and yellow. The creation of each of these colors depended on the glassmaker's choice of sand, as these colors were due to the varying amounts of iron impurities in different types of sand. But glassmakers could also add organic substances to achieve more brilliant

GLORY HOLE

**A modern glass blower at work in the Corning Glass Center, Corning, New York. The procedure he is following is described on p. 114.**

colors. These additional colors were most often used just for decoration, frequently by trailing thin lines of molten glass onto a finished vessel, rather like piping colored icing onto a fancy cake. The bowl on page 100 (top right) is a mosaic bowl of the Hellenistic type, in which short

sections cut from multicolored canes of glass were placed side by side around a mold, then heated in a glass furnace until they fused.

Late in the first century B.C., in Palestine or Syria, a new invention completely changed the glassmaking industry. The glassmakers discovered that instead of forming bottles around a core or casting bowls in or around molds, they could pick them up on the end of a hollow pipe and shape them by blowing down the pipe. Glass-blowing is illustrated in the photograph on p. 113. The modern workman in the Corning, New York Glass Center has dipped his pipe into the crucible (the porcelain box which has been pulled forward out of the fire) in the furnace at his left and has lifted out a blob of molten glass. He is blowing steadily down the pipe in order to shape the glass into a hollow bubble. By careful reheating and repeated blowing, the glass bubble can be made, as here, quite big. Many different shapes can be produced by swinging the bubble gently during the blowing, or by using special tools for shaping and cutting. Handles, bases, and decorations can then be added.

After the invention of glass blowing, glassmakers were able to produce many different shapes and sizes of vessels quickly and efficiently. From then on, glass could be used not only for making luxury goods but for producing large quantities of ordinary household objects for everyday use. The use of glass spread everywhere in the Roman empire and among all classes of society. Glassmakers and glass-sellers, including those in Alexandria, prospered.

# Egypt

South of Alexandria stretched the fertile valley of the river Nile. Every year the Nile flooded, watering the land and depositing rich new soil on the fields. This produced not only enough wheat to supply the whole of Egypt but also a large surplus to be sold abroad, in particular at Rome. However, the profits from the wheat trade benefited only a small number of people.

Before the Romans came to Egypt, the country had been ruled by Egyptian "pharaohs" (kings), then by Greeks. These rulers had worked out a system for making the fullest possible use of the land for their own advantage. They regarded the whole country as their own property, and treated the peasant farmers as their private force of workers. They had drawn up a detailed list of all the farms in Egypt and the crops grown on them, and in every village lived government officials whose job was to keep the list up-to-date and check up on the peasants who worked on each farm.

The peasants had no choice but to work hard all year around. They were not allowed to leave their village without permission; they had to plant whatever crop they were told; and they did not receive their share of the harvest until the ruler had received his. They were also responsible for the upkeep and repair of the country's canals and dykes. Everything the peasants did was checked by the officials. The following certificate, for example, was issued by an official called Dioscurus:

> "Certificate. Year 16 of the Emperor Caesar Traianus Hadrianus Augustus. Zoilus son of Peteusuchus son of Elites, his mother being Taorsenuphis, has worked on the embankment operations for four days at the canal of Patsontis in Bacchias. I, Dioscurus, signed this."

Such careful checking-up gave the peasants little chance of going unnoticed or avoiding work. All they could do was complain. Many letters have been found addressed by peasants to government officials, and they usually say the same thing: "We are worn out; we shall run away."

When the Romans came, they did nothing to improve the life of the peasants. The certificate quoted above was issued in the reign of the Emperor Hadrian, more than a hundred and fifty years after the

**Farm workers in modern Egypt.**

**Sphinx and pyramid at Giza, near Cairo.**

Romans' arrival in Egypt. Like the previous rulers, the Romans were more concerned to use the land for their own benefit than to improve the working conditions of peasant farmers. Above all, they wanted to make sure of a steady supply of grain to Rome.

Further money was needed by the government in order to maintain the Alexandrian fleet of merchant ships, the Pharos, the police and the huge numbers of officials. This money was raised by taxation. There were taxes, for example, on vineyards, slaves, dovecotes, and imported and exported goods. Government officials checked continually on the day-to-day activities of the Egyptians. If a man went fishing, an official went with him to register the catch; if anyone sailed out of Alexandria without a permit, he might be fined one third of his property. Licenses were required for such activities as brewing, beekeeping, and pig-breeding.

Under these conditions, it is not surprising that bribery and corruption were common. Here is an extract from the private accounts kept by a Greek living in Egypt:

| gift | 240 drachmas |
| to the guard | 20 drachmas |
| bribes | 2,200 drachmas |
| to two police agents | 100 drachmas |
| to Hermias, police agent | 100 drachmas |
| to a soldier | 500 drachmas |

Although such payments were illegal, they were regarded as a normal part of daily life, and the government usually ignored them.

# Words and Phrases Checklist

Adjectives from now on are usually listed as in the Language Information Section of this Unit (see p. 198 for details).

→

| | |
|---|---|
| aliquid | *something* |
| audeō, audēre | *dare* |
| caput, capitis | *head* |
| coepī | *I began* |
| cognōscō, cognōscere, cognōvī | *find out, get to know* |
| cōnsistō, cōnsistere, cōnstitī | *stand one's ground, stand firm* |
| dea, deae | *goddess* |
| dēmōnstrō, dēmōnstrāre, dēmōnstrāvī | *point out, show* |
| discēdō, discēdere, discessī | *depart, leave* |
| fortasse | *perhaps* |
| fortūna, fortūnae | *fortune, luck* |
| frangō, frangere, frēgī | *break* |
| ibi | *there* |
| invītus, invīta, invītum | *unwilling* |
| libenter | *gladly* |
| longus, longa, longum | *long* |
| manus, manūs | *hand* |
| mīles, mīlitis | *soldier* |
| nam | *for* |
| nēmō | *no one* |
| nox, noctis | *night* |
| obstō, obstāre, obstitī | *obstruct, block the way* |
| pars, partis | *part* |
| perīculōsus, perīculōsa, perīculōsum | *dangerous* |
| petō, petere, petīvī | *beg for, ask for* |
| posteā | *afterwards* |
| postrēmō | *finally, lastly* |
| praesidium, praesidiī | *protection* |
| prō | *in front of* |
| prōcumbō, prōcumbere, prōcubuī | *fall down* |
| quō? | *where, where to?* |
| recūsō, recūsāre, recūsāvī | *refuse* |
| resistō, resistere, restitī | *resist* |
| sacer, sacra, sacrum | *sacred* |
| saeviō, saevīre, saeviī | *be in a rage* |

# Word Search

decapitate, demonstrable, manually, militant, nocturnal, petition, sacrilege

1 . . . . .: an offense against something sacred
2 . . . . .: to behead
3 . . . . .: able to be shown or proven
4 . . . . .: by hand, without mechanical assistance
5 . . . . .: aggressive; forcefully insistent
6 . . . . .: to make a formal request
7 . . . . .: active by night

# Stage 19

# Īsis

hic vir est Aristō.
Aristō est amīcus Barbillī.
in vīllā splendidā habitat,
sed miserrimus est.

haec fēmina est Galatēa.
Galatēa est uxor Aristōnis.
Galatēa marītum saepe castīgat,
numquam laudat.

haec puella est Helena.
Helena est fīlia Aristōnis et Galatēae.
multī iuvenēs hanc puellam amant,
quod pulcherrima est.

pompa splendida per viās
Alexandrīae prōcēdit.
omnēs Alexandrīnī hanc
pompam spectāre volunt.

hī virī sunt sacerdōtēs deae
Īsidis. Aristō hōs virōs intentē
spectat. sacerdōtēs statuam
deae per viās portant.

hae puellae prō pompā currunt.
Helena hās puellās intentē
spectat. puellae corōnās
rosārum gerunt.

pompa ad templum Serāpidis
advenit. prope hoc templum
stant duo iuvenēs. hī iuvenēs
tamen pompam nōn spectant.

# Aristō

Aristō vir miserrimus est, quod vītam dūram vīvit. pater Aristōnis scrīptor nōtissimus erat, quī in Graeciā habitābat. tragoediās optimās scrībēbat. Aristō, quod ipse tragoediās scrībere vult, vītam quiētam quaerit; sed uxor et fīlia eī obstant.

Galatēa, uxor Aristōnis, amīcōs ad vīllam semper invītat. amīcī    5
Galatēae sunt tībīcinēs et citharoedī. amīcī in vīllā Aristōnis semper cantant et iocōs faciunt. Aristō amīcōs uxōris semper fugit.

Helena quoque, fīlia Aristōnis et Galatēae, patrem vexat. multōs iuvenēs ad vīllam patris invītat. amīcī Helenae sunt poētae. in vīllā Aristōnis poētae versūs suōs recitant. Aristō hōs versūs nōn amat,    10
quod scurrīlēs sunt. saepe poētae inter sē pugnant. saepe Aristō amīcōs fīliae ē vīllā expellit. difficile est Aristōnī tragoediās scrībere.

| | |
|---|---|
| vīvit: vīvere | *live* |
| scrīptor | *writer* |
| tragoediās: tragoedia | *tragedy* |
| tībīcinēs: tībīcen | *pipe player* |
| citharoedī: citharoedus | *cithara player* |
| expellit: expellere | *throw out* |

When you have read this story, answer the questions at the end.

# diēs fēstus

cīvēs laetī erant. nam hiems erat cōnfecta, et vēr aderat. iam prīmus diēs vēris erat. iam sacerdōtēs deam Īsidem per viās urbis portāre solēbant. sacerdōtēs effigiem deae ad portum quotannīs ferēbant. pompa, quam plūrimī Alexandrīnī spectāre volēbant, splendida erat.    5

hanc pompam tamen Barbillus spectāre nōlēbat.

"nōn commodum est mihi hodiē ad urbem īre," inquit. "ego hanc pompam saepe vīdī, tū tamen numquam. amīcus meus igitur, Aristō, tē ad pompam dūcere vult."

Barbillō grātiās ēgī, et cum Aristōne ad portum ībam. Galatēa et    10
fīlia, Helena, nōbīscum ībant. viās urbis iam complēbant cīvēs
Alexandrīnī. ubi portuī appropinquābāmus, Galatēa fīliam et
marītum assiduē castīgābat:

"Helena! nōlī festīnāre! tolle caput! Aristō! ēmovē hanc turbam!
turba Alexandrīnōrum tōtam viam complet. in magnō perīculō    15
sumus."

postquam ad templum Augustī vēnimus, locum petīvimus, unde
pompam vidēre poterāmus.

"locum optimum nōvimus, unde spectāculum vidēre solēmus,"
inquit Galatēa. "illinc pompam et nāvem sacram vidēre possumus.    20
servus nōbīs illum locum servat. Aristō! nōnne servum māne
ēmīsistī?"

"ēheu!" Aristō sibi dīxit.

ubi ad illum locum, quem Galatēa ēlēgerat, tandem pervēnimus,
Galatēa duōs iuvenēs cōnspexit. hī iuvenēs locum tenēbant, ubi    25
Galatēa stāre volēbat.

"marīte!" exclāmāvit, "ēmovē hōs iuvenēs! ubi est servus noster?
nōnne servum ēmīsistī?"

"cārissima," respondit Aristō, quī anxius circumspectābat,
"melius est nōbīs locum novum quaerere. iste servus sānē neglegēns    30
erat."

Galatēa tamen, quae iam īrātissima erat, Aristōnem incitāvit. ille
igitur iuvenibus appropinquāvit et cōmiter locum poscēbat. uxor
tamen vehementer clāmāvit,

"iuvenēs! cēdite! nōlīte nōbīs obstāre!"    35

iuvenēs, quamquam rem graviter ferēbant, cessērunt. iuvenēs
Galatēam spectābant timidī, Helenam avidī.

subitō spectātōrēs pompam cōnspexērunt. statim multitūdō
spectātōrum clāmōrem sustulit.

"ecce pompa! ecce! dea Īsis!"    40

| diēs fēstus | *festival, holiday* |
| cōnfecta: cōnfectus | *finished* |
| vēr | *spring* |
| assiduē | *continually* |
| castīgābat: castīgāre | *scold, nag* |
| tolle! | *hold up!* |
| unde | *from where* |
| illinc | *from there* |
| sānē | *obviously* |
| cōmiter | *politely, courteously* |
| avidī: avidus | *eager* |

1 Why were the citizens happy?
2 What ceremony took place in Alexandria every year at this time?
3 What arrangement had Barbillus made for Quintus to see the ceremony? Why did Barbillus not go himself?
4 Why did Aristo say "ēheu!" to himself (line 23)?
5 What did Galatea tell her husband to do, when she saw the young men? What did her husband suggest instead?
6 Why did the young men move?
7 How would you describe Galatea's behavior in this story?

# pompa

pompa adveniēbat. prō pompā currēbant multae puellae, quae flōrēs in canistrīs ferēbant. puellae flōrēs spectātōribus dabant, et in viam spargēbant. post multitūdinem puellārum tubicinēs et puerī prōcēdēbant. puerī carmen dulce cantābant. tubicinēs tubās īnflābant. nōs, quī pompam plānē vidēre poterāmus, assiduē    5
plaudēbāmus. Helena, ubi tot flōrēs vīdit sparsōs, Galatēae dīxit,

"spectā illās rosās, quās fēminae in viam spargunt! rosās pulchriōrēs quam illās numquam vīdī."

duo iuvenēs tamen, quōs Galatēa ē locō ēmōverat, pompam vidēre vix poterant.    10

"pompam vidēre nōn possum," inquit iuvenis. "sed spectā illam puellam! puellam pulchriōrem quam illam rārō vīdī."

Galatēa, simulatque hunc iuvenem audīvit, "Helena! hūc venī!" clāmāvit. "stā prope mē! Aristō! cūr fīliam tuam in tantā multitūdine nōn servās?"    15

subitō omnēs tubicinēs tubās vehementer īnflābant. sonitus tubārum mīrābilis erat.

"ō mē miseram! ō caput meum!" clāmāvit Galatēa. "audīte illōs tubicinēs! audīte sonitum! quam raucus est sonitus tubārum!"

"tubicinēs vix audīre possum," clāmāvit alter iuvenis. "quam    20
raucae sunt vōcēs fēminārum Graecārum!"

post turbam puerōrum tubicinumque vēnit dea ipsa. quattuor sacerdōtēs effigiem deae in umerīs ferēbant.

"spectā illam stolam croceam!" clāmāvit Galatēa. "pulcherrima

est illa stola, pretiōsissima quoque. ēheu! vīlēs sunt omnēs stolae    25
meae, quod marītus avārus est."

subitō iuvenēs, quī effigiem vidēre nōn poterant, Galatēam
trūsērunt. iuvenis forte pedem Galatēae calcāvit. illa, postquam
valdē exclāmāvit, eum vituperāvit,

"ō iuvenem īnsolentissimum! nōlī mē vexāre! nōn decōrum est    30
mātrōnam trūdere. num bēstia es?"

Helena "māter!" inquit "hic iuvenis tibi forte nocuit. spectātōrēs
nōs premunt, quod pompam vidēre cupiunt."

Galatēa tamen fīliam castīgāvit, quod iuvenem dēfendēbat. tum
marītum quoque castīgāre coepit.    35

"Aristō! cūr mē nōn servās? uxōrem fīliamque floccī nōn facis.
miserrima sum!"

Aristō, postquam uxōrem lēnīvit, mihi dīxit,

"ēheu! facile est mihi tragoediās scrībere. uxor mē vexat, fīlia
mātrem. tōta vīta mea est tragoedia."    40

| | | |
|---|---|---|
| spargēbant: spargere | *scatter* | |
| tubicinēs: tubicen | *trumpeter* | |
| carmen | *song* | |
| dulce: dulcis | *sweet* | |
| īnflābant: īnflāre | *blow* | |
| plānē | *clearly* | |
| sparsōs: sparsus | *scattered* | |
| rosās: rosa | *rose* | |
| rārō | *rarely* | |
| sonitus | *sound* | |
| raucus | *harsh* | |
| vīlēs: vīlis | *cheap* | |
| trūsērunt: trūdere | *push, shove* | |
| calcāvit: calcāre | *step on* | |
| nocuit: nocēre | *hurt* | |
| premunt: premere | *push* | |
| lēnīvit: lēnīre | *soothe, calm down* | |

**Roman statue of the goddess Isis with sistrum
and water jug.**

# nāvis sacra

sacerdōtēs, ubi ad portum pervēnērunt, effigiem deae Īsidis dēposuērunt. in portū stābat nāvis, quae ōrnātissima erat. tōta puppis erat aurāta. corōna rosārum dē mālō nāvis pendēbat. nūllī tamen nautae in nāve erant.

sacerdōtēs cum effigiē deae ad hanc nāvem prōcessērunt. deinde 5
pontifex ipse deae Īsidī precēs adhibēbat. cīvēs sacerdōtēsque rosās in nāvem et in mare iēcērunt. tum nautae rudentēs solvere coepērunt. ventus secundus nāvem in altum lentē impellēbat. spectātōrēs iterum iterumque plaudēbant. clāmor spectātōrum precēsque sacerdōtum aurēs nostrās implēbant. 10

"nunc nāvis solūta est; nunc mare placidum. dea Īsis nōbīs favet. dea cīvibus Alexandrīnīs favet."

sacerdōtēs, postquam nāvem sacram ita ēmīsērunt, effigiem deae ad templum reportāvērunt. cīvēs per viās urbis laetī currēbant.

ad vīllam Aristōnis lentē reveniēbāmus. Helena cum illīs 15
iuvenibus ambulābat, quōs Galatēa ē locō ēmōverat. hoc tamen Galatēa nōn sēnsit, quod assiduē marītum castīgābat:

"in hāc urbe diūtius manēre nōlō. tū nihil facis, nihil cūrās. servum nōn ēmīsistī, quamquam tē saepe monuī. ēheu! cīvēs Alexandrīnī sunt bēstiae. fīliam nostram vexābant illī iuvenēs. 20
Helena ērubēscēbat; paene lacrimābat. cūr eam numquam servās? mihi semper necesse est fīliam nostram cūrāre."

"ubi est Helena?" rogāvit Aristō.

"nōnne tēcum ambulābat?" respondit Galatēa. "ēheu! illī iuvenēs columbam meam iterum agitant." 25

"stultissima es, uxor!" respondit ille. "columba iuvenēs agitat, nōn iuvenēs columbam."

| | | | |
|---|---|---|---|
| puppis | *stern* | ventus | *wind* |
| corōna | *garland, wreath* | secundus | *favorable, following* |
| dē mālō | *from the mast* | in altum | *towards the open sea* |
| pendēbat: pendēre | *hang* | impellēbat: impellere | *carry* |
| pontifex | *high priest* | implēbant: implēre | *fill* |
| precēs adhibēbat | *offered prayers to* | solūta: solūtus | *untied, cast off* |
| iēcērunt: iacere | *throw* | placidum: placidus | *calm, peaceful* |
| rudentēs: rudēns | *cable, rope* | reportāvērunt: reportāre | *carry back* |
| solvere | *untie, cast off* | ērubēscēbat: ērubēscere | *blush* |

# About the Language

**1** You have now met the following forms of the Latin word for *this* (plural *these*):

|  | SINGULAR | | PLURAL | |
|---|---|---|---|---|
|  | NOMINATIVE | ACCUSATIVE | NOMINATIVE | ACCUSATIVE |
| MASCULINE | hic | hunc | hī | hōs |
| FEMININE | haec | hanc | hae | hās |
| NEUTER | hoc | hoc | | |

**hic** vir est Barbillus.      ***This*** *man is Barbillus.*
**hanc** gemmam invēnī.      *I've found **this** jewel.*
**hae** stolae sunt sordidae!      ***These*** *dresses are dirty!*
tibi **hōs** flōrēs trādō.      *I hand **these** flowers to you.*

**2** Further examples:
1 haec cēna est optima.
2 operae hunc mercātōrem vexant.
3 hoc templum prope forum est.
4 hī servī sunt Aegyptiī.

---

# vēnātiō

---

Barbillus mē et Aristōnem ad vēnātiōnem invītāvit. māne vīlicum
Phormiōnem cum multīs servīs ēmīsit. Phormiō sēcum duōs haedōs
dūxit. sed, ubi ē vīllā discēdēbāmus, astrologus Barbillī commōtus
ad nōs cucurrit.

    "domine, quō festīnās?" clāmāvit. "cūr ē vīllā hodiē exīre vīs?"     5
    "ad praedium meum iter facimus," Barbillus astrologō respondit.
    "sed, domine," inquit astrologus, "immemor es. perīculōsum est
tibi hodiē ē vīllā exīre, quod hodiē sōl Arietī appropinquat."
    ubi hoc audīvī, astrologum dērīsī. Barbillus, quamquam eī

| | |
|---|---|
| haedōs: haedus *kid, young goat* | praedium *estate* |
| astrologus *astrologer* | immemor *forgetful* |
| commōtus *alarmed, excited* | |

    Arietī: Ariēs *the Ram (sign of the zodiac)*

---

crēdēbat, mē offendere nōluit. postquam rem diū cōgitāvit, 10
astrologō dīxit, "mihi placet exīre."

astrologus igitur, ubi dominō persuādēre nōn potuit, amulētum,
quod Chaldaeī fēcerant, eī dedit. tum sēcūrī ad praedium Barbillī
contendimus. per partem praediī flūmen Nīlus lēniter fluēbat.

ubi illūc advēnimus, multōs servōs vīdimus collēctōs. in hāc 15
multitūdine servōrum erant nōnnūllī Aethiopes, quī hastās in
manibus tenēbant. prope Aethiopas stābat Phormiō, vīlicus
Barbillī.

Phormiō "salvē, domine!" inquit. "omnēs rēs tibi parāvimus.
Aethiopes, quōs postulāvistī, īnstrūctī et parātī sunt. tibi scaphās 20
quoque decem comparāvimus."

"haedōs cecīdistis?" rogāvit Barbillus.

"duōs haedōs cecīdimus, domine," respondit vīlicus. "eōs in
scaphās iam posuimus."

tum Phormiō nōs ad rīpam flūminis dūxit, ubi scaphae, quās 25
comparāverat, dēligātae erant. postquam scaphās cōnscendimus,
ad palūdem, in quā crocodīlī latēbant, cautē nāvigāvimus. ubi
palūdī appropinquāvimus, aqua līmōsior fīēbat, harundinēsque
dēnsiōrēs. postquam ad mediam palūdem nāvigāvimus, Barbillus
Phormiōnī signum dedit. haedōs Phormiō in aquam iniēcit. 30

**Mosaic from Pompeii of the River Nile, with Egyptian animals, including a hippopotamus and a crocodile.**

crocodīlī, ubi haedōs caesōs cōnspexērunt, praecipitēs eōs petēbant.
sanguis haedōrum crocodīlōs trahēbat. tum Aethiopes crocodīlōs
agitāre coepērunt. hastās ēmittēbant et crocodīlōs interficiēbant.
magna erat fortitūdō crocodīlōrum, maior tamen perītia
Aethiopum. mox multī crocodīlī mortuī erant.                               35
    subitō ingentem clāmōrem audīvimus.

| | | | |
|---|---|---|---|
| offendere | *displease* | dēligātae: dēligātus | *tied up, moored* |
| persuādēre | *persuade* | palūdem: palūs | *marsh, swamp* |
| amulētum | *amulet, lucky charm* | crocodīlī: crocodīlus | *crocodile* |
| flūmen | *river* | līmōsior: līmōsus | *muddy* |
| lēniter | *gently* | fīēbat | *became* |
| collēctōs: collēctus | *assembled* | harundinēs: harundō | *reed* |
| īnstrūctī: īnstrūctus | *drawn up* | iniēcit: inicere | *throw in* |
| scaphās: scapha | *small boat* | praecipitēs: praeceps | *headlong* |
| cecīdistis: caedere | *kill* | fortitūdō | *courage* |
| rīpam: rīpa | *bank* | perītia | *skill* |

| | |
|---|---|
| Chaldaeī | *Chaldeans, an ancient people of Babylon* |
| flūmen Nīlus | *river Nile* |
| Aethiopes | *Ethiopians* |

"domine!" clāmāvit Phormiō. "hippopotamus, quem Aethiopes ē palūde excitāvērunt, scapham Barbillī ēvertit. Barbillum et trēs servōs in aquam dēiēcit."

quamquam ad Barbillum et ad servōs, quī in aquā natābant, 40 celeriter nāvigāvimus, crocodīlī iam eōs circumvēnerant. hastās in crocodīlōs statim ēmīsimus. ubi crocodīlōs dēpulimus, Barbillum et ūnum servum servāre potuimus. sed postquam Barbillum ex aquā trāximus, eum invēnimus vulnerātum. hasta, quam servus ēmīserat, umerum Barbillī percusserat. Barbillus ā servō suō 45 graviter vulnerātus erat.

| | | | |
|---|---|---|---|
| hippopotamus | *hippopotamus* | dēpulimus: dēpellere | *drive off* |
| ēvertit: ēvertere | *overturn* | ā servō suō | *by his own slave* |

# About the Language

**1** In each of the following sentences, one or more people are being told to do something:

| | |
|---|---|
| māter! **spectā** nāvem! | *Mother!* **Look at** *the ship!* |
| māter! pater! **spectāte** nāvem! | *Mother! Father!* **Look at** *the ship!* |
| Helena! **venī** ad mē! | *Helena!* **Come** *to me!* |
| servī! **venīte** ad mē! | *Slaves!* **Come** *to me!* |

The form of the verb in boldface is known as the *imperative*. If only one person is being told to do something, the *imperative singular* is used; if more than one person, the *imperative plural* is used.

**2** Compare the imperative forms with the infinitive:

| | INFINITIVE | IMPERATIVE | |
|---|---|---|---|
| | | SINGULAR | PLURAL |
| FIRST CONJUGATION | portāre | portā! | portāte! |
| | *to carry* | *carry!* | *carry!* |
| SECOND CONJUGATION | docēre | docē! | docēte! |
| | *to teach* | *teach!* | *teach!* |
| THIRD CONJUGATION | trahere | trahe! | trahite! |
| | *to drag* | *drag!* | *drag!* |
| FOURTH CONJUGATION | audīre | audī! | audīte! |
| | *to listen* | *listen!* | *listen!* |

**3** Translate the following examples:

festīnā!    respondē!    labōrāte!    curre!
date mihi pecūniam!    sedē!

In each example, is the order being given to one person only, or to more than one?

**4** Notice the way in which people are ordered *not* to do things:

SINGULAR:    nōlī currere!    *don't run!*
             nōlī cantāre!    *don't sing!*

PLURAL:    nōlīte festīnāre!    *don't hurry!*
           nōlīte trūdere!    *don't push!*

**5** Translate the following examples:

tacēte!    labōrā!    tacē!    currite!
nōlī dormīre!    nōlīte pugnāre!

In each example, is the order being given to one person only, or to more than one?

# Practicing the Language

**1** Complete each sentence with the right word and then translate.

1 astrologus, ubi dē vēnātiōne audīvit, Barbillō amulētum . . . . . .
  (dedit, dedērunt)
2 Barbillus et amīcus ad praedium, quod situm erat prope Nīlum,
  . . . . . .(contendit, contendērunt)
3 Aethiopes, quī hastās tenēbant, Barbillum . . . . . . (exspectābat, exspectābant)
4 multī servī, quōs vīlicus collēgerat, in ōrdinibus longīs . . . . . .
  (stābat, stābant)
5 ubi Barbillus Aethiopas servōsque īnspexit, omnēs ad rīpam Nīlī
  iter . . . . . . (fēcit, fēcērunt)

situm: situs *situated*

**2** This exercise is based on the story "diēs fēstus" on pages 122-23. Read the story again. Complete each of the sentences below with one of the following groups of words and then translate. Use each group of words once only.

postquam ad illum locum pervēnērunt
quod pompam vidēre volēbat
simulac prīmus diēs vēris advēnit
postquam marītum vituperāvit
quamquam Galatēa eum saepe monuit
quod valdē īrāta erat

1 sacerdōtēs . . . . . deam Īsidem ad portum ferre solēbant.
2 Galatēa Aristōnem iussit servum māne ēmittere et locum
   servāre . . . . . .
3 sed Aristō . . . . . servum nōn ēmīsit.
4 Aristō et Galatēa . . . . . duōs iuvenēs ibi cōnspexērunt.
5 Galatēa marītum vituperāre coepit . . . . . .
6 Galatēa . . . . . iuvenēs ēmōvit.

**3** With the help of the table of nouns on pages 162–63 of the Review Grammar, complete the sentences of this exercise with the right form of each unfinished word and then translate. For example:

mercātor in viā stābat. amīcī mercātōr. . . salūtāvērunt.
mercātor in viā stābat. amīcī mercātōrem salūtāvērunt.
*A merchant was standing in the street. The friends greeted the merchant.*

1 puella stolam habēbat. stola puell. . . erat splendidissima.
2 servus leō. . . in silvā vīdit. leō dormiēbat.
3 puellae tabernam intrāvērunt. mercātor puell. . . multās stolās ostendit.
4 cīvēs rēgem laudāvērunt, quod rēx cīv. . . magnum spectāculum dederat.
5 serv. . ., quod dominum timēbant, fūgērunt.
6 mercātōrēs gemmās vēndēbant. gemmae mercātōr. . . Clēmentem dēlectāvērunt.
7 rēx mēcum cēnābat. ego rē. . . pōculum vīnī obtulī.
8 multī cīvēs in casīs habitābant. casae cīv. . . erant sordidae.
9 servī dīligenter labōrāvērunt. serv. . . igitur praemium dedī.

10 puer perterritus ad templum cucurrit et iānuam templ. . . pulsāvit.

11 rē. . ., quī in aulā sedēbat, tubam audīvit.

12 Salvius puer. . ., quī amphorās portābant, vehementer vituperāvit.

# About the Language

1 In each of the following sentences, somebody is being spoken to:

| | |
|---|---|
| **Aristō**! quam stultus es! | *Aristo! How stupid you are!* |
| quid accidit, **Barbille**? | *What happened, **Barbillus?*** |
| contendite, **amīcī**! | *Hurry, **friends!*** |
| cūr rīdētis, **cīvēs**? | *Why are you laughing, **citizens?*** |

The words in boldface are in the *vocative* case. If only one person is spoken to, the *vocative singular* is used; if more than one person, the *vocative plural* is used.

2 Compare the nominative singular and vocative singular of the second declension nouns like **servus** and **Salvius**:

| NOMINATIVE | VOCATIVE |
|---|---|
| **servus** labōrat. | cūr labōrās, **serve**? |
| **amīcus** gladium habet. | dā mihi gladium, **amīce**! |
| **Eutychus** est in viā. | ubi sunt operae, **Eutyche**? |
| **fīlius** currit. | cūr curris, **fīlī**? |
| **Salvius** est īrātus. | quid accidit, **Salvī**? |
| **Holcōnius** in lectō recumbit. | **Holcōnī**! surge! |

**Coin portraying Isis holding a billowing sail and standing before the Pharos at Alexandria.**

**3** In all other nouns, the vocative singular has the same form as the nominative singular:

NOMINATIVE
**iuvenis** clāmat.
**Helena** cibum cōnsūmit.

VOCATIVE
tacē, **iuvenis!**
placetne tibi, **Helena**?

**4** The vocative plural always has the same form as the nominative plural:

NOMINATIVE
**custōdēs** dormiunt.
**puerī** in forō stant.

VOCATIVE
vōs semper dormītis, **custōdēs.**
ubi est theātrum, **puerī**?

# The Worship of Isis

Isis was one of Egypt's oldest and most important goddesses. According to the Egyptians, she had loved and married the god Osiris, who appeared on earth in the form of a man. However, Osiris was murdered; his body was cut up and the pieces were scattered throughout the world. Overcome with grief, Isis set out on a search for the pieces of her husband's corpse. When at last she had found them all, a miracle took place; the dead Osiris was given new life and became the father of the child Horus. The Egyptians worshiped Isis for her power to give new life; they believed that just as she had given new life to Osiris, she was also responsible for the new life which appeared in springtime, or which followed the annual flooding of the Nile waters. They believed also that she offered a hope of life after death for those who became her followers.

One of the most important festivals of Isis was held at the beginning of spring. It took place on March 5th each year, when the sailing season opened and the large grain ships could once again set off safely across the Mediterranean to Rome. A statue of Isis was carried in procession down to the Great Harbor.

At the front of the procession came the dancers and musicians playing pipes, trumpets, and castanets. Female attendants scattered roses in the roadway and over the tightly packed crowd. The statue of Isis was carried high on the shoulders of her priests, so that everyone could get a glimpse of the goddess and her splendid robe. Next came more priests

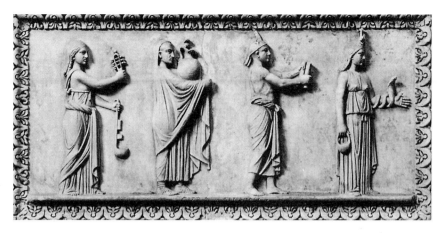

**Procession of priests and priestesses carrying sacred objects in the worship of Isis.**

and more trumpeters and finally the high priest, wearing garlands of roses and shaking a sacred rattle known as a **sistrum** (like that held by the statue on page 125, and the last priestess in the procession above).

At the harbor, a special newly built ship was moored. Its stern was shaped like a goose's neck and covered with gold plate. First the high priest dedicated the ship to Isis and offered prayers; then the priests and people loaded it with gifts of spices and flowers; finally the mooring-ropes were unfastened and the wind carried the ship out to sea.

After the ceremony at the harbor, the statue of Isis was taken back to the temple. The spectators crowded into the open area in front of the temple, and the priests replaced the statue in the **cella** or sanctuary. Then a priest on a raised platform read to the people from a sacred book, and recited prayers for the safety of the Roman people and their emperor, and for sailors and ships.

The festival was noisy, colorful, and spectacular. Everybody had the day off, and although the religious ceremony was serious, it was also good entertainment. When the ceremony was over, the Alexandrians continued to enjoy themselves in a lively and high-spirited way. Their behavior was sometimes criticized, for example by the writer Philo who attacked them in these words: "They give themselves up to heavy drinking, noisy music, amusements, feasting, luxury, and rowdy behavior, eager for what is shameful and neglecting what is decent. They wake by night and sleep by day, turning the laws of nature upside down."

But in spite of these words of Philo, a festival of Isis was not just an excuse for a holiday. The worship of the goddess was taken seriously by

Wall painting for Heculaneum, showing a cermony being performed in the worship of Isis. Notice four Nubian, or African, priests.

Blue faience hippopotamus from Egypt, now known as "William": in the Metropolitan Museum of Art, New York City.

many Egyptians, who went regularly to her temple, prayed to her statue, and made offerings. Some of them, like Clemens in Stage 18, went further and became **Īsiacī**, or members of the special brotherhood of Isis; this involved a long period of preparation leading up to a secret initiation ceremony in the temple.

Those who wished to join the brotherhood of Isis had to begin with an act of repentance for the sins they had committed in the past; for example, they might offer a sacrifice, or fast from food, or go on a pilgrimage. The poet Juvenal mockingly describes the behavior of a Roman woman cleansing herself of her previous sins in the following unpleasant manner: "On a winter morning she'll break the ice, lower herself into the river Tiber, and duck her head three times under the swirling waters. Then out she'll crawl, naked and trembling, and creep on bleeding knees across the Campus Martius."

In a Latin novel known as *The Golden Ass*, the chief character becomes a follower of Isis. He explains to his readers how he prepared to be admitted to the brotherhood. First his body was washed by the priests in a ceremony of baptism; next he was instructed about the sacred mysteries of the goddess, and forbidden to reveal them to anyone outside the brotherhood; then he fasted from food for ten days; and finally he underwent the initiation ceremony in the temple.

This was a ceremony of mystery and magic, full of strange and emotional experiences for the worshipers: those who were initiated believed that they had personally met Isis and that by dedicating themselves as her followers they could hope for life after death. But the exact details of the ceremony were kept strictly secret, as the narrator of *The Golden Ass* explains: "If you are interested in my story, you may want to know what was said and done in the temple. I would tell you if I were allowed to tell, you would learn if you were allowed to hear; but your ears and my tongue would suffer for your foolish curiosity."

The worship of Isis spread from Alexandria across the ancient world. Temples to Isis have been found in places as far apart as London and the Black Sea area. A group of priests serving in a temple of Isis at Pompeii suffered a miserable death when the city was destroyed in the eruption of Vesuvius. They collected the sacred objects and treasures, and fled from the temple, but by then it was too late. Their bodies were found along the route of their flight across the city, each corpse surrounded by the valuables he had tried to save. The food shown in the picture on page 28 of Unit 1 was found in the temple.

# Words and Phrases Checklist

| | |
|---|---|
| amō, amāre, amāvī | *love, like* |
| caedō, caedere, cecīdī | *kill* |
| cārus, cāra, cārum | *dear* |
| castīgō, castīgāre, castīgāvī | *scold, nag* |
| cautē | *cautiously* |
| cōgitō, cōgitāre, cōgitāvī | *think, consider* |
| comparō, comparāre, comparāvī | *obtain* |
| cōnficiō, cōnficere, cōnfēcī | *finish* |
| cūrō, cūrāre, cūrāvī | *take care of, supervise* |
| dē | *from, down from* |
| dēfendō, dēfendere, dēfendī | *defend* |
| dulcis | *sweet* |
| fīlia, fīliae | *daughter* |
| fluō, fluere, flūxī | *flow* |
| forte | *by chance* |
| grātiās agō | *I thank, give thanks* |
| illūc | *there, to that place* |
| iter, itineris | *journey, trip* |
| locus, locī | *place* |
| māne | *in the morning* |
| neglegēns, *gen.* neglegentis | *careless* |
| nōvī | *I know* |
| perīculum, perīculī | *danger* |
| plūrimus, plūrima, plūrimum | *very much* (plūrimī  *very many*) |
| pompa, pompae | *procession* |
| poscō, poscere, poposcī | *demand, ask for* |
| sonitus, sonitūs | *sound* |
| stola, stolae | *long dress* |
| tot | *so many* |
| umerus, umerī | *shoulder* |
| vexō, vexāre, vexāvī | *annoy* |
| vīvō, vīvere, vīxī | *live* |
| vix | *hardly, scarcely* |
| vōx, vōcis | *voice* |

# Word Search

allocate, cogitation, curator, dulcet, fortuitous, itinerant, vex

1 . . . . .: the administrative director of an institution such as a museum
2 . . . . .: melodious; sweet
3 . . . . .: traveling or wandering
4 . . . . .: thoughtful consideration, meditation
5 . . . . .: to designate
6 . . . . .: to bother, annoy
7 . . . . .: happening by chance or accident

# Stage 20

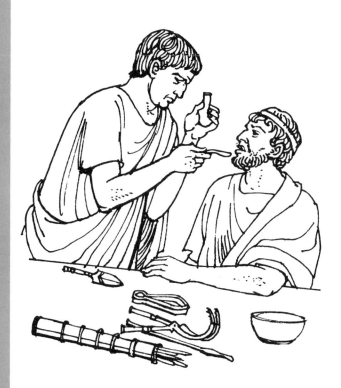

# medicus

servī ad vīllam revēnērunt,
Barbillum portantēs.

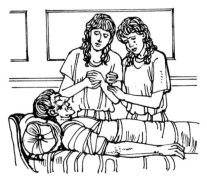

ancillae prope lectum
stābant, lacrimantēs.

astrologus in cubiculum
irrūpit, clāmāns.

Barbillus, in lectō recumbēns,
astrologum audīvit.

Phormiō ad urbem contendit,
medicum quaerēns.

# remedium astrologī

quattuor servī Barbillum exanimātum ad vīllam portāvērunt. multus sanguis ex vulnere effluēbat. Phormiō, quī servōs vulnerātōs sānāre solēbat, tunicam suam sciderat; partem tunicae circum umerum Barbillī dēligāverat. fluēbat tamen sanguis.

servī, quī Barbillum portābant, ubi cubiculum intrāvērunt, in 5 lectum eum lēniter posuērunt. duae ancillae prope lectum stābant lacrimantēs. Phormiō ancillās ē cubiculō ēmīsit et servōs ad sē vocāvit.

"necesse est vōbīs," inquit "arāneās quaerere. magnum

| | |
|---|---|
| remedium | *cure* |
| vulnere: vulnus | *wound* |
| effluēbat: effluere | *pour out, flow out* |
| sānāre | *heal, cure* |
| sciderat: scindere | *tear up* |
| dēligāverat: dēligāre | *bind, tie* |
| lectum: lectus | *bed* |
| arāneās: arānea | *spider's web, cobweb* |

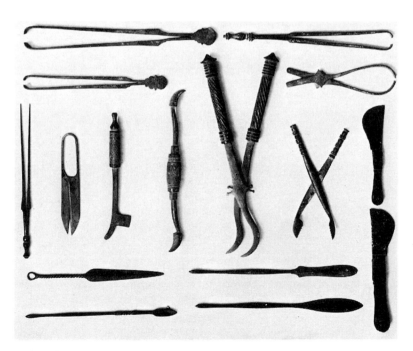

**Medical instruments.**

numerum arāneārum accipere volō. ubi sanguis effluit, nihil melius 10
est quam arāneae."

servī per tōtam vīllam contendēbant, arāneās quaerentēs;
magnum clāmōrem tollēbant. Phormiō, postquam servī multās
arāneās ad cubiculum tulērunt, in umerum dominī eās collocāvit.

astrologus ancillās lacrimantēs vīdit, servōsque clāmantēs 15
audīvit. statim in cubiculum Barbillī irrūpit, exclāmāns:

"nōnne hoc prōvīdī? ō nefāstum diem! ō dominum īnfēlīcem!"

"habēsne remedium?" rogāvī anxius.

"remedium certum habeō," respondit astrologus. "facile est mihi
Barbillum sānāre, quod nōs astrologī sumus vērī medicī. remedium 20
igitur Barbillō comparāre possum. est remedium, quod Chaldaeī
nōbīs trādidērunt. prīmō necesse est mihi mūrem nigrum capere.
deinde mūrem captum dissecāre volō. postrēmō eum in umerum
Barbillī pōnere volō. hoc sōlum remedium est."

subitō, Barbillus, quī astrologum audīverat, oculōs aperuit. 25
postquam mihi signum languidum dedit, in aurem meam
susurrāvit,

"quaere Petrōnem, medicum bonum!"

Phormiōnem, quī Petrōnem bene nōverat, ē vīllā statim ēmīsī.
itaque vīlicus medicum quaerēbat, astrologus mūrem. 30

| | | | | |
|---|---|---|---|---|
| numerum: numerus | *number* | | medicī: medicus | *doctor* |
| tollēbant: tollere | *raise* | | mūrem: mūs | *mouse* |
| collocāvit: collocāre | *place* | | nigrum: niger | *black* |
| prōvīdī: prōvidēre | *foresee* | | captum: captus | *captured, caught* |
| nefāstum: nefāstus | *terrible* | | dissecāre | *cut up* |
| certum: certus | *certain, infallible* | | languidum: languidus | *weak, feeble* |
| vērī: vērus | *true, real* | | | |

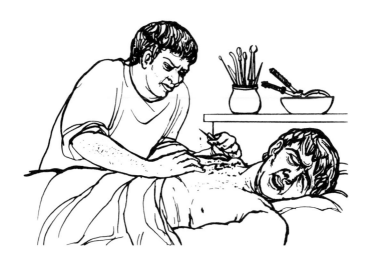

# Petrō

Petrō, postquam dē vulnere Barbillī audīvit, statim ad vīllam eius festīnāvit. ubi cubiculum intrāvit, astrologum vīdit, quī Barbillum sānāre temptābat. astrologus mūrem dissectum in vulnus dominī collocābat, versum magicum recitāns. Petrō, simulac mūrem cōnspexit, īrātissimus erat; astrologum verberāvit et ē cubiculō  5
expulit.

tum Petrō, postquam umerum Barbillī īnspexit, spongiam cēpit et in acētō summersit. eam in vulnus collocāvit. Barbillus exanimātus reccidit.

Petrō ad mē sē vertit.  10

"necesse est tibi mē adiuvāre," inquit. "difficile est mihi Barbillum sānāre. dē vītā eius dēspērō, quod tam multus sanguis etiam nunc effluit."

itaque medicō auxilium dedī. Petrō, postquam aquam ferventem postulāvit, manūs forcipemque dīligenter lāvit. deinde, forcipem  15

| | | | |
|---|---|---|---|
| eius | *his* | acētō: acētum | *vinegar* |
| dissectum: dissectus | *cut up, dismembered* | summersit: summergere | *dip* |
| versum magicum: | | reccidit: recidere | *fall back* |
| versus magicus | *magic spell* | ferventem: fervēns | *boiling* |
| spongiam: spongia | *sponge* | forcipem: forceps | *doctors' tongs, forceps* |

firmē tenēns, vulnus cum summā cūrā īnspexit. postquam hoc
cōnfēcit, umerum Barbillī lāvit; cutem, quam hasta servī secuerat,
perītē cōnseruit. dēnique fasciam lātam cēpit, umerumque firmē
dēligāvit.

mē ita monuit Petrō: 20
"nunc necesse est Barbillō in hōc lectō manēre; necesse est eī
quiēscere et dormīre. nātūra sōla eum sānāre potest, nōn
astrologus."

Petrōnī grātiās maximās ēgī. apud Barbillum diū manēbam,
negōtium eius administrāns. Barbillus enim mihi sōlī cōnfīdēbat. 25
cotīdiē ad cubiculum, ubi iacēbat aeger, veniēbam. multōs
sermōnēs cum Barbillō habēbam, prope lectum sedēns. postquam
Barbillum familiārissimē cognōvī, ille mihi dē vītā suā multum
nārrāvit. sine dubiō fortūna eum graviter afflīxerat.

| firmē | *firmly* | monuit: monēre | *advise* |
|---|---|---|---|
| cutem: cutis | *skin* | quiēscere | *rest* |
| perītē | *skillfully* | nātūra | *nature* |
| cōnseruit: cōnserere | *stitch* | familiārissimē: familiāriter | *closely, intimately* |
| fasciam: fascia | *bandage* | afflīxerat: afflīgere | *afflict, hurt* |
| lātam: lātus | *wide* | | |

**Reconstruction of a Roman bed.**

# About the Language

**1** Study the following sentences:

medicus, per forum **ambulāns**, Phormiōnem cōnspexit.
*The doctor, **walking** through the forum, caught sight of Phormio.*

in mediā viā stābat Eutychus, **rīdēns**.
*In the middle of the street stood Eutychus, **laughing**.*

servī, Barbillum **portantēs**, vīllam intrāvērunt.
*The slaves, **carrying** Barbillus, entered the house.*

amīcī, in tabernā **dormientēs**, clāmōrem nōn audīvērunt.
*The friends, **sleeping** in the inn, didn't hear the noise.*

The words in boldface are *present participles*.

**2** A present participle is used to describe a noun. For example, in the first sentence, **ambulāns** describes the doctor.

**3** Translate the following examples:

1 astrologus in cubiculum irrūpit, lacrimāns.
2 puerī, per urbem currentēs, Petrōnem cōnspexērunt.
3 sacerdōtēs, solemniter cantantēs, ad āram prōcessērunt.
4 Galatēa, in locō optimō stāns, pompam vidēre poterat.

Pick out the present participle in each sentence and find the noun which it describes.

**4** A present participle changes its ending to agree with the noun it describes. For example:

SINGULAR: Phormiō exiit, **clāmāns**. *Phormio went out, **shouting**.*
PLURAL: iuvenēs exiērunt, *The young men went out,*
**clāmantēs.** ***shouting**.*

5 Translate the following examples and pick out the present participle in each sentence:

1 fūr ē vīllā effūgit, cachinnāns.
2 mīlitēs, prō templō sedentēs, rēgem spectābant.
3 Eutychus, in lectō recumbēns, Clēmentem salūtāvit.
4 gladiātōrēs, in arēnā pugnantēs, nūbem mīrābilem vīdērunt.

Find the noun which each present participle is describing, and say whether each noun-and-participle pair is singular or plural.

6 A present participle is part of a verb. For example, **portantēs** (*carrying*) is part of the verb **portāre** (*to carry*); **dormientēs** (*sleeping*) is part of the verb **dormīre** (*to sleep*).

# fortūna crūdēlis

Barbillus uxōrem fidēlem fīliumque optimum habēbat. Plōtīna, uxor Barbillī, erat fēmina placida, quae domī manēbat contenta. Rūfus, fīlius Barbillī et Plōtīnae, erat iuvenis impiger. ad palaestram cum amīcīs saepe adībat; in dēsertīs equitāre solēbat, bēstiās ferōcissimās agitāns. aliquandō, sīcut aliī iuvenēs, 5 contentiōnēs cum parentibus habēbat. sed parentēs Rūfī eum maximē amābant, et ille eōs.

inter amīcōs Rūfī erat iuvenis Athēniēnsis, Eupor. hic Eupor ad urbem Alexandrīam vēnerat et medicīnae studēbat. saepissimē domum Barbillī vīsitābat. tandem ad urbem Athēnās rediit, ubi 10 artem medicīnae exercēbat. Eupor mox epistulam scrīpsit, in quā Rūfum parentēsque ad nūptiās suās invītāvit. Rūfus ad Graeciam īre valdē cupiēbat, sed Barbillus nāvigāre timēbat, quod hiems iam appropinquābat. astrologum suum igitur arcessīvit, et sententiam eius rogāvit. astrologus, postquam diū cōgitāvit, Rūfō 15 parentibusque respōnsum dedit.

"rem perīculōsam suscipitis. lūna Scorpiōnem iam intrat. tūtius est vōbīs domī manēre."

Barbillus et uxor astrologō, quī erat vir doctissimus, libenter crēdidērunt, sed Rūfus rem graviter ferēbat. ubi Barbillus aberat, Rūfus saepe ad mātrem ībat, patrem dēplōrāns:

"pater stultissimus est, quod astrologō crēdit. astrologī nōn sunt nautae. nihil dē arte nāvigandī sciunt."

itaque Rūfus Plōtīnae persuāsit, sed patrī persuādēre nōn poterat. Barbillus obstinātus nāvigāre nōluit. Rūfus igitur et Plōtīna Barbillum domī relīquērunt, et ad Graeciam nāvigābant. ubi tamen nāvis, quae eōs vehēbat, Graeciae appropinquābat, ingēns tempestās eam obruit. Rūfus ad lītus natāre poterat, sed Plōtīna, quam Barbillus valdē amābat, in magnīs undīs periit.

ubi Barbillus dē naufragiō, in quō uxor perierat, audīvit, maximē commōtus erat. fīlium iterum vidēre nōlēbat. Rūfus, quamquam domum redīre volēbat, patrī pārēbat. in Graeciā diū manēbat; sed tandem iter ad Britanniam fēcit, ubi in exercitū Rōmānō mīlitāvit.

| | |
|---|---|
| domī | *at home* |
| impiger | *lively, energetic* |
| aliquandō | *sometimes* |
| medicīnae: medicīna | *medicine* |
| studēbat: studēre | *study* |
| artem: ars | *art* |
| nūptiās: nūptiae | *wedding* |
| respōnsum | *answer* |
| tūtius est | *it would be safer* |
| nāvigandī | *of sailing* |
| vehēbat: vehere | *carry* |
| tempestās | *storm* |
| obruit: obruere | *overwhelm* |
| commōtus | *upset, distressed* |
| pārēbat: pārēre | *obey* |
| exercitū: exercitus | *army* |
| | |
| Athēniēnsis | *Athenian* |
| Scorpiōnem: Scorpiō | *the Scorpion (sign of the zodiac)* |

# astrologus victor

astrologus, quī in vīllā Barbillī habitābat, erat vir ingeniī prāvī.
astrologus et Petrō inimīcī erant. astrologus Syrius, medicus
Graecus erat. Petrō artem medicīnae in urbe diū exercuerat. multī
Alexandrīnī, quōs Petrō sānāverat, artem eius laudābant.

astrologus tamen in vīllā Barbillī habitābat, Petrō in urbe       5
Alexandrīā. facile igitur erat astrologō Barbillum vīsitāre. ad
cubiculum, in quō dominus aeger iacēbat, saepe veniēbat. ubi Petrō
aberat, astrologus in aurem dominī dīcēbat,

"in perīculō maximō es, domine. Petrō medicus pessimus est.
paucōs sānāvit. multōs aegrōs ad mortem mīsit. num Petrōnī       10
cōnfīdis? Petrō est vir avārissimus, nēmō est avārior quam ille.
pecūniam tuam cupit. necesse est tibi eum ē vīllā expellere."

Barbillus astrologum anxius audīvit. sed, quamquam dolor
cotīdiē ingravēscēbat, medicō etiam crēdēbat. ubi medicum
expellere Barbillus nōlēbat, astrologus cōnsilium cēpit. in       15
cubiculum dominī māne irrūpit, clāmāns:

"domine! tibi nūntium optimum ferō. tē sānāre possum! dea Īsis,
quae precēs meās semper audit, noctū somnium ad mē mīsit. in
somniō per viās urbis Alexandrīae ambulābam. subitō puerum vīdī
in triviīs stantem. puer erat servus tuus, quem Aegyptiī in tumultū   20
necāvērunt. mihi dē medicāmentō exquīsītissimō nārrāvit."

Barbillus, ubi hoc audīvit, astrologō sē tōtum trādidit. ille igitur,
postquam medicāmentum composuit, umerum dominī aperuit et
ūnxit. sed medicāmentum astrologī pessimum erat. ingravēscēbat
vulnus Barbillī.                                                 25

astrologus, ubi hoc sēnsit, ē vīllā fūgit perterritus. Barbillus, dē
vītā suā dēspērāns, mē ad cubiculum arcessīvit.

"mī Quīnte," inquit, in aurem susurrāns, "nōlī lacrimāre!
moritūrus sum. id plānē intellegō. necesse est omnibus mortem
obīre. hoc ūnum ā tē postulō. fīlium meum in Britanniā quaere!   30
refer eī hanc epistulam! ubi Rūfum ē vīllā expulī īrātus, eī magnam
iniūriam intulī. nunc tandem veniam ā Rūfō petō."

ubi hoc audīvī, Petrōnem arcessere volēbam, sed Barbillus
obstinātus recūsābat. arcessīvī tamen illum. sed ubi advēnit,
Barbillus iam mortuus erat.                                      35

| | |
|---|---|
| vir ingeniī prāvī | *a man of evil character* |
| dolor | *pain* |
| ingravēscēbat: | |
|   ingravēscere | *grow worse* |
| etiam | *also* |
| noctū | *by night* |
| somnium | *dream* |
| medicāmentō: | |
|   medicāmentum | *ointment* |
| exquīsītissimō: exquīsītus | *special* |
| composuit: compōnere | *put together, mix, make up* |
| ūnxit: unguere | *anoint, smear* |
| obīre | *meet* |
| refer: referre | *carry, deliver* |
| iniūriam intulī: | |
|   iniūriam īnferre | *do an injustice to, bring injury to* |

**Papyrus letter from Alexandria,
written in Greek in the first
century A.D.**

# About the Language

**1** You have now met various forms of the Latin word for *him, her, them,* etc.:

|  | SINGULAR | | | PLURAL | |
|---|---|---|---|---|---|
|  | GENITIVE | DATIVE | ACCUSATIVE | DATIVE | ACCUSATIVE |
| MASCULINE | eius | eī | eum ⎱ | eīs | eōs ⎱ |
| FEMININE |  |  | eam ⎰ |  | eās ⎰ |

Barbillus mē ad cēnam invītāvit. ego ad vīllam **eius** contendī.
*Barbillus invited me to dinner. I hurried to **his** house.*

operae celeriter convēnērunt. Eutychus **eīs** fūstēs trādidit.
*The thugs assembled quickly. Eutychus handed out clubs **to them**.*

Clēmēns officīnam intrāvit. Eutychus **eum** salūtāvit.
*Clemens entered the workshop. Eutychus greeted **him**.*

servī ingentēs erant. Clēmēns tamen **eōs** neglēxit.
*The slaves were huge. However, Clemens ignored **them**.*

**2** Further examples:

1 Barbillus in cubiculō iacēbat. Quīntus eī vīnum dedit.
2 Galatēa marītum castīgābat. tōta turba eam audīvit.
3 puellae suāviter cantābant. Aristō eās laudāvit.
4 ubi Petrō advēnit, Phormiō eum ad cubiculum dūxit.

# Practicing the Language

1 Translate into English:

Aristō: Galatēa! fortūna nōbīs favet! iuvenis Narcissus, quem heri vīdimus, Helenae dōnum mīsit. dōnum, quod iuvenis mīsit, pretiōsissimum est. dōnum mihi quoque mīsit. iuvenis Narcissus Helenam nostram amat.

Galatēa: quid dīcis, asine? iuvenis, quī prope nōs stābat, fīliae    5
nostrae dōnum mīsit? ēheu! marītum habeō, quī nihil intellegit. Narcissus humilis est. māter Narcissī est Aegyptia.

Aristō: fēminam, quam vituperās, nōn nōvī. sed Narcissum bene nōvī. iuvenis optimus est, quem omnēs laudant.    10

Galatēa: sed pater Narcissī est caupō. taberna, quam tenet, sordida est. vīnum, quod vēndit, pessimum est.

Aristō: tabernam patris nōn floccī faciō. Narcissus ipse probus et benignus est. iuvenis etiam līberālis est. dōnum, quod mihi mīsit, libellus est. (*Aristō libellum īnspicere*    15 *incipit.*) ēheu! Narcissus poēta est. suōs versūs scurrīlēs mihi mīsit.

Galatēa: fortūna nōbīs favet! nunc marītus meus illī iuvenī Helenam dare nōn vult.

| | |
|---|---|
| humilis | *low-born, of low class* |
| libellus | *little book* |
| incipit: incipere | *begin* |

# testāmentum Tiberiī Claudiī Barbillī

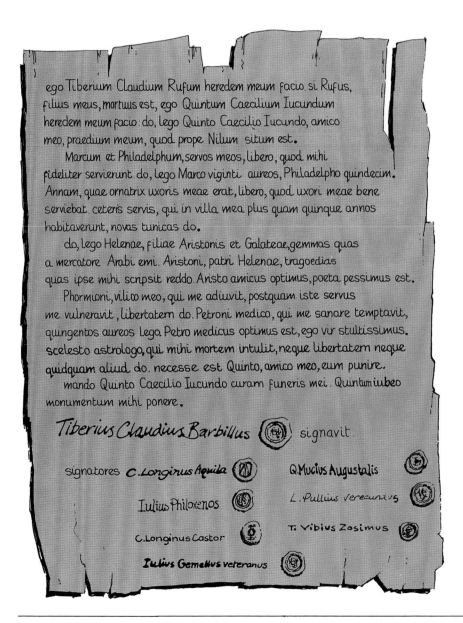

ego Tiberium Claudium Rufum heredem meum facio si Rufus,
filius meus, mortuus est, ego Quintum Caecilium Iucundum
heredem meum facio: do, lego Quinto Caecilio Iucundo, amico
meo, praedium meum, quod prope Nilum situm est.

Marcum et Philadelphum, servos meos, libero, quod mihi
fideliter servierunt. do, lego Marco viginti aureos, Philadelpho quindecim.
Annam, quae ornatrix uxoris meae erat, libero, quod uxori meae bene
serviebat. ceteris servis, qui in villa mea plus quam quinque annos
habitaverunt, novas tunicas do.

do, lego Helenae, filiae Aristonis et Galateae, gemmas quas
a mercatore Arabi emi. Aristoni, patri Helenae, tragoedias
quas ipse mihi scripsit reddo. Aristo amicus optimus, poeta pessimus est.

Phormioni, vilico meo, qui me adiuvit, postquam iste servus
me vulneravit, libertatem do. Petroni medico, qui me sanare temptavit,
quingentos aureos lego. Petro medicus optimus est, ego vir stultissimus.
scelesto astrologo, qui mihi mortem intulit, neque libertatem neque
quidquam aliud do. necesse est Quinto, amico meo, eum punire.

mando Quinto Caecilio Iucundo curam funeris mei. Quintum iubeo
monumentum mihi ponere.

Tiberius Claudius Barbillus  signavit

signatores  C. Longinus Aquila          Q. Mucius Augustalis

Iulius Philoxenos          L. Pullius Verecundus

C. Longinus Castor          T. Vibius Zosimus

Iulius Gemellus veteranus

| testāmentum | *will* |
|---|---|
| hērēdem: hērēs | *heir* |
| sī | *if* |
| dō, lēgō | *I give and bequeath* |
| fidēliter | *faithfully* |
| serviērunt: servīre | *serve (as a slave)* |
| plūs | *more* |
| quīngentōs: quīngentī | *five hundred* |
| mortem intulit: mortem īnferre | *bring death upon* |
| quidquam aliud | *anything else* |
| mandō: mandāre | *entrust* |
| fūneris: fūnus | *funeral* |
| signāvit: signāre | *sign, seal* |
| signātōrēs: signātor | *witness* |

1 Who is Barbillus' heir?
2 What is to happen if the heir chosen by Barbillus is dead?
3 What legacy does Barbillus leave to Quintus?
4 What instructions does Barbillus give about his slaves?
5 What does Barbillus leave to Helena?
6 What does he leave to Aristo? What is Barbillus' opinion of Aristo?
7 Barbillus mentions three people besides Quintus who took care of him when he was ill. What does he give to each of them?
8 In his will, Barbillus asks Quintus to do three things. What are they?
9 Judging from this will, what sort of person do you think Barbillus was?
10 Barbillus leaves nothing to Aristo's wife. Suggest possible reasons for this.

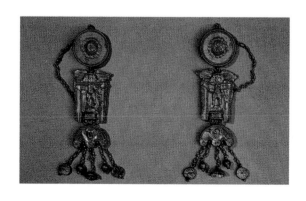

# Medicine and Science

Soon after its foundation, Alexandria became famous as a center of science and learning. The Museum and its library, which were set up and financed by the Greek rulers of Egypt, attracted intelligent men from all over the Greek world, who quickly began to make discoveries in all the sciences, including medicine. A good beginning had already been made in medicine by the Greek, Hippocrates, who had attempted to remove magic and superstition from the treatment of disease by observing his patients' symptoms carefully and trying to discover their causes. Hippocrates, who lived on the island of Cos in the fifth century B.C., was rightly regarded as the founder of medical science. He and his followers pledged themselves to high standards of conduct in a famous oath known as the Hippocratic oath. Part of it reads as follows:

"Into whatever houses I enter, I will go into them for the benefit of the sick, and will abstain from every voluntary act of mischief and corruption. Whatever in my professional practice I see or hear, which ought not to be spoken abroad, I will not divulge."

But Hippocrates and his Greek followers usually investigated only the surface of the body and not its interior; this was because the Greeks felt the idea of dissecting a body was disagreeable and perhaps wicked. The Egyptians, however, with their ancient custom of mummifying corpses, had a somewhat different attitude to the body, and dissections of corpses were frequently performed by Egyptian doctors. Alexandria was therefore a good place for studying anatomy. Herophilus, the most famous Alexandrian anatomist, gave a detailed description of the brain, explained the differences between tendons and nerves, arteries and veins, and described the optic nerve and the eye, including the retina. He also measured the frequency of the pulse and used this to diagnose fever. Like earlier doctors, he laid great stress on the importance of hygiene, diet, exercise, and bathing.

In addition to general advice of this kind, an experienced doctor of the first century A.D. would treat minor ailments with drugs, only some of which would be effective. The juice of the wild poppy, which contains opium, was used to relieve pain. Unwashed sheep's wool, containing lanolin, was often applied to wounds and swellings to soothe the irritation. Many prescriptions, however, would have been useless. For example, one account of the treatment of chilblains begins: "In the first place the chilblains are to be fomented thoroughly with boiled turnips . . . ." Any benefit felt by the patient would be due not to the turnips, but to the heat of the fomentation or the patient's own belief that the treatment would do him or her good.

Some prescriptions are rather alarming, such as this for severe toothache: "When a tooth decays, there is no great need to remove it, but if the pain compels its removal, a peppercorn or an ivy berry should be inserted into the cavity of the tooth, which will then split and fall out in bits."

Minor surgery was regularly practiced: "Tonsils are covered by a thin layer of skin. If they become hardened after inflammation, they should be scratched around with a finger and drawn out. If they cannot be drawn out in this way they should be gripped with a hook and cut out with a scalpel. The hollow should then be swilled out with vinegar and the wound smeared with something to check the blood."

Fractures and wounds presented greater problems. Nevertheless, doctors were able to make incisions, tie veins and arteries, reset broken bones with splints, and stitch up wounds. Difficult or very delicate operations were sometimes attempted, such as operations on the eye to relieve cataracts. Amputation of limbs was undertaken as a last resort.

Like Petro in the story on page 143, Greek doctors insisted on high standards of cleanliness in operations, to reduce the risk of infection. Although the quality of medical treatment in the ancient world would naturally vary considerably from one doctor to another, it is probably true that the standards of the best doctors were not improved upon in the western world until about a hundred years ago.

Astronomy, which had begun in Babylon, developed further at Alexandria. There the first attempts were made to calculate the distances between the Earth and the Sun, and between the Earth and the Moon. The idea was also put forward that the Earth was round, rotated on its axis and, with the other planets, circled the Sun. After the end of the western Roman Empire in the fifth century A.D., this idea was forgotten until Copernicus rediscovered it in the fifteenth century. It is remarkable that Alexandrian astronomers devised their theories and made their calculations without the aid of telescopes or other accurate instruments.

The Museum was also famous for the study of mathematics. Euclid, who worked at Alexandria in the third century B.C., wrote a book known as the *Elements*, in which he summarized all previous knowledge of

**A reconstruction of the Great Hall of the ancient Library of Alexandria.**

**Hero's steam turbine.**

geometry; it continued to be used as a school textbook almost down to the present day. In applying the mathematical knowledge to the world around them, the Greeks at Alexandria reached some very accurate conclusions. For example, Eratosthenes calculated that the circumference of the Earth was 24,662 miles; this is remarkably close to the true figure of 24,857.

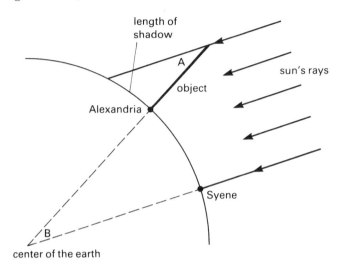

**Diagram of Eratosthenes' experiment**

At noon, when Eratosthenes had calculated that the sun was directly overhead in Syene, he measured the length of the shadow of an object in Alexandria. From this he could calculate the angle A between the sun's rays and the object. Since the sun's rays are parallel, by simple geometry angle B is the same size as angle A. Knowing angle B and the distance between Syene and Alexandria (which was north of Syene), he was able to calculate the circumference of the earth.

Hero of Alexandria invented the first steam turbine, in the form of a toy, in which a hollow ball was mounted on two brackets on the lid of a vessel of boiling water. One bracket was hollow and conducted steam from the vessel into the ball. The steam escaped from the ball by means of two bent pipes, thus creating a force which made the ball spin around. He also made a hollow altar, where, when a fire was lit, hot air streamed through four bent pipes to make puppets dance.

Ctesibius, an engineer who lived and worked in the Museum, invented the flap valve and force pump.

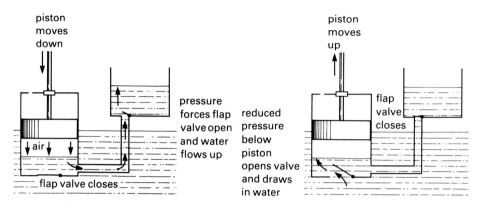

**Ctesibius' pump for raising water to a higher chamber**

This technology was used by Ctesibius in the original musical organ, which he called *hydraulis*, meaning "water-flute" in Greek—the source of the word *hydraulics*. When the pistons (C) move up, they pump air into the central bell (B), displacing some of the water into the tank (A). When the pistons move down again, flap valves (D) fall closed; the water in the bell (B) rises to find its level and forces the air through the flap valve (E) which opens, and to the pipes above the keyboard (F).

The Alexandrians did not take advantage of their scientific discoveries to build complicated and powerful machines for use in industry. Perhaps they felt they had no need for such machines, as they had a large work-force of slaves and free men available; perhaps they regarded trade and manufacturing as less dignified than scientific research and investigation; or perhaps they were prevented from developing industrial machinery by their lack of technical skills, such as the ability to make large metal containers and hold them together with screws and welds. Whatever the reason, some of the discoveries made by the Alexandrians were not put to practical use until several centuries later.

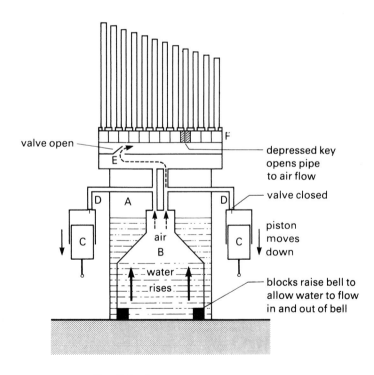

valve open

E

depressed key
opens pipe
to air flow

F

D A D

valve closed

piston
moves
down

C C

air
B

water
rises

blocks raise bell to
allow water to flow
in and out of bell

**Ctesibius' water organ.**

# Words and Phrases Checklist

| | |
|---|---|
| adeō, adīre, adiī | *approach, go up to* |
| arcessō, arcessere, arcessīvī | *summon, send for* |
| ars, artis | *art, skill* |
| auris, auris | *ear* |
| collocō, collocāre, collocāvī | *place, put* |
| crūdēlis | *cruel* |
| dēnique | *at last, finally* |
| doctus, docta, doctum | *educated, learned* |
| domus, domūs | *home* |
| equitō, equitāre, equitāvī | *ride (a horse)* |
| hiems, hiemis | *winter* |
| īnferō, īnferre, intulī | *bring in, bring on* |
| irrumpō, irrumpere, irrūpī | *burst in* |
| lātus, lāta, lātum | *wide* |
| līberō, līberāre, līberāvī | *free, set free* |
| lūna, lūnae | *moon* |
| medicus, medicī | *doctor* |
| mors, mortis | *death* |
| oculus, oculī | *eye* |
| parēns, parentis | *parent* |
| persuādeō, persuādēre, persuāsī | *persuade* |
| pessimus, pessima, pessimum | *very bad, worst* |
| precēs, precum | *prayers* |
| relinquō, relinquere, relīquī | *leave* |
| remedium, remediī | *cure* |
| sermō, sermōnis | *conversation* |
| sīcut | *like* |
| tam | *so* |
| temptō, temptāre, temptāvī | *try* |
| vulnus, vulneris | *wound* |

| | | | | | |
|---|---|---|---|---|---|
| ūnus | *one* | sex | *six* | vīgintī | *twenty* |
| duo | *two* | septem | *seven* | trīgintā | *thirty* |
| trēs | *three* | octō | *eight* | quadrāgintā | *forty* |
| quattuor | *four* | novem | *nine* | quīnquāgintā | *fifty* |
| quīnque | *five* | decem | *ten* | | |

# Word Search

aural, domesticate, imprecation, irremediable, latitude, pessimist, relinquish

1 . . . . .: extent, breadth
2 . . . . .: to tame
3 . . . . .: pertaining to the ear
4 . . . . .: one who habitually expects the worst
5 . . . . .: a curse
6 . . . . .: to abandon, leave behind
7 . . . . .: unable to be corrected; incurable

---

# Language
# Information
# Section

# PART ONE: Review Grammar

## Nouns

**1**   You have learned five of the six cases of the noun:

|  | *first declension* | *second declension* |  |  |
|---|---|---|---|---|
| gender | f. | m. | m. | n. |
| SINGULAR |  |  |  |  |
| *nominative* and *vocative* | **puella** | **servus** (*voc.* **serve**) | **puer** | **templum** |
| *genitive* | **puellae** | **servī** | **puerī** | **templī** |
| *dative* | **puellae** | **servō** | **puerō** | **templō** |
| *accusative* | **puellam** | **servum** | **puerum** | **templum** |
| *ablative (not yet learned)* |  |  |  |  |
| PLURAL |  |  |  |  |
| *nominative* and *vocative* | **puellae** | **servī** | **puerī** | *(not* |
| *genitive* | **puellārum** | **servōrum** | **puerōrum** | *yet* |
| *dative* | **puellīs** | **servīs** | **puerīs** | *learned)* |
| *accusative* | **puellās** | **servōs** | **puerōs** |  |
| *ablative (not yet learned)* |  |  |  |  |

*Notes*

1  The vocative case is used to name someone who is being spoken to directly, e.g. "**ubi es, serve?**" "*Where are you, slave?*"

2  Some 2nd declension nouns like **puer** have a nominative and vocative singular ending in **-er**. All their other cases are formed with endings like those of **servus**.

3  1st declension nouns like **puella, pecūnia**, and **via** are usually feminine. 2nd declension nouns are usually either masculine like **servus, cibus**, and **equus,** or neuter like **templum** and **aedificium**. 3rd declension nouns may be either masculine like **mercātor**, or feminine like **urbs**, or neuter like **nōmen**. (Sometimes in English the

*third declension*

| m. | m. | m.f. | m. | f. | n. | *gender* |
|---|---|---|---|---|---|---|
| | | | | | | SINGULAR |
| **mercātor** | **leō** | **cīvis** | **rēx** | **urbs** | **nōmen** | *nominative* and *vocative* |
| **mercātōris** | **leōnis** | **cīvis** | **rēgis** | **urbis** | **nōminis** | *genitive* |
| **mercātōrī** | **leōnī** | **cīvī** | **rēgī** | **urbī** | **nōminī** | *dative* |
| **mercātōrem** | **leōnem** | **cīvem** | **rēgem** | **urbem** | **nōmen** | *accusative* |
| | | | | | | *(not yet learned)* ablative |
| | | | | | | PLURAL |
| **mercātōrēs** | **leōnēs** | **cīvēs** | **rēgēs** | **urbēs** | *(not* | *nominative* and *vocative* |
| **mercātōrum** | **leōnum** | **cīvium** | **rēgum** | **urbium** | *yet* | *genitive* |
| **mercātōribus** | **leōnibus** | **cīvibus** | **rēgibus** | **urbibus** | *learned)* | *dative* |
| **mercātōrēs** | **leōnēs** | **cīvēs** | **rēgēs** | **urbēs** | | *accusative* |
| | | | | | | *(not yet learned)* ablative |

reasons for the gender of some of these nouns may not be clear: for example, **pecūnia** may not seem to us particularly feminine, nor **cibus** particularly masculine.)

4 Study the two nouns **templum** and **nōmen**. Notice that the form **templum** can be either nominative or accusative; so can the form **nōmen**. This is because **templum** and **nōmen** are *neuter*. Every neuter noun uses the same form for both its nominative and accusative singular. (You have not yet learned the nominative and accusative plural of neuter nouns.)

**2** Translate each sentence, then change the words in boldface from the singular to the plural, and translate again. Notice that in these examples *two* words in each sentence have to be changed.

For example: **agricola** in fundō **labōrābat.**
The **farmer was working** on the farm.

This becomes: **agricolae** in fundō **labōrābant.**
The **farmers were working** on the farm.

1 **servus** ferrum ē terrā **effodiēbat.**
2 **mercātor** ad urbem **contendēbat.**
3 **ancilla** in templō manēre **volēbat.**
4 **centuriō** fūrem ferōciter **pulsābat.**
5 **lībertus** saepe dē rēge Cogidubnō **audiēbat.**
6 cūr **canis** prope iānuam **lātrābat?**
7 **domina** coquum in culīnā **exspectābat.**
8 **hospes** cibum **gustābat.**
9 **custōs** servōs **spectābat.**
10 **servus** ad āream celeriter **currēbat.**

**3** Translate each sentence, then change the words in boldface from the plural to the singular, and translate again.

For example: **centuriōnēs** rēgem **salūtābant.**
The **centurions were greeting** the king.

This becomes: **centuriō** rēgem **salūtābat.**
The **centurion was greeting** the king.

1 **leōnēs** aquam **bibēbant.**
2 **servī** epistulās longās **scrībēbant.**
3 **ancillae** prope iānuam **stābant.**
4 **pictōrēs** Herculem **pingēbant.**
5 **mātrōnae** multās ancillās **habēbant.**
6 **candidātī** in forō **ambulābant.**
7 **iuvenēs** in viā **stābant.**
8 **fēminae** cum prīncipibus **sedēbant.**
9 **nāvēs** magnō saxō **appropinquābant.**
10 **servī** ursam **custōdiēbant.**

**4** Translate sentences 1–10, then change their meaning by turning:
each nominative into an accusative, *and*
each accusative into a nominative,
and then translate again.

For example:   dominus ancillās salūtāvit.
                     *The master greeted the slave-girls.*
This becomes:  ancillae dominum salūtāvērunt.
                     *The slave-girls greeted the master.*

Notice that in some sentences, as in the example above, you will have
to change the verb from singular to plural or from plural to singular.

  1  puerī leōnēs audīvērunt.
  2  puella coquum amāvit.
  3  Belimicus ursam cōnspexit.
  4  barbarī mīlitēs necāvērunt.
  5  rēx cīvēs laudāvit.
  6  fēminae mercātōrem vīsitāvērunt.
  7  mātrōnam pictor spectāvit.
  8  Rōmānōs Britannī interfēcērunt.
  9  imperātor honōrāvit victōrēs.
10  nautam vulnerāvit mīles.


**5** Translate the following sentences, which contain several examples of
the dative case. If you are not sure whether a word is dative singular or
plural, use the table in paragraph 1 for help.

  1  imperātor lībertīs et cīvibus spectāculum dedit.
  2  Salvius vīlicō et agricolae canem ostendit.
  3  puer iuvenibus et senī rem nārrāvit.
  4  ancillae mercātōrī et mīlitibus triclīnium parāvērunt.
  5  coquus dominō et amīcīs respondit.
  6  nūntius cīvī et nautae crēdēbat.

In Latin, dative forms often appear with verbs of "giving," "showing,"
and "telling" (e.g. above, **dedit, ostendit,** and **nārrāvit**). What other
kinds of verbs with the dative are illustrated in the sentences above?

---

**6** From Stage 17 onwards, you learned the *genitive* case:

puer ad tabernam **Clēmentis** cucurrit.
*The boy ran to Clemens' store.*

spectātōrēs clāmābant, sed rēx clāmōrēs **spectātōrum** nōn audīvit.
*The spectators were shouting, but the king did not hear the shouts of the spectators.*

iuvenis vōcem **fēminae** laudāvit.
*The young man praised the woman's voice.*

Further examples:

1 Quīntus, quī prope nāvem stābat, vōcēs nautārum audīvit.
2 Īsis erat dea. sacerdōtēs ad templum deae cotīdiē ībant.
3 magna multitūdō mīlitum in triviīs nōbīs obstābat.
4 in vīllā amīcī meī saepe cēnābam.
5 clāmōrēs puerōrum senem vexābant.
6 prīncipēs ad aulam rēgis quam celerrimē contendērunt.
7 umerus fabrī erat sordidus.
8 mīlitēs quī appropinquābant vōcēs cīvium audīre poterant.

# Adjectives

**1** In Stages 14 and 18, you learned how an adjective changes its endings to agree with the noun it describes in:
1 case,
2 number, *and*
3 gender.

**2** Most adjectives in Latin belong either to the 1st and 2nd declension or to the 3rd declension. The adjective **bonus** *good* is one that belongs to the 1st and 2nd declension:

|  | singular | | | plural | | |
|---|---|---|---|---|---|---|
|  | *masculine* (*2nd decl.*) | *feminine* (*1st decl.*) | *neuter* (*2nd decl.*) | *masculine* (*2nd decl.*) | *feminine* (*1st decl.*) | *neuter* (*2nd decl.*) |
| *nominative* and *vocative* | **bonus** (*voc.***bone**) | **bona** | **bonum** | **bonī** | **bonae** | |
| *genitive* | **bonī** | **bonae** | **bonī** | **bonōrum** | **bonārum** | *(not yet* |
| *dative* | **bonō** | **bonae** | **bonō** | **bonīs** | **bonīs** | *learned)* |
| *accusative* | **bonum** | **bonam** | **bonum** | **bonōs** | **bonās** | |
| *ablative* | (*not yet learned*) | | | | | |

Compare the endings of **bonus** with the endings of the 1st and 2nd declension nouns **servus**, **puella**, and **templum** listed on p. 162.

**3** The adjective **fortis** (*brave*) is one that belongs to the 3rd declension:

|  | *singular* | | *plural* | |
|---|---|---|---|---|
|  | *masc. and fem.*<br>*(3rd decl.)* | *neuter*<br>*(3rd decl.)* | *masc. and fem.*<br>*(3rd decl.)* | *neuter*<br>*(3rd decl.)* |
| *nominative*<br>and *vocative* | **fortis** | | **fortēs** | |
| *genitive* | **fortis** | *(not* | **fortium** | *(not* |
| *dative* | **fortī** | *yet* | **fortibus** | *yet* |
| *accusative* | **fortem** | *learned)* | **fortēs** | *learned)* |
| *ablative (not yet learned)* | | | | |

Compare the endings of **fortis** with the endings of the 3rd declension noun **cīvis** listed on p. 163.

**4** With the help of paragraphs 2 and 3, find the Latin words for *good* and *brave* in each of the following sentences:

1 The merchant praised his good daughter.
2 The king greeted the brave soldiers.
3 The good men were working hard.
4 A brave woman resisted the enemy.
5 The jewels of good merchants are genuine.
6 The citizens gave their support to the brave soldiers.
7 The enemy could not break the swords of the brave young men.

# Comparison of Adjectives (i.e. comparative and superlative forms)

**1** In Stage 8 of Unit 1, you learned the *superlative* form of the adjective:

Clēmēns est **laetissimus**.  coquus est **stultissimus**.
*Clemens is **very happy**.*  *The cook is **very stupid**.*

**2** In Stage 10, you learned the *comparative* form:

gladiātor erat **fortior** quam leō.  estis **stultiōrēs** quam asinī!
*The gladiator was **braver** than a lion.*  *You are **more stupid** than donkeys!*

**3** Study the difference between the positive (nominative and accusative), comparative and superlative forms of the following adjectives:

| positive | | comparative nominative | superlative nominative |
|---|---|---|---|
| nominative singular masculine | accusative singular masculine | | |
| **longus** *long* | **longum** | **longior** *longer* | **longissimus** *longest, very long* |
| **pulcher** *beautiful* | **pulchrum** | **pulchrior** *more beautiful* | **pulcherrimus** *most/very beautiful* |
| **fortis** *brave* | **fortem** | **fortior** *braver* | **fortissimus** *bravest, very brave* |
| **fēlīx** *lucky* | **fēlīcem** | **fēlīcior** *luckier* | **fēlīcissimus** *luckiest, very lucky* |

**4** The comparative and superlative forms change their endings in the usual way to indicate case, number, and gender:

*nominative:* leō **saevissimus** intrāvit.
A **very fierce** *lion entered.*

*accusative:* leōnem **saevissimum** interfēcī.
*I killed a* **very fierce** *lion.*

*singular:* Dumnorix est **callidior** quam Belimicus.
*Dumnorix is* **smarter** *than Belimicus.*

*plural:* Rēgnēnsēs sunt **callidiōrēs** quam Cantiacī.
*The Regnenses are* **smarter** *than the Cantiaci.*

*masculine:* dominus meus est **īrātissimus**.
*My master is* **very angry**.

*feminine:* uxor mea est **īrātissima**.
*My wife is* **very angry**.

3rd declension forms of adjectives (e.g. **fortis**, **fēlīx**, and all the comparative **-ior** forms) usually have the same form for both the masculine and feminine gender:

*masculine:* puer est **pulchrior** quam puella.
*The boy is* **more beautiful** *than the girl.*

*feminine:* puella est **pulchrior** quam puer.
*The girl is* **more beautiful** *than the boy.*

**5** Some important adjectives form their comparative and superlative in an irregular way:

| **bonus** | **melior** | **optimus** |
|---|---|---|
| *good* | *better* | *best, very good* |
| **magnus** | **maior** | **maximus** |
| *big* | *bigger* | *biggest, very big* |

and

| **multus** | **plūs** | **plūrimus** |
|---|---|---|
| *much* | *more* | *most, very much* |

which becomes in the plural:

| **multī** | **plūrēs** | **plūrimī** |
|---|---|---|
| *many* | *more* | *most, very many* |

*Note:* **plūs** is a neuter noun.

**6** Further examples:

1 leō erat maior quam Herculēs.
2 Clēmēns plūrēs amīcōs quam Eutychus habēbat.
3 Barbillus plūrēs gemmās quam Quīntus habēbat.
4 Aristō erat poēta melior quam Barbillus.
5 Petrō erat medicus melior quam iste astrologus.
6 Quīntus numquam gemmās maiōrēs vīderat.

**7** Translate each sentence below, then change the adjective in boldface
into the superlative form, and then translate again.

For example:   ātrium **magnum** erat.   *The atrium was **big***.
This becomes:  ātrium **maximum** erat. *The atrium was **very big***.

1 rhētor puerōs **bonōs** laudāvit.
2 **multī** cīvēs in flammīs periērunt.
3 Quīntus servīs **bonīs** lībertātem dedit.
4 Herculēs erat **magnus**, et **magnum** fūstem habēbat.

**8** Translate the first (a) sentence of each pair below.
Complete the second (b) sentence with a comparative and superlative
adjective, using the first sentence as a guide, and then translate. The
positive form of the adjective is given in parentheses after each
sentence.

1a Cerberus est ferōcissimus; canem ferōciōrem numquam vīdī.
   (ferōx)
1b gladiātor est . . . . . ; virum . . . . . numquam vīdī. (audāx)
2a frāter meus est sapientior quam tū; sapientissimus est. (sapiēns)
2b Bregāns est . . . . . quam Loquāx; . . . . . est. (īnsolēns)
3a mīlitēs sunt fortiōrēs quam cīvēs; fortissimī sunt. (fortis)
3b servī sunt . . . . . quam lībertī; . . . . . sunt. (trīstis)
4a Melissa vōcem suāvissimam habēbat; vōcem suāviōrem
   numquam audīvī. (suāvis)
4b Caecilius servum . . . . . habēbat; servum . . . . . numquam vīdī.
   (fidēlis)

# Pronouns

**1** In Unit 1, you learned the Latin words for *I, you* (singular), *me*, etc.:

|  | *I* | *you* |
|---|---|---|
| SINGULAR | | |
| *nominative* | **ego** | **tū** |
| *genitive (not yet learned)* | | |
| *dative* | **mihi** | **tibi** |
| *accusative* | **mē** | **tē** |
| *ablative (not yet learned)* | | |

senex **mihi** illum equum dedit.
*The old man gave that horse **to me**.*

iuvenis **tibi** hunc ānulum ostendit.
*The young man showed this ring **to you**.*

rhētor **tē** laudāvit.
*The teacher praised **you**.*

dominus **mē** vituperāvit.
*The master found fault with **me**.*

**2** You also learned the words for *we, you* (plural), *us*, etc.:

|  | *we* | *you* |
|---|---|---|
| PLURAL | | |
| *nominative* | **nōs** | **vōs** |
| *genitive (not yet learned)* | | |
| *dative* | **nōbīs** | **vōbīs** |
| *accusative* | **nōs** | **vōs** |
| *ablative (not yet learned)* | | |

**nōs** Rōmānī sumus mīlitēs.
***We** Romans are soldiers.*

**vōs** Graecī estis servī.
***You** Greeks are slaves.*

centuriōnēs **nōbīs** gladiōs dedērunt.
*The centurions gave the swords **to us**.*

servī **vōbīs** vīllam custōdiunt.
*The slaves are guarding the house **for you**.*

puer **nōs** vituperābat.
*The boy was cursing **us**.*

dominus **vōs** īnspicere vult.
*The master wants to inspect **you**.*

---

**3** Notice the Latin for *with me, with you*, etc.:

Salvius **mēcum** ambulābat.      Rūfilla **tēcum** cēnābat.
*Salvius was walking **with me**.*      *Rufilla was having dinner **with you**.*

rēx **nōbīscum** vēnit.      iuvenēs **vōbīscum** pugnābant?
*The king came **with us**.*      *Were the young men fighting **with you**?*

Compare this with the usual Latin way of saying *with*:

rēx **cum Salviō** ambulābat.      mīlitēs **cum iuvenibus** pugnābant.
*The king was walking **with Salvius**. The soldiers were fighting **with the
young men.***

Can you describe in your own words when **cum** should *follow* the word
for the person accompanied and when it should come *before*? If you
can't, study the above sentences again.

**4** Further examples:

1  ego tibi pecūniam dedī.
2  rēx nōs ad aulam invītāvit.
3  Cogidubnus nōbīscum sedēbat.
4  cūr mē accūsās?
5  nōs servī semper labōrāmus.
6  necesse est vōbīs mēcum venīre.
7  vōs Quīntō crēditis, sed Salvius mihi crēdit.
8  tē pūnīre possum quod ego sum dominus.
9  decōrum est mihi Quīntum invītāre.
10  vōs nautae, postquam tuba sonuit, diū clāmāvistis.
11  ubi prīnceps nōbīs signum dedit, exiimus.
12  quid tū fēcistī?

**5** The words **ego, tū**, etc. belong to a group of words called *pronouns*. Pronouns are used in sentences in a way similar to nouns. For example, this sentence uses the noun **Salvius**:

**Salvius** est dominus.               *Salvius is the master.*

But if Salvius himself were the speaker of the sentence, he would use not the noun **Salvius** but the pronoun **ego**:

**ego** sum dominus               *I am the master.*

Somebody speaking to Salvius would replace the noun **Salvius** with the pronoun **tū**:

**tū** es dominus.               *You are the master.*

And somebody speaking about Salvius, without facing him, could say:

**hic** est dominus.               *This man is the master.*
**ille** est dominus.               *That man is the master.*

The pronouns **hic** and **ille** are a special kind of pronoun called *demonstrative pronouns*. Another demonstrative pronoun that you have met is **iste** *that person*—angrily.

**6** You have also learned the pronoun **sē**, meaning *himself, herself,* or *themselves*. It has the same form for both singular and plural, both masculine and feminine. It does not have a nominative case:

|                          | *singular* | *plural* |
|--------------------------|-----------|----------|
| *nominative (none)*      |           |          |
| *genitive (not yet learned)* |       |          |
| *dative*                 | **sibi**  | **sibi** |
| *accusative*             | **sē**    | **sē**   |
| *ablative (not yet learned)* |       |          |

Dumnorix in ursam **sē** coniēcit.     rēgīna **sē** interfēcit.
*Dumnorix threw **himself** at the bear.*     *The queen killed **herself**.*

mercātor **sibi** vīllam ēmit.
*The merchant bought the house **for himself**.*
or *The merchant bought himself a house.*

mīlitēs in longīs ōrdinibus **sē** īnstrūxērunt.
*The soldiers drew* **themselves** *up in long lines.*

candidātī quoque **sibi** crēdēbant.
*The candidates too had faith* **in themselves**.

**7** In Stages 15 and 16, you learned various forms of the *relative pronoun*
**quī**, which is placed at the start of a *relative clause* and means *who, which,*
etc.:

| | singular | | | plural | | |
|---|---|---|---|---|---|---|
| | *masculine* | *feminine* | *neuter* | *masculine* | *feminine* | *neuter* |
| *nominative* | **quī** | **quae** | **quod** | **quī** | **quae** | *(not yet learned)* |
| *genitive (not yet learned)* | | | | | | |
| *dative (not yet learned)* | | | | | | |
| *accusative* | **quem** | **quam** | **quod** | **quōs** | **quās** | |
| *ablative (not yet learned)* | | | | | | |

ursa, **quam** Quīntus vulnerāvit, nunc mortua est.
*The bear* **which** *Quintus wounded is now dead.*

ubi est templum, **quod** Augustus Caesar aedificāvit?
*Where is the temple* **which** *Augustus Caesar built?*

in mediō ātriō stābant mīlitēs, **quī** rēgem custōdiēbant.
*In the middle of the atrium stood the soldiers,* **who** *were guarding the king.*

The noun described by a relative clause is known as the *antecedent* of the
relative pronoun. For example, in the first Latin sentence above, **ursa**
is the antecedent of **quam**.

**8** In Stage 19, the following forms of the *demonstrative pronoun* **hic** *this* (plural: *these*) were listed:

| | singular | | | plural | | |
|---|---|---|---|---|---|---|
| | *masculine* | *feminine* | *neuter* | *masculine* | *feminine* | *neuter* |
| *nominative* | **hic** | **haec** | **hoc** | **hī** | **hae** | *(not* |
| *genitive (not yet learned)* | | | | | | *yet* |
| *dative (not yet learned)* | | | | | | *learned)* |
| *accusative* | **hunc** | **hanc** | **hoc** | **hōs** | **hās** | |
| *ablative (not yet learned)* | | | | | | |

**hae** stolae sunt sordidae!      **hunc** servum pūnīre volō.
*These dresses are dirty!*      *I want to punish **this** slave.*

**9** You have also learned the following forms of the *demonstrative pronoun* **ille** *that* (plural: *those*):

| | singular | | | plural | | |
|---|---|---|---|---|---|---|
| | *masculine* | *feminine* | *neuter* | *masculine* | *feminine* | *neuter* |
| *nominative* | **ille** | **illa** | *(not* | **illī** | **illae** | *(not* |
| *genitive (not yet learned)* | | | *yet* | | | *yet* |
| *dative (not yet learned)* | | | | | | |
| *accusative* | **illum** | **illam** | *learned)* | **illōs** | **illās** | *learned)* |
| *ablative (not yet learned)* | | | | | | |

**illa** taberna nunc est mea.
*That store is now mine.*

**ille** diēs quem timēbat Cephalus tandem advēnit.
*That day which Cephalus feared arrived at last.*

spectā **illōs** hominēs!      audīvit **illās** precēs dea Īsis.
*Look at **those** men!*      *The goddess Isis heard **those** prayers.*

**illae** sunt fēminae quās vīdī rosās in viam spargentēs.
*Those are the women whom I saw scattering roses on the street.*

**10** In Stage 20, the following forms of the *determinative pronoun* **eum** *him /* **eam** *her* (nominative: **is** *he*) were listed:

|  | singular | | | plural | | |
|---|---|---|---|---|---|---|
|  | masculine | feminine | neuter | masculine | feminine | neuter |
| nominative (not yet learned) | | | | | | |
| genitive | **eius** | **eius** | *(not* | *(not yet* | *learned)* | *(not* |
| dative | **eī** | **eī** | *yet* | **eīs** | **eīs** | *yet* |
| accusative | **eum** | **eam** | *learned)* | **eōs** | **eās** | *learned)* |
| ablative (not yet learned) | | | | | | |

imperātor **eōs** laudāvit.     dominus **eī** praemium dedit.
*The emperor praised **them**.*     *The master gave a reward **to him** (or **her**).*
         or     *The master gave him (or her) a reward.*

**11** Further examples:

1 postquam senex hoc dīxit, Barbillus eum laudāvit.
2 in palaestrā erant multī āthlētae, quī sē exercēbant.
3 quamquam puellae prope mē stābant, eās vidēre nōn poteram.
4 hoc est vīnum quod Cogidubnus ex Ītaliā importat.
5 simulac mercātōrēs advēnērunt, Clēmēns eīs pecūniam trādidit.
6 dā mihi illum fūstem!
7 mīlitēs quōs imperātor mīserat nōbīscum sedēbant.
8 Barbillus hās gemmās sibi ēmit.
9 rēgīna, quae tē honōrāvit, nōs castīgāvit.
10 illa stola quam ēmistī est pulcherrima.
11 prīncipēs quōs Cogidubnus vocāverat convēnērunt.
12 simulac Eutychus hanc tabernam intrāvit, vōcem eius audīvī.

**12** The various forms of the demonstrative pronouns **hic** and **ille** can also be used to mean *he, him* (masculine), *she, her* (feminine), and *they, them* (plural):

**hic** dēcidit exanimātus; **illa** tamen nōn erat perterrita.
**He** *fell down unconscious;* **she**, *however, was not terrified.*

**illam** vīdī.     mē vīdit **illa**.
*I saw **her**.*     **She** *saw me.*

# Verbs

**1** You have learned the following forms of the verb:

| first conjugation | second conjugation | third conjugation | third -iō conjugation | fourth conjugation |
|---|---|---|---|---|
| PRESENT INFINITIVE | | | | |
| *to carry* | *to teach* | *to drag* | *to take* | *to hear* |
| **portāre** | **docēre** | **trahere** | **capere** | **audīre** |
| PRESENT TENSE | | | | |
| *I carry,* | *I teach,* | *I drag,* | *I take,* | *I hear,* |
| *you carry, etc.* | *you teach, etc.* | *you drag, etc.* | *you take, etc.* | *you hear, etc.* |
| **portō** | **doceō** | **trahō** | **capiō** | **audiō** |
| **portās** | **docēs** | **trahis** | **capis** | **audīs** |
| **portat** | **docet** | **trahit** | **capit** | **audit** |
| **portāmus** | **docēmus** | **trahimus** | **capimus** | **audīmus** |
| **portātis** | **docētis** | **trahitis** | **capitis** | **audītis** |
| **portant** | **docent** | **trahunt** | **capiunt** | **audiunt** |
| IMPERFECT TENSE | | | | |
| *I was carrying,* | *I was teaching,* | *I was dragging,* | *I was taking,* | *I was hearing,* |
| *etc.* | *etc.* | *etc.* | *etc.* | *etc.* |
| **portābam** | **docēbam** | **trahēbam** | **capiēbam** | **audiēbam** |
| **portābās** | **docēbās** | **trahēbās** | **capiēbās** | **audiēbās** |
| **portābat** | **docēbat** | **trahēbat** | **capiēbat** | **audiēbat** |
| **portābāmus** | **docēbāmus** | **trahēbāmus** | **capiēbāmus** | **audiēbāmus** |
| **portābātis** | **docēbātis** | **trahēbātis** | **capiēbātis** | **audiēbātis** |
| **portābant** | **docēbant** | **trahēbant** | **capiēbant** | **audiēbant** |
| PERFECT TENSE | | | | |
| *I (have)* | *I (have)* | *I (have)* | *I (have)* | *I (have)* |
| *carried, etc.* | *taught, etc.* | *dragged, etc.* | *taken, etc.* | *heard, etc.* |
| **portāvī** | **docuī** | **trāxī** | **cēpī** | **audīvī** |
| **portāvistī** | **docuistī** | **trāxistī** | **cēpistī** | **audīvistī** |
| **portāvit** | **docuit** | **trāxit** | **cēpit** | **audīvit** |
| **portāvimus** | **docuimus** | **trāximus** | **cēpimus** | **audīvimus** |
| **portāvistis** | **docuistis** | **trāxistis** | **cēpistis** | **audīvistis** |
| **portāvērunt** | **docuērunt** | **trāxērunt** | **cēpērunt** | **audīvērunt** |

| *first* conjugation | *second* conjugation | *third* conjugation | *third* -iō conjugation | *fourth* conjugation |
|---|---|---|---|---|

PLUPERFECT TENSE

| *I had carried, etc.* | *I had taught, etc.* | *I had dragged, etc.* | *I had taken, etc.* | *I had heard, etc.* |
|---|---|---|---|---|
| portāveram | docueram | trāxeram | cēperam | audīveram |
| portāverās | docuerās | trāxerās | cēperās | audīverās |
| portāverat | docuerat | trāxerat | cēperat | audīverat |
| portāverāmus | docuerāmus | trāxerāmus | cēperāmus | audīverāmus |
| portāverātis | docuerātis | trāxerātis | cēperātis | audīverātis |
| portāverant | docuerant | trāxerant | cēperant | audīverant |

IMPERATIVE

| *carry!* | *teach!* | *drag!* | *take!* | *hear!* |
|---|---|---|---|---|
| portā | docē | trahe | cape | audī |
| portāte | docēte | trahite | capite | audīte |

**2** Translate the following examples:
1. portāvī; audīvī; portābam; audiēbam.
2. portābant; docēbant; portāvimus; trāximus.
3. trahēbās; capiēbāmus; audiēbātis; audiebam.
4. docuit; trāxit; cēpērunt; cēpit; trāxērunt.
5. portāvistī; audīvistī; audīvistis; cēpistī.
6. docuerās; audīverās; audīverātis; trāxerātis.
7. capiēbat; cēperat; audīverat; audiēbat.
8. portātis; docēbātis; trāxistis; audīverātis.
9. portābāmus; audiēbāmus; portāvimus; audīvimus.
10. docueram; portābam; cēperam; trahēbam.
11. trahō; cēpī; audiēbam; portāveram.
12. portāmus; audiēbāmus; cēpimus; docuerāmus.

**3** In paragraph 1, find the Latin words for:
I was carrying; I was dragging; you (singular) were hearing; you (plural) were taking.

What would be the Latin for the following?

we carried; we heard; we took; we taught; you (plural) had heard; they taught; they dragged; you (plural) dragged.

**4** Translate the following examples, then change them from the singular to the plural, so that they mean *we* . . . . . instead of *I* . . . . ., and translate again:

trahō; audīvī; docēbam; labōrābam; faciēbam; scrīpsī; iubeō; īnspiciō. (Remember that **īnspiciō** is third conjugation "-iō")

**5** Translate the following examples, then change them from the plural to the singular, so that they mean *I* . . . . . instead of *we* . . . . ., and then translate again:

portāvimus; trahimus; audīverāmus; facimus; docēmus; laudāmus; capiēbāmus; intellēximus.

**6** Translate the following examples, then change them to mean *I* . . . . . instead of *he* . . . . ., and translate again:

trahēbat; īnspiciēbat; docet; intrāvit; dormiēbat; sedet; īnspexit.

**7** Translate the following examples, then change them to mean *we* . . . . . instead of *they* . . . . ., and translate again:

nāvigāvērunt; scrīpsērunt; īnspiciunt; terrent; vēndēbant; faciunt; complēverant.

**8** The forms of the verb that indicate *I, you* (singular), and *he* (or *she* or *it*) are known as the *1st, 2nd, and 3rd persons singular*; the forms that indicate *we, you* (plural), and *they* are known as the *1st, 2nd, and 3rd persons plural*. The table below summarizes the Latin personal endings and the English translations that are used to indicate the different persons:

|  | *Latin personal ending* | | *English* |
|---|---|---|---|
|  | *present, imperfect, and pluperfect* | *perfect* |  |
| *1st person singular* | **-ō** *or* **-m** | **-ī** | I |
| *2nd person singular* | **-s** | **-istī** | you |
| *3rd person singular* | **-t** | **-it** | s/he, it |
| *1st person plural* | **-mus** | **-imus** | we |
| *2nd person plural* | **-tis** | **-istis** | you |
| *3rd person plural* | **-nt** | **-ērunt** | they |

Thus, a word like **trāxerant** can be both translated (*they had dragged*) and described (*3rd person plural pluperfect*). Two further examples, **portāvī** and **docent**, are described and translated as follows:

| **portāvī** | 1st person singular perfect | *I carried* |
|---|---|---|
| **docent** | 3rd person plural present | *they teach* |

**9** Translate and describe the following examples:

trāxī; audīs; portābāmus; capis; docuerant; ambulāvistī; dīxerat.

# Irregular Verbs

**1** You have learned the following forms of five irregular verbs:

PRESENT INFINITIVE

| **esse** | **posse** | **velle** | **īre** | **ferre** |
|---|---|---|---|---|
| *to be* | *to be able* | *to want* | *to go* | *to bring* |

PRESENT TENSE

| *I am,* | *I am able,* | *I want,* | *I go,* | *I bring,* |
|---|---|---|---|---|
| *you are,* | *you are able,* | *you want,* | *you go,* | *you bring,* |
| *etc.* | *etc.* | *etc.* | *etc.* | *etc.* |
| **sum** | **possum** | **volō** | **eō** | **ferō** |
| **es** | **potes** | **vīs** | **īs** | **fers** |
| **est** | **potest** | **vult** | **it** | **fert** |
| **sumus** | **possumus** | **volumus** | **īmus** | **ferimus** |
| **estis** | **potestis** | **vultis** | **ītis** | **fertis** |
| **sunt** | **possunt** | **volunt** | **eunt** | **ferunt** |

IMPERFECT TENSE

| *I was,* | *I was able,* | *I was wanting,* | *I was going,* | *I was bringing,* |
|---|---|---|---|---|
| *etc.* | *etc.* | *etc.* | *etc.* | *etc.* |
| **eram** | **poteram** | **volēbam** | **ībam** | **ferēbam** |
| **erās** | **poterās** | **volēbās** | **ībās** | **ferēbās** |
| **erat** | **poterat** | **volēbat** | **ībat** | **ferēbat** |
| **erāmus** | **poterāmus** | **volēbāmus** | **ībāmus** | **ferēbāmus** |
| **erātis** | **poterātis** | **volēbātis** | **ībātis** | **ferēbātis** |
| **erant** | **poterant** | **volēbant** | **ībant** | **ferēbant** |

PERFECT TENSE

| *I was* | *I was able* | *I (have)* | *I have gone* | *I (have)* |
|---|---|---|---|---|
| *(have been),* | *(have been able),* | *wanted,* | *I went,* | *brought,* |
| *etc.* | *etc.* | *etc.* | *etc.* | *etc.* |
| **fuī** | **potuī** | **voluī** | **iī** | **tulī** |
| **fuistī** | **potuistī** | **voluistī** | **iistī** | **tulistī** |
| **fuit** | **potuit** | **voluit** | **iit** | **tulit** |
| **fuimus** | **potuimus** | **voluimus** | **iimus** | **tulimus** |
| **fuistis** | **potuistis** | **voluistis** | **iistis** | **tulistis** |
| **fuērunt** | **potuērunt** | **voluērunt** | **iērunt** | **tulērunt** |

*Note:* **tulī**, the perfect tense of **ferō**, is very different from the present tense. Compare this kind of difference with *I went* and *I go* in English.

**2** The negative forms of **volō** *I want* are formed in an irregular way. Compare the forms of **volō** *I want* with those of **nōlō** *I don't want:*

| I want, <br> you want, <br> etc. | I don't want, <br> you don't want, <br> etc. |
|---|---|
| **volō** | **nōlō** |
| **vīs** | **nōn vīs** |
| **vult** | **nōn vult** |
| **volumus** | **nōlumus** |
| **vultis** | **nōn vultis** |
| **volunt** | **nōlunt** |

**3** **sum** and **possum** also form their *imperfect* tense in an irregular way:

| I was, <br> you were, <br> etc. | I was able, <br> you were able, <br> etc. |
|---|---|
| **eram** | **poteram** |
| **erās** | **poterās** |
| **erat** | **poterat** |
| **erāmus** | **poterāmus** |
| **erātis** | **poterātis** |
| **erant** | **poterant** |

**4** Using paragraphs 1, 2, and 3, translate the following examples:

ferunt; es; potes; ībat; erāmus; poterāmus; fert; nōn vultis; tulit; sumus; ferēbant; vīs.

**5** In paragraph 1 find the Latin for:

he wants; they go; I was bringing; he went; you (plural) could; to bring; they wanted.

**6** In paragraphs 2 and 3, find the Latin for:

they were; he doesn't want; we were able; you (singular) are able; they want; they can; we were; they could.

**7** The verbs **adsum** *I am present* and **absum** *I am absent* are formed by adding **ad** and **ab** to the forms of **sum.**

| *I am,* | *I am present,* | *I am absent,* |
| --- | --- | --- |
| *you are,* | *you are present,* | *you are absent,* |
| *etc.* | *etc.* | *etc.* |
| **sum** | **adsum** | **absum** |
| **es** | **ades** | **abes** |
| **est** | **adest** | **abest** |
| **sumus** | **adsumus** | **absumus** |
| **estis** | **adestis** | **abestis** |
| **sunt** | **adsunt** | **absunt** |

**8** In paragraph 7, find the Latin for:

he is present; we are absent; they are present; you (plural) are absent; you (singular) are present; she is present.

# Word Order

**1** Notice the word order in the following sentences:

| clāmābant Rēgnēnsēs. | *The Regnenses were shouting.* |
| --- | --- |
| intrāvit Cogidubnus. | *Cogidubnus entered.* |

Further examples:

1 saltābant ancillae.
2 labōrābat Clēmēns.
3 dormiēbat rēx.

**2** From Stage 7 (in Unit 1) onwards, you have met the following word order:

| amīcum salūtāvit. | *He greeted his friend.* |
| --- | --- |
| ancillās laudāvimus. | *We praised the slave-girls.* |

Further examples:

1 rēgem salūtāvērunt.
2 dominōs audīvimus.
3 pecūniam invēnit.

**3** From Stage 18 onwards, you have met the following word order:

discum petīvit āthlēta.      *The athlete looked for the discus.*
nautās vituperāvit Belimicus.      *Belimicus cursed the sailors.*

Further examples:

1 amphoram portābat vīlicus.
2 vīnum bibēbant prīncipēs.
3 gladiātōrēs laudāvit nūntius.

**4** From Stage 17 onwards, you have also met the following word order:

mercātōrem rēx dēcēpit.      *The king deceived the merchant.*
equum agricola vēndidit.      *The farmer sold the horse.*

Further examples:

1 puellās iuvenis spectāvit.
2 gladiātōrem leō interfēcit.
3 āctōrēs rēgīna honōrāvit.

**5** The following sentences include all the different kinds of word order illustrated in paragraphs 1–4:

1 surrēxērunt prīncipēs.      5 rēgem cīvēs vīdērunt.
2 fīlium pater vituperābat.      6 plausērunt lībertī.
3 togam gerēbat.      7 deōs laudāvimus.
4 multitūdinem incitābat senex.      8 mē dēcēpistī.

**6** The following examples each contain a noun in the dative case:

nūntiō epistulam dedī.      *I gave a letter to the messenger.*
hospitibus agrum ostendit.      *He showed the field to the guests.*
amīcīs crēdēbat.      *He believed his friends.*

Further examples:

1 mercātōrī pecūniam reddidit.
2 mīlitibus cibum parāvī.
3 dominō resistēbant.
4 tibi faveō.

# Longer Sentences—I
# (with "postquam," "simulac," etc.)

**1** From Stage 6 (in Unit 1) onwards, you have met sentences like this:

Salvius, postquam fundum īnspexit, ad vīllam revēnit.
*Salvius, after he inspected the farm, returned to the house.*
   Or, in more natural English,
*After Salvius inspected the farm, he returned to the house.*

**2** From Stage 12 (in Unit 1) onwards, you have met sentences which are like the one above, but also contain a noun in the dative case. Study the following examples:

1  Rūfilla, postquam Salviō rem nārrāvit, surrēxit.
   *Rūfilla, after she told the story to Salvius, stood up.*
      Or, in more natural English,
   *After Rūfilla told Salvius the story, she stood up.*

2  imperātor, postquam gladiātōribus lībertātem dedit, ex amphitheātrō exiit.
   *After the emperor gave freedom to the gladiators, he went out of the amphitheater.*

**3** Further examples:

1  geminī, postquam coquō cibum trādidērunt, ē culīnā discessērunt.
2  nūntius, postquam cīvibus spectāculum nūntiāvit, ad tabernam festīnāvit.
3  rēx, postquam gladiātōrī pecūniam dedit, leōnem mortuum īnspexit.

**4** From Stage 13 onwards, you have met sentences with **quamquam**, **simulac**, and **ubi** *when*. Study the following examples:

1a  Pompēius custōdēs interfēcit.
   *Pompeius killed the guards.*
1b  Pompēius, quamquam invītus erat, custōdēs interfēcit.
   *Pompeius, although he was unwilling, killed the guards.*
      Or, in more natural English,
   *Although Pompeius was unwilling, he killed the guards.*

---

2a puer ē triclīniō contendit.

*The boy hurried out of the dining-room.*

2b simulac Salvius signum dedit, puer ē triclīniō contendit.

*As soon as Salvius gave the signal, the boy hurried out of the dining-room.*

3a Bregāns fūgit.

*Bregans ran away.*

3b ubi Salvius revēnit īrātus, Bregāns fūgit.

*When Salvius came back angry, Bregans ran away.*

**5** Translate the following examples of sentences with **quamquam**, **simulac**, **ubi** *when*, and **quod** *because*:

1 senex, quamquam uxor pompam vidēre volēbat, ex urbe discessit.

2 amīcī, simulac tabernam vīdērunt dīreptam, ad Clēmentem cucurrērunt.

3 iuvenēs, ubi Helenam cōnspexērunt, appropinquāvērunt.

4 simulac nāvem vīdit, Quīntus "ecce!" clāmāvit.

5 Salvius, quamquam servī dīligenter labōrābant, nōn erat contentus.

6 Clēmēns, quod Eutychus tabernae iam appropinquābat, amīcōs arcessīvit.

7 servus, simulac multitūdō ērūpit turbulenta, ad templum Serāpidis cucurrit.

8 Quīntus, quod amīcus Barbillus ad vēnātiōnem īre volēbat, in vīllā eius manēre nōn potuit.

**6** Complete each sentence with the most suitable group of words from the list below, and then translate. Use each group of words once only.

ubi saxō appropinquant
quamquam servī dīligenter labōrābant
simulac sacerdōtēs ē cellā templī prōcessērunt
postquam hospitī cubiculum ostendit
ubi iuvenēs laetī ad theātrum contendērunt
quod turbam īnfestam audīre poterat

1 . . . . ., dominus nōn erat contentus.

2 necesse est nautīs, . . . . ., cursum tenēre rēctum.

3 puer timēbat ē casā exīre, . . . . . .

4 . . . . ., tacuērunt omnēs.

5 māter, . . . . ., cibum in culīnā gustāvit.

6 . . . . ., senex in tablīnō manēbat occupātus.

**7** From Stage 15 onwards, you met sentences containing *relative clauses* introduced by such words as **quī** and **quae**:

sacerdōtēs quī prope āram stābant victimās īnspexērunt.
*The priests who were standing near the altar inspected the victims.*

**8** Translate the following examples, and pick out the relative clause if there is one. Find the noun that is being described by each relative clause.

1 flōrēs rēgem dēlectāvērunt.
2 flōrēs quī in hortō erant rēgem dēlectāvērunt.
3 nāvis ad mētam advēnit.
4 nāvis quam Belimicus dīrigēbat ad mētam advēnit.
5 prīncipēs quī in aulā sedēbant "vīnum!" clāmāvērunt.
6 fēminae quae in aulā cum prīncipibus sedēbant servōs spectābant.
7 faber ex Ītaliā vēnit.
8 faber quī lectum faciēbat ex Ītaliā vēnit.
9 omnēs prīncipēs ad aulam contendērunt.
10 omnēs prīncipēs quī in amīcitiā cum Cogidubnō erant ad aulam contendērunt.
11 ursa servum ferōciter percussit.
12 ursa, quam terruerant clāmōrēs, servum ferōciter percussit.
13 Quīntus et Clēmēns ad Graeciam iērunt.
14 Quīntus et Clēmēns, quī nāvem cōnscenderant, ad Graeciam iērunt.

# Longer sentences—II (with verbs understood)

**1** You have met several examples of this kind of sentence:

Rēgnēnsēs erant laetī, Cantiacī miserī.
*The Regnenses were happy, the Cantiaci were miserable.*

Britannī cibum laudāvērunt, Rōmānī vīnum.
*The Britons praised the food, the Romans praised the wine.*

**2** Further examples:

1 ūnus servus est fūr, cēterī innocentēs.
2 Cantiacī Belimicum spectābant, Rēgnēnsēs Dumnorigem.

**3** The following examples are slightly different:

sacerdōs templum, poēta tabernam quaerēbat.
*The priest was looking for a temple, the poet was looking for an inn.*

iuvenis Aegyptius, senex Graecus erat.
*The young man was Egyptian, the old man was Greek.*

**4** Further examples:
1 Clēmēns attonitus, Quīntus īrātus erat.
2 mercātor stolās, caupō vīnum vēndēbat.
3 puer ad portum, ancillae ad theātrum contendērunt.
4 Cogidubnus magnum taurum, Salvius parvum agnum sacrificāvit.
5 Galatēa stolam, iuvenēs Helenam spectābant.

# PART TWO: Reference Grammar

(Including some forms introduced later in the course)

## I Nouns

|  | *first declension* | *second declension* |  |  |
|---|---|---|---|---|
|  | *f.* | *m.* | *m.* | *n.* |
| **SINGULAR** |  |  |  |  |
| *nominative* and *vocative* | puella | servus (*voc.* **serve**) | puer | templum |
| *genitive* | puellae | servī | puerī | templī |
| *dative* | puellae | servō | puerō | templō |
| *accusative* | puellam | servum | puerum | templum |
| *ablative* | puellā | servō | puerō | templō |
| **PLURAL** |  |  |  |  |
| *nominative* and *vocative* | puellae | servī | puerī | templa |
| *genitive* | puellārum | servōrum | puerōrum | templōrum |
| *dative* | puellīs | servīs | puerīs | templīs |
| *accusative* | puellās | servōs | puerōs | templa |
| *ablative* | puellīs | servīs | puerīs | templīs |

|  | *third declension* |  |  |  |  |  |
|---|---|---|---|---|---|---|
|  | *m.* | *m.* | *m.f.* | *m.* | *f.* | *n.* |
| **SINGULAR** |  |  |  |  |  |  |
| *nominative* and *vocative* | mercātor | leō | cīvis | rēx | urbs | nōmen |
| *genitive* | mercātōris | leōnis | cīvis | rēgis | urbis | nōminis |
| *dative* | mercātōrī | leōnī | cīvī | rēgī | urbī | nōminī |
| *accusative* | mercātōrem | leōnem | cīvem | rēgem | urbem | nōmen |
| *ablative* | mercātōre | leōne | cīve | rēge | urbe | nōmine |
| **PLURAL** |  |  |  |  |  |  |
| *nominative* and *vocative* | mercātōrēs | leōnēs | cīvēs | rēgēs | urbēs | nōmina |
| *genitive* | mercātōrum | leōnum | cīvium | rēgum | urbium | nōminum |
| *dative* | mercātōribus | leōnibus | cīvibus | rēgibus | urbibus | nōminibus |
| *accusative* | mercātōrēs | leōnēs | cīvēs | rēgēs | urbēs | nōmina |
| *ablative* | mercātōribus | leōnibus | cīvibus | rēgibus | urbibus | nōminibus |

# II Adjectives

## 1 FIRST AND SECOND DECLENSION

|  | *singular* | | | *plural* | | |
|---|---|---|---|---|---|---|
|  | *masculine* | *feminine* | *neuter* | *masculine* | *feminine* | *neuter* |
| *nominative* and *vocative* | **bonus** (voc. **bone**) | **bona** | **bonum** | **bonī** | **bonae** | **bona** |
| *genitive* | **bonī** | **bonae** | **bonī** | **bonōrum** | **bonārum** | **bonōrum** |
| *dative* | **bonō** | **bonae** | **bonō** | **bonīs** | **bonīs** | **bonīs** |
| *accusative* | **bonum** | **bonam** | **bonum** | **bonōs** | **bonās** | **bona** |
| *ablative* | **bonō** | **bonā** | **bonō** | **bonīs** | **bonīs** | **bonīs** |

## 2 THIRD DECLENSION

|  | *singular* | | | *plural* | | |
|---|---|---|---|---|---|---|
|  | *masculine* | *feminine* | *neuter* | *masculine* | *feminine* | *neuter* |
| *nominative* and *vocative* | **fortis** | **fortis** | **forte** | **fortēs** | **fortēs** | **fortia** |
| *genitive* | **fortis** | **fortis** | **fortis** | **fortium** | **fortium** | **fortium** |
| *dative* | **fortī** | **fortī** | **fortī** | **fortibus** | **fortibus** | **fortibus** |
| *accusative* | **fortem** | **fortem** | **forte** | **fortēs** | **fortēs** | **fortia** |
| *ablative* | **fortī** | **fortī** | **fortī** | **fortibus** | **fortibus** | **fortibus** |

# III Pronouns

## 1 PERSONAL PRONOUNS (*I*, *you*, etc.)

|  | *singular* | | *plural* | |
|---|---|---|---|---|
|  | *first person* | *second person* | *first person* | *second person* |
| *nominative* | **ego** | **tū** | **nōs** | **vōs** |
| *genitive* | **meī** | **tuī** | **nostrum** | **vestrum** |
| *dative* | **mihi** | **tibi** | **nōbīs** | **vōbīs** |
| *accusative* | **mē** | **tē** | **nōs** | **vōs** |
| *ablative* | **mē** | **tē** | **nōbīs** | **vōbīs** |

## 2 REFLEXIVE PRONOUN (*herself, himself, itself, themselves*)

|  | *singular and plural* |
|---|---|
| *nominative (no forms)* | |
| *genitive* | **suī** |
| *dative* | **sibi** |
| *accusative* | **sē** |
| *ablative* | **sē** |

## 3 RELATIVE PRONOUN (*who, which,* etc.)

| | singular | | | plural | | |
|---|---|---|---|---|---|---|
| | *masculine* | *feminine* | *neuter* | *masculine* | *feminine* | *neuter* |
| *nominative* | quī | quae | quod | quī | quae | quae |
| *genitive* | cuius | cuius | cuius | quōrum | quārum | quōrum |
| *dative* | cui | cui | cui | quibus | quibus | quibus |
| *accusative* | quem | quam | quod | quōs | quās | quae |
| *ablative* | quō | quā | quō | quibus | quibus | quibus |

## 4 DEMONSTRATIVE PRONOUNS

| | singular | | | plural | | |
|---|---|---|---|---|---|---|
| | *masculine* | *feminine* | *neuter* | *masculine* | *feminine* | *neuter* |
| **hic** (*this, these,* etc.) | | | | | | |
| *nominative* | hic | haec | hoc | hī | hae | haec |
| *genitive* | huius | huius | huius | hōrum | hārum | hōrum |
| *dative* | huic | huic | huic | hīs | hīs | hīs |
| *accusative* | hunc | hanc | hoc | hōs | hās | haec |
| *ablative* | hōc | hāc | hōc | hīs | hīs | hīs |
| **ille** (*that, those,* etc.) | | | | | | |
| *nominative* | ille | illa | illud | illī | illae | illa |
| *genitive* | illīus | illīus | illīus | illōrum | illārum | illōrum |
| *dative* | illī | illī | illī | illīs | illīs | illīs |
| *accusative* | illum | illam | illud | illōs | illās | illa |
| *ablative* | illō | illā | illō | illīs | illīs | illīs |

## 5 DETERMINATIVE PRONOUN (*he, she, it; that, those,* etc.)

| | singular | | | plural | | |
|---|---|---|---|---|---|---|
| | *masculine* | *feminine* | *neuter* | *masculine* | *feminine* | *neuter* |
| *nominative* | is | ea | id | eī | eae | ea |
| *genitive* | eius | eius | eius | eōrum | eārum | eōrum |
| *dative* | eī | eī | eī | eīs | eīs | eīs |
| *accusative* | eum | eam | id | eōs | eās | ea |
| *ablative* | eō | eā | eō | eīs | eīs | eīs |

# IV Verbs

See Review Grammar, pp 178–79, for grammatical tables of infinitive, present, imperfect, perfect, pluperfect, and imperative.

**PRESENT PARTICIPLE** (*carrying, teaching, dragging, taking, hearing*)

|  | *first conj.* | *second conj.* | *third conj.* | *third conj. -iō* | *fourth conj.* |
|---|---|---|---|---|---|
| SINGULAR |  |  |  |  |  |
| *nominative* and *vocative* | portāns | docēns | trahēns | capiēns | audiēns |
| *genitive* | portantis | docentis | trahentis | capientis | audientis |
| *dative* | portantī | docentī | trahentī | capientī | audientī |
| *accusative* | portantem | docentem | trahentem | capientem | audientem |
| *ablative* | portantī/-e | docentī/-e | trahentī/-e | capientī/-e | audientī/-e |
| PLURAL |  |  |  |  |  |
| *nominative* and *vocative* | portantēs | docentēs | trahentēs | capientēs | audientēs |
| *genitive* | portantium | docentium | trahentium | capientium | audientium |
| *dative* | portantibus | docentibus | trahentibus | capientibus | audientibus |
| *accusative* | portantēs | docentēs | trahentēs | capientēs | audientēs |
| *ablative* | portantibus | docentibus | trahentibus | capientibus | audientibus |

See Review Grammar, pp. 182–83, for tables of some irregular verbs: **esse** *to be*, **posse** *to be able*, **velle** *to want*, **īre** *to go*, **ferre** *to bring*, and **nōlle** *not to want*.

# V The Infinitive

In Stage 13, you met the *infinitive* of the verb (e.g. **portāre** *to carry*, **dormīre** *to sleep*). You have met two types of infinitive constructions.

1 Complementary Infinitive

A complementary infinitive *complements* or *completes* a sentence which generally contains an auxiliary (helping) verb such as **volō** *I want*, **nōlumus** *we do not want*, or **potes** *you are able*. The following sentences contain a helping verb and a complementary infinitive:

**amphoram magnam portāre potes**.  *You are able to carry a large wine-jar.*
**ad urbem redīre nōlēbam**.  *I did not want to return to the city.*

2 Subject Infinitive

A subject infinitive is similar to a noun in that it is described by an adjective, such as **necesse** *necessary* or **decōrum** *proper*. The following sentences are examples of how the subject infinitive may be used in English:

To err is human. ("To err" is the infinitive, and "human" is the adjective that describes it.)
To resist is useless. ("To resist" is the infinitive, and "useless" is the adjective.)

The following are examples of the use of the subject infinitive in Latin:

**necesse est cubiculum ōrnāre**.  *It is necessary to decorate the bedroom.*
**hospitem nostrum vexāre nōn decōrum est**.  *It is not proper to annoy our guest.*

# VI  Agreement of Nouns and Adjectives

## 1 Case and Number

In Stage 14, you learned that an adjective must agree with the noun it describes in *case* and *number*. Study the following sentence:

**magnus servus iānuam custōdiēbat.**    *The large slave was guarding the door.*

The adjective **magnus** and the noun **servus** are both in the nominative case and they are both singular. Here is another example:

**nautae nāvēs pulchrās cōnspexērunt.**    *The sailors caught sight of the beautiful ships.*

The noun **nāvēs** and the adjective **pulchrās** are both accusative plural.

## 2 Gender

In Stage 18, you learned about the *gender* of nouns: every Latin noun is masculine, feminine, or neuter (a few, such as **cīvis** *citizen*, can be either masculine or feminine). An adjective must agree with the noun it describes in gender, as well as in case and number. Study again the examples shown in paragraph VI.1 above. In the first example, **magnus** is masculine to agree with **servus**, a masculine noun. In the second example, **pulchrās** is feminine to agree with **nāvēs**, a feminine noun. Refer to the noun and adjective tables on pp. 190 and 191 to review the endings for all three genders.

# VII  Relative Clauses

In Stage 15, you were introduced to a type of subordinate clause known as a *relative clause*, which is generally introduced by a relative pronoun and ends with a verb that is subordinate to the verb in the main clause.

## 1 Function of the Relative Clause

A relative clause can be substituted for an adjective, and it provides information about the noun it describes in the same way that an adjective does: by answering such questions as "who?", "which?", "what kind of?", etc. In Latin, the relative clause frequently occupies the usual position of the adjective—that is, following the noun it describes. For example, compare the following sentences:

**fēlēs sacra ad Clēmentem accurrit.**
*The sacred cat ran up to Clemens.*

**fēlēs, quae in templō habitābat, ad Clēmentem accurrit.**
*The cat, which was living in the temple, ran up to Clemens.*

Note that in the first sentence **fēlēs** *the cat* is described by an adjective, **sacra**. In the second sentence, **fēlēs** is described by the relative clause **quae in templō habitābat**. The adjective and the relative clause occupy the same position in the two sentences.

## 2 The Relative Pronoun

It is the relative pronoun (see p. 192 for a table of forms of the relative pronoun) that distinguishes the relative clause from other types of subordinate clause. The relative pronoun refers directly to the noun which the whole clause describes, and that noun is known as the *antecedent* of the relative pronoun. A relative pronoun (like an adjective) must agree with its antecedent in number and gender, but (unlike an adjective) it need not agree in case. This is because the case of the relative pronoun is determined by its function within the relative clause, not by the case of the noun in the main clause. Study the following example:

**pompa, quam Aristō Galatēaque spectābant, magnifica erat.**
*The procession, which Aristo and Galatea were watching, was magnificent.*

The noun **pompa**, which is being described by the relative clause, is feminine and singular. It is nominative, because it is the subject of the main verb **erat**. The relative pronoun **quam** is also feminine and singular, as it must be to agree with **pompa**, but it is in the accusative case, because it is the direct object of the verb **spectābant** in the relative clause.

# VIII  Participial Phrases

In Stage 14, you were introduced to the present participle, a part of a verb (see § IV above). A participle, like an adjective, agrees with a noun in case, number, and gender; like a verb, it describes the action or state of the noun with which it agrees.

An adjective, a relative clause, and a participial phrase (so far made up of a participle and its adverbial modifiers) can all be used to express a similar idea. For example, compare the following sentences:

**Barbillus in mediō cubiculō ancillās trīstēs vīdit.**
*Barbillus saw the sad slave-girls in the middle of his room.*

**Barbillus ancillās, quae in mediō cubiculō lacrimābant, vīdit.**
*Barbillus saw the slave-girls, who were weeping in the middle of his room.*

**Barbillus ancillās in mediō cubiculō lacrimantēs vīdit.**
*Barbillus saw the slave-girls weeping in the middle of his room.*

# IX  The Genitive Case

In Stage 17, you met the *genitive* case of the noun. You have seen the genitive case used in two types of construction.

1 Genitive of Possession

The genitive case is commonly used to indicate possession, as in the following expressions:

**vīlla Barbillī**     *the house of Barbillus* or *Barbillus' house*
**pēs leōnis**     *the paw of the lion* or *the lion's paw*

2 Genitive of Description

Sometimes the genitive case is used, like an adjective, to describe a noun, as in the following expression:

**multitūdō Aegyptiōrum**     *a crowd of Egyptians*

---

## X Principal Parts of a Verb

In the Complete Vocabulary, pp. 198–213, you will find that most verbs are listed with three forms, e.g. **capiō, capere, cēpī**. These forms are the first three of a total of four *principal parts* which your teacher may eventually want you to learn for **capiō**. Many Latin verbs—not just **capiō**—have four principal parts. The fourth principal part is the *perfect participle*. You will meet this at the beginning of Unit 3.

Principal parts are called "principal" because they are like building blocks, out of which all forms of a given verb are made. English verbs, too, have their own kind of principal parts that serve as building blocks: e.g. *take, took, taken*. With these three words, one can make any form of the English verb: "I *take*," for example, or "they *took*," or "the victim was *taken* to the hospital."

Knowing the principal parts of a verb can help you distinguish third conjugation "-iō" verbs from fourth conjugation verbs. The verbs below have similar endings in the first principal part (listed in the first column), but only third conjugation "-iō" verbs have, in the second column of matching infinitives, a short "e" before the "-re" termination.

| *third conjugation -iō*<br>*1* | *2* | *3* | *4* |
|---|---|---|---|
| **capiō**<br>*I take* | **capere**<br>*to take* | **cēpī**<br>*I took* | captus |
| **cōnspiciō**<br>**faciō**<br>**īnspiciō** | **cōnspicere**<br>**facere**<br>**īnspicere** | **cōnspexī**<br>**fēcī**<br>**īnspexī** | cōnspectus<br>factus<br>īnspectus |
| *fourth conjugation*<br>**audiō**<br>*I hear* | **audīre**<br>*to hear* | **audīvī**<br>*I heard* | audītus |
| **custōdiō**<br>**dormiō**<br>**sentiō** | **custōdīre**<br>**dormīre**<br>**sentīre** | **custōdīvī**<br>**dormīvī**<br>**sēnsī** | custōdītus<br>*(none)*<br>sēnsus |

Knowing the principal parts of a verb can help you distinguish first conjugation verbs from third conjugation verbs. The verbs below have similar endings in the first principal part (listed in the first column), but only third conjugation verbs have, in the second column of matching infinitives, a short "e" before the "-re" termination.

| *first conjugation*<br>**exspectō**<br>*I wait for* | **exspectāre**<br>*to wait for* | **exspectāvī**<br>*I waited for* | exspectātus |
|---|---|---|---|
| **pugnō**<br>**vituperō** | **pugnāre**<br>**vituperāre** | **pugnāvī**<br>**vituperāvī** | *(none)*<br>vituperātus |
| *third conjugation*<br>**intellegō**<br>*I understand* | **intellegere**<br>*to understand* | **intellēxī**<br>*I understood* | intellēctus |
| **reddō**<br>**scrībō** | **reddere**<br>**scrībere** | **reddidī**<br>**scrīpsī** | redditus<br>scrīptus |

# XI  Sentence Patterns

Below are some of the most important sentence patterns which you have met in Unit 2.
The patterns are shown on the left, with examples given on the right.
Key: NOM = nominative; ACC = accusative; DAT = dative; GEN = genitive; V = verb;
ADJ = adjective; INF = infinitive; RC = relative clause.

| PATTERNS | EXAMPLES |
|---|---|
| **V.1** (NOM) + INF + V | ancilla dormīre vult. |
| | *The slave-girl wants to sleep.* |
| **V.2** ADJ (decōrum, etc.) + est | facile est dominō servum pūnīre. |
| + DAT + (ACC) + INF | *It is easy for the master to punish the slave.* |
| **V.3** NOM + RC + V | nāvis, quam Dumnorix dīrigēbat, crocea erat. |
| | *The ship which Dumnorix was steering was yellow.* |
| **V.4** DAT + ACC + V | Vespasiānō multum auxilium dedī. |
| | *I gave much assistance to Vespasian.* |
| **V.5** ACC + NOM + V | hominēs scelestōs deī semper pūniunt. |
| | *The gods always punish wicked people.* |
| **V.6** NOM/ACC + GEN + V | taberna Clēmentis ardēbat. |
| | *Clemens' store was burning.* |
| **V.7** ACC + V + NOM | Clēmentem servāvit fēlēs sacra. |
| | *The sacred cat protected Clemens.* |
| **V.8** "nesting" of one subordinate | postquam Clēmēns, quī Eutychum operāsque nōn |
| clause inside another | timēbat, hoc dīxit, Eutychus vehementer saeviēbat. |
| | *After Clemens, who was not afraid of Eutychus and* |
| | *the thugs, said this, Eutychus was in a violent* |
| | *rage.* |

# PART THREE: Complete Vocabulary

**1** Nouns are listed in the following way:

the nominative case, e.g. servus (*slave*);
the genitive case, e.g. servī (*of a slave*, explained in Stage 17);
the gender of the noun (explained in Stage 18: m. = masculine,
f. = feminine, n. = neuter);
the meaning.

Thus, if the following information is given:

pāx, pācis, f. *peace*

**pāx** means *peace*, **pācis** means *of peace*, and the word is feminine.

**2** Adjectives are listed in the following way:

1st and 2nd declension adjectives are listed with the masculine,
feminine, and neuter forms of the nominative singular, as follows:

bonus, bona, bonum *good*

3rd declension adjectives are usually listed with the masculine form
only of the nominative singular, e.g. **fortis, trīstis**. (Often the
masculine form will also serve as the feminine form, e.g. **fortis vir** and
**fortis fēmina**.) Sometimes the genitive singular (which is always the
same for all genders) is added, e.g. ferōx, *gen.* ferōcis; ingēns, *gen.*
ingentis.

**3** Verbs are usually listed in the following way:

The *I* form of the present tense, e.g. parō (*I prepare*);
the present infinitive, e.g. parāre (*to prepare*);
the *I* form of the perfect tense, e.g. parāvī (*I prepared*);
and the meaning.

So, if the first three of the usual four principal parts are listed:

āmittō, āmittere, āmīsī *lose*

**āmittō** means *I lose*
**āmittere** means *to lose*
**āmīsī** means *I lost*.

**4** All words that are given in the "Words and Phrases Checklists" for
Stages 1–20 are marked with an asterisk.

# a

*ā, ab *from; by*

* abeō, abīre, abiī *go away*

abiciō, abicere, abiēcī *throw away*

* absum, abesse, āfuī *be gone, be absent,
   be away*

accidō, accidere, accidī *happen*

* accipiō, accipere, accēpī *accept,
   take in, receive*

accurrēns, *gen.* accurrentis *running up*

accūsō, accūsāre, accūsāvī *accuse*

acētum, acētī, n. *vinegar*

ācriter *keenly, fiercely*

āctor, āctōris, m. *actor*

* ad *to*

* adeō, adīre, adiī *approach, go up to*

adeō *so much, so greatly*

adhibeō, adhibēre, adhibuī *use, apply*
   precēs adhibēre *offer prayers to*

adiuvō, adiuvāre, adiūvī *help*

administrāns, *gen.* administrantis
   *managing*

administrō, administrāre,
   administrāvī *manage*

admittō, admittere, admīsī *admit, let in*

adōrō, adōrāre, adōrāvī *worship*

* adsum, adesse, adfuī *be here, be present*

* adveniō, advenīre, advēnī *arrive*

* aedificium, aedificiī, n. *building*

* aedificō, aedificāre, aedificāvī *build*

* aeger, aegra, aegrum *sick, ill*

Aegyptius, Aegyptia, Aegyptium
   *Egyptian*

Aegyptus, Aegyptī, f. *Egypt*

aēneus, aēnea, aēneum *made of bronze*

aequus, aequa, aequum *fair*

Aethiopes, Aethiopum, m.f.pl.
   *Ethiopians*

afflīgō, afflīgere, afflīxī *afflict, hurt*

ager, agrī, m. *field*

agilis *agile, nimble*

agitāns, *gen.* agitantis *chasing, hunting*

* agitō, agitāre, agitāvī *chase, hunt*

* agmen, agminis, n. *column (of people),
   procession*

* agnōscō, agnōscere, agnōvī *recognize*

agnus, agnī, m. *lamb*

* agō, agere, ēgī *do, act*
   age! *come on!*
   fābulam agere *act in a play*
* grātiās agere *thank, give thanks*

* negōtium agere *do business, work*
* quid agis? *how are you?*

* agricola, agricolae, m. *farmer*

āla, ālae, f. *wing*

Alexandrīnus, Alexandrīna,
   Alexandrīnum *Alexandrian*

aliquandō *sometimes*

* aliquid *something*

* alius, alia, aliud *other, another, else*

* alter, altera, alterum *the other, the second*

altus, alta, altum *deep*
   in altum *towards the open sea*

* ambulō, ambulāre, ambulāvī *walk*

amīca, amīcae, f. *friend*

* amīcē *in a friendly way*

amīcitia, amīcitiae, f. *friendship*

* amīcus, amīcī, m. *friend*

* āmittō, āmittere, āmīsī *lose*

* amō, amāre, amāvī *love, like*

amphora, amphorae, f. *wine-jar*

amulētum, amulētī, n. *amulet, lucky
   charm*

* ancilla, ancillae, f. *slave-girl, slave-woman*

animal, animālis, n. *animal*

* animus, animī, m. *spirit, soul*
   animum recipere *recover consciousness*

annus, annī, m. *year*

anteā *before*

* antīquus, antīqua, antīquum *old, ancient*

* ānulus, ānulī, m. *ring*

anus, anūs, f. *old woman*

anxius, anxia, anxium *anxious*

aperiō, aperīre, aperuī *open*

appāreō, appārēre, appāruī *appear*

* appropinquō, appropinquāre,
   appropinquāvī *approach, come near to*

* apud *among, at the house of*

* aqua, aquae, f. *water*

aquila, aquilae, f. *eagle*

* āra, ārae, f. *altar*

Arabs, *gen.* Arabis *Arabian*

arānea, arāneae, f. *spider's web, cobweb*

arātor, arātōris, m. *plowman*

arca, arcae, f. *strong-box, chest*

* accessō, arcessere, arcessīvī *summon,
   send for*

architectus, architectī, m. *builder,
   architect*

ardeō, ardēre, arsī *burn, be on fire*

ārea, āreae, f. *courtyard*

arēna, arēnae, f. *arena*

---

*argenteus, argentea, argenteum *made of silver*
armārium, armāriī, n. *chest, cupboard*
* ars, artis, f. *art, skill*
ascendō, ascendere, ascendī *climb, rise*
asinus, asinī, m. *ass, donkey*
assiduē *continually*
astrologus, astrologī, m. *astrologer*
Athēnae, Athēnārum, f.pl. *Athens*
Athēniēnsis *Athenian*
āthlēta, āthlētae, m. *athlete*
* ātrium, ātriī, n. *atrium, reception hall*
* attonitus, attonita, attonitum *astonished*
audāx, *gen.* audācis *bold, daring*
* audeō, audēre *dare*
* audiō, audīre, audīvī *hear, listen to*
* aula, aulae, f. *palace*
aurātus, aurāta, aurātum *gilded, gold-plated*
aureus, aurea, aureum *golden, made of gold*
aureus, aureī, m. *gold coin, gold piece*
* auris, auris, f. *ear*
* auxilium, auxiliī, n. *help*
avārus, avāra, avārum *miserly, stingy*
* avārus, avārī, m. *miser*
avidus, avida, avidum *eager*

# b

bālō, bālāre, bālāvī *bleat*
barbarus, barbarī, m. *barbarian*
* bene *well*
benignitās, benignitātis, f. *kindness*
* benignus, benigna, benignum *kind*
bēstia, bēstiae, f. *wild animal, beast*
* bibō, bibere, bibī *drink*
* bonus, bona, bonum *good*
Britannī, Britannōrum, m.pl. *Britons*
Britannia, Britanniae, f. *Britain*
Britannicus, Britannica, Britannicum *British*

# c

cachinnāns, *gen.* cachinnantis *laughing, cackling*
cachinnō, cachinnāre, cachinnāvī *laugh, cackle, roar with laughter*
cachinnus, cachinnī, m. *laughter*
cadō, cadere, cecidī *fall*
* caedō, caedere, cecīdī *kill*

caelum, caelī, n. *sky*
caerimōnia, caerimōniae, f. *ceremony*
caeruleus, caerulea, caeruleum *blue*
caesus, caesa, caesum *killed*
calcō, calcāre, calcāvī *step on*
* callidus, callida, callidum *clever, smart*
candēlābrum, candēlābrī, n. *lamp-stand, candelabrum*
candidātus, candidātī, m. *candidate*
* canis, canis, m. *dog*
canistrum, canistrī, n. *basket*
cantāns, *gen.* cantantis *singing, chanting*
* cantō, cantāre, cantāvī *sing, chant*
capillī, capillōrum, m.pl. *hair*
* capiō, capere, cēpī *take, catch, capture*
cōnsilium capere *make a plan, have an idea*
captus, capta, captum *taken, caught, captured*
* caput, capitis, n. *head*
carmen, carminis, n. *song*
carnifex, carnificis, m. *executioner*
* cārus, cāra, cārum *dear*
casa, casae, f. *small house, cottage*
* castīgō, castīgāre, castīgāvī *scold, nag*
caudex, caudicis, m. *blockhead, idiot*
caupō, caupōnis, m. *innkeeper*
* cautē *cautiously*
cecidī *see* cadō
cecīdī *see* caedō
cēdō, cēdere, cessī *give in, yield*
* celebrō, celebrāre, celebrāvī *celebrate*
* celeriter *quickly, fast*
celerius *faster*
celerrimē *very quickly*
quam celerrimē *as quickly as possible*
cella, cellae, f. *sanctuary*
cellārius, cellāriī, m. *(house) steward*
cēlō, cēlāre, cēlāvī *hide*
* cēna, cēnae, f. *dinner*
* cēnō, cēnāre, cēnāvī *eat dinner, dine*
centum *a hundred*
* centuriō, centuriōnis, m. *centurion*
cēpī *see* capiō
* cēra, cērae, f. *wax, wax tablet*
cērātus, cērāta, cērātum *wax, made of wax*
certāmen, certāminis, n. *struggle, contest*
certāmen nāvāle *boat race*
certō, certāre, certāvī *compete*
certus, certa, certum *certain, infallible*

cessī *see* cēdō

* cēterī, cēterae, cētera *the others, the rest*

Chaldaeī, Chaldaeōrum, m.pl.
*Chaldeans*

* cibus, cibī, m. *food*

* cinis, cineris, m. *ash*

circum *around*

* circumspectō, circumspectāre,
circumspectāvī *look around*

circumveniō, circumvenīre,
circumvēnī *surround*

citharoedus, citharoedī, m. *cithara
player*

* cīvis, cīvis, m.f. *citizen*

clādēs, clādis, f. *disaster*

clam *secretly, in private*

clāmāns, *gen.* clāmantis *shouting*

* clāmō, clāmāre, clāmāvī *shout*

* clāmor, clāmōris, m. *shout, uproar,
racket*

claudicō, claudicāre, claudicāvī
*be lame, limp*

* claudō, claudere, clausī *shut, close, block*

* coepī *I began*

* cōgitō, cōgitāre, cōgitāvī *think, consider*

* cognōscō, cognōscere, cognōvī, *find out,
get to know*

collēctus, collēcta, collēctum *gathered,
assembled*

colligō, colligere, collēgī *gather, collect,
assemble*

* collocō, collocāre, collocāvī *place, put*

columba, columbae, f. *dove, pigeon*

comes, comitis, m.f. *comrade, companion*

cōmis *polite, courteous, friendly*

cōmiter *politely, courteously*

commemorō, commemorāre,
commemorāvī *talk about*

* commodus, commoda, commodum
*convenient*

commōtus, commōta, commōtum
*moved, upset, affected, alarmed, excited,
distressed*

* comparō, comparāre, comparāvī
*obtain*

competītor, competītōris, m. *competitor*

* compleō, complēre, complēvī *fill*

compōnō, compōnere, composuī *put
together, arrange, mix, make up*

condūcō, condūcere, condūxī *hire*

cōnfectus, cōnfecta, cōnfectum *finished*

* cōnficiō, cōnficere, cōnfēcī *finish*

cōnfīdō, cōnfīdere *trust*

coniciō, conicere, coniēcī *hurl, throw*

coniungō, coniungere, coniūnxī *join*
sē coniungere *join*

* coniūrātiō, coniūrātiōnis, f. *plot,
conspiracy*

coniūrō, coniūrāre, coniūrāvī *plot,
conspire*

cōnscendō, cōnscendere, cōnscendī
*embark on, go on board*

cōnscius, cōnsciī, m. *accomplice*

cōnsecrō, cōnsecrāre, cōnsecrāvī
*dedicate*

* cōnsentiō, cōnsentīre, cōnsēnsī *agree*

cōnserō, cōnserere, cōnseruī *stitch*

cōnsīdō, cōnsīdere, cōnsēdī *sit down*

* cōnsilium, cōnsiliī, n. *plan, idea*
cōnsilium capere *make a plan, have an
idea*

* cōnsistō, cōnsistere, cōnstitī *stand one's
ground, stand firm*

* cōnspiciō, cōnspicere, cōnspexī *catch
sight of*

* cōnsūmō, cōnsūmere, cōnsūmpsī *eat*

* contendō, contendere, contendī *hurry*

contentiō, contentiōnis, f. *argument*

* contentus, contenta, contentum
*satisfied*

contrā *against*

contrōversia, contrōversiae, f. *debate*

* conveniō, convenīre, convēnī *come
together, gather, meet*

convertō, convertere, convertī *turn*
sē convertere *turn*

* coquō, coquere, coxī *cook*

* coquus, coquī, m. *cook*

corōna, corōnae, f. *garland, wreath*

* cotīdiē *every day*

* crēdō, crēdere, crēdidī *trust, believe,
have faith in*

crīnēs, crīnium, m.pl. *hair*

croceus, crocea, croceum *yellow*

crocodīlus, crocodīlī, m. *crocodile*

* crūdēlis *cruel*

* cubiculum, cubiculī, n. *bedroom*

cucurrī *see* currō

culīna, culīnae, f. *kitchen*

* cum *with*

cumulus, cumulī, m. *pile*

* cupiō, cupere, cupīvī *want*

* cūr? *why?*

cūra, cūrae, f. *care*

* cūrō, cūrāre, cūrāvī *take care of, supervise*
nihil cūrō *I don't care*
currēns, *gen.* currentis *running*
* currō, currere, cucurrī *run*
cursus, cursūs, m. *course*
* custōdiō, custōdīre, custōdīvī *guard*
* custōs, custōdis, m. *guard*
cutis, cutis, f. *skin*

# d

dare *see* dō
* dē *from, down from; about*
* dea, deae, f. *goddess*
* dēbeō, dēbēre, dēbuī *owe, ought, should, must*
* decem *ten*
* dēcidō, dēcidere, dēcidī *fall down*
dēcipiō, dēcipere, dēcēpī *deceive, trick*
* decōrus, decōra, decōrum *right, proper*
dedī *see* dō
* dēfendō, dēfendere, dēfendī *defend*
dēiciō, dēicere, dēiēcī *throw down, throw*
* deinde *then*
* dēlectō, dēlectāre, dēlectāvī *delight, please*
* dēleō, dēlēre, dēlēvī *destroy*
dēliciae, dēliciārum, f.pl. *darling*
dēligātus, dēligāta, dēligātum *tied up, moored*
dēligō, dēligāre, dēligāvī *bind, tie, tie up*
* dēmōnstrō, dēmōnstrāre, dēmōnstrāvī *point out, show*
dēnārius, dēnāriī, m. *a denarius (small coin worth four sesterces)*
* dēnique *at last, finally*
dēns, dentis, m. *tooth, tusk*
* dēnsus, dēnsa, dēnsum *thick*
dēpellō, dēpellere, dēpulī *drive off*
dēplōrāns, *gen.* dēplōrantis *complaining about*
dēplōrō, dēplōrāre, dēplōrāvī *complain about*
dēpōnō, dēpōnere, dēposuī *put down, take off*
* dērīdeō, dērīdēre, dērīsī *mock, make fun of*
dēscendēns, *gen.* dēscendentis *coming down*
dēscendō, dēscendere, dēscendī *come down*
dēserō, dēserere, dēseruī *desert*

dēsertus, dēserta, dēsertum *deserted*
in dēsertīs *in the desert*
* dēsiliō, dēsilīre, dēsiluī *jump down*
dēspērāns, *gen.* dēspērantis *despairing*
* dēspērō, dēspērāre, dēspērāvī *despair*
dēstringō, dēstringere, dēstrīnxī *draw (a sword), pull out*
* deus, deī, m. *god*
dexter, dextra, dextrum *right*
ad dextram *to the right*
diadēma, *gen.* diadēmatis, n. *diadem, crown*
* dīcō, dīcere, dīxī *say*
* dictō, dictāre, dictāvī *dictate*
* diēs, diēī, m. *day*
diēs fēstus, diēī fēstī, m. *festival, holiday*
* diēs nātālis, diēī nātālis, m. *birthday*
* difficilis *difficult*
dignitās, dignitātis, f. *dignity*
* dīligenter *carefully*
* dīmittō, dīmittere, dīmīsī *send away, dismiss*
dīreptus, dīrepta, dīreptum *torn apart, ransacked*
dīrigō, dīrigere, dīrēxī *steer*
dīripiō, dīripere, dīripuī *tear apart, ransack*
dīrus, dīra, dīrum *dreadful, awful*
* discēdō, discēdere, discessī *depart, leave*
dissecō, dissecāre, dissecuī *cut up*
dissectus, dissecta, dissectum *cut up, dismembered*
* diū *for a long time*
diūtius *any longer*
dīves, *gen.* dīvitis *rich*
dīxī *see* dīcō
* dō, dare, dedī *give*
doceō, docēre, docuī *teach*
* doctus, docta, doctum *educated, learned, skillful*
dolor, dolōris, m. *pain*
* domina, dominae, f. *lady (of the house), mistress*
* dominus, dominī, m. *master (of the house)*
* domus, domūs, f. *home*
domī *at home*
domum redīre *return home*
* dōnum, dōnī, n. *present, gift*
dormiēns, *gen.* dormientis *sleeping*

*dormiō, dormīre, dormīvī *sleep*
dubitō, dubitāre, dubitāvī *be doubtful, hesitate*
dubium, dubiī, n. *doubt*
ducentī, ducentae *two hundred*
*dūcō, dūcere, dūxī *lead*
*dulcis *sweet*
mī dulcissime! *my good man!*
*duo *two*
dūrus, dūra, dūrum *harsh, hard*

# e

*ē, ex *from, out of*
eam *her*
eās *them*
eburneus, eburnea, eburneum *ivory*
*ecce! *see! look!*
*effigiēs, effigiēī, f. *image, statue*
effluō, effluere, efflūxī *pour out, flow out*
effodiō, effodere, effōdī *dig*
effringō, effringere, effrēgī *break down*
*effugiō, effugere, effūgī *escape*
effundō, effundere, effūdī *pour out*
ēgī *see* agō
*ego, meī *I, me*
mēcum *with me*
ehem! *well, well!*
*ēheu! *alas! oh dear!*
eī *to him, to her, to it*
eīs *to them, for them*
eius *his*
ēlegāns, *gen.* ēlegantis *elegant*
ēligō, ēligere, ēlēgī *choose*
ēlūdō, ēlūdere, ēlūsī *slip past*
*ēmittō, ēmittere, ēmīsī *throw, send out*
*emō, emere, ēmī *buy*
ēmoveō, ēmovēre, ēmōvī *move, clear away*
enim *for*
*eō, īre, iī *go*
eōs *them*
*epistula, epistulae, f. *letter*
eques, *gen.* equitis, m. *horseman*
*equitō, equitāre, equitāvī *ride (a horse)*
*equus, equī, m. *horse*
eram *see* sum
ērubēscēns, *gen.* ērubēscentis *blushing*
ērubēscō, ērubēscere, ērubuī *blush*
ērumpō, ērumpere, ērūpī *break away*
est *see* sum
*et *and*

*etiam *even, also*
*euge! *hurrah!*
*eum *him*
ēvellēns, *gen.* ēvellentis *wrenching off*
ēvertō, ēvertere, ēvertī *overturn*
ēvolō, ēvolāre, ēvolāvī *fly out*
ēvulsus, ēvulsa, ēvulsum *wrenched off*
*ex, ē *from, out of*
*exanimātus, exanimāta, exanimātum *unconscious*
*excitō, excitāre, excitāvī *arouse, wake up*
*exclāmāns, *gen.* exclāmantis *exclaiming, shouting*
*exclāmō, exclāmāre, exclāmāvī *exclaim, shout*
*exeō, exīre, exiī *go out*
*exerceō, exercēre, exercuī *exercise*
exercitus, exercitūs, m. *army*
expellō, expellere, expulī *throw out*
explōrātor, explōrātōris, m. *scout, spy*
exquīsītus, exquīsīta, exquīsītum *special*
exspectātus, exspectāta, exspectātum *welcome*
*exspectō, exspectāre, exspectāvī *wait for*
extendō, extendere, extendī *stretch out*
extorqueō, extorquēre, extorsī *extort*
extrā *outside*
extrahō, extrahere, extrāxī *pull out, take out*

# f

*faber, fabrī, m. *craftsman*
*fābula, fābulae, f. *play, story*
*facile *easily*
*facilis *easy*
*faciō, facere, fēcī *make, do*
floccī nōn faciō *I don't give a hoot about*
*familiāris, familiāris, m. *relative, relation*
*familiāriter *closely, intimately*
fascia, fasciae, f. *bandage*
*faveō, favēre, fāvī *favor, support*
fax, facis, f. *torch*
fēcī *see* faciō
fēlēs, fēlis, f. *cat*
*fēmina, fēminae, f. *woman*
fenestra, fenestrae, f. *window*

* ferō, ferre, tulī *bring, carry*
   graviter ferre *take badly*
* ferōciter *fiercely*
* ferōx, *gen.* ferōcis *fierce, ferocious*
  ferrum, ferrī, n. *iron*
  fervēns, *gen.* ferventis *boiling*
* fessus, fessa, fessum *tired*
* festīnō, festīnāre, festīnāvī *hurry*
  fēstus, fēsta, fēstum *festival, holiday*
* fidēlis *faithful, loyal*
  fidēliter *faithfully, loyally*
* fīlia, fīliae, f. *daughter*
* fīlius, fīliī, m. *son*
  fīō *I become*
  firmē *firmly*
* flamma, flammae, f. *flame*
  floccī nōn faciō *I don't give a hoot about*
* flōs, flōris, m. *flower*
  flūmen, flūminis, n. *river*
* fluō, fluere, flūxī *flow*
  foedus, foeda, foedum *foul, horrible*
  fōns, fontis, m. *fountain*
  forceps, forcipis, m. *doctors' tongs, forceps*
* fortasse *perhaps*
* forte *by chance*
* fortis *brave, strong*
* fortiter *bravely*
  fortitūdō, fortitūdinis, f. *courage*
* fortūna, fortūnae, f. *fortune, luck*
  fortūnātus, fortūnāta, fortūnātum
    *lucky*
* forum, forī, n. *forum, business center*
* fossa, fossae, f. *ditch*
* frāctus, frācta, frāctum *broken*
  frangēns, *gen.* frangentis *breaking*
* frangō, frangere, frēgī *break*
* frāter, frātris, m. *brother*
  frequentō, frequentāre, frequentāvī
    *crowd, fill*
* frūmentum, frūmentī, n. *grain*
* frūstrā *in vain*
* fugiō, fugere, fūgī *run away, flee (from)*
  fuī *see* sum
  fulgēns, *gen.* fulgentis *shining, glittering*
* fulgeō, fulgēre, fulsī *shine, glitter*
  fundō, fundere, fūdī *pour*
* fundus, fundī, m. *farm*
  funebris, *funereal, of the funeral*
  fūnus, fūneris, n. *funeral*
* fūr, fūris, m. *thief*
  furēns, *gen.* furentis *furious, in a rage*
  fūstis, fūstis, m. *club, stick*

# g

  garriēns, *gen.* garrientis *chattering,*
    *gossiping*
  garriō, garrīre, garrīvī *chatter, gossip*
  garum, garī, n. *sauce*
* geminī, geminōrum, m.pl. *twins*
  gemitus, gemitūs, m. *groan*
* gemma, gemmae, f. *jewel, gem*
* gēns, gentis, f. *family, tribe*
  Germānicus, Germānica,
    Germānicum *German*
  gerō, gerere, gessī *wear*
  gladiātor, gladiātōris, m. *gladiator*
* gladius, gladiī, m. *sword*
  Graecia, Graeciae, f. *Greece*
  Graecus, Graeca, Graecum *Greek*
  grātiae, grātiārum, f.pl. *thanks*
*  grātiās agere *thank, give thanks*
  gravis *heavy*
* graviter *seriously*
  graviter ferre *take badly*
  gubernātor, gubernātōris, m.
    *helmsman*
* gustō, gustāre, gustāvī *taste*

# h

* habeō, habēre, habuī *have*
* habitō, habitāre, habitāvī *live*
  hāc *this*
  hae *these*
  haec *this*
  haedus, haedī, m. *young goat, kid*
* haereō, haerēre, haesī *stick, cling*
  hanc *this*
  harundō, harundinis, f. *reed*
  hās *these*
* hasta, hastae, f. *spear*
* hauriō, haurīre, hausī *drain, drink up*
* hercle! *by Hercules!*
  hērēs, hērēdis, m.f. *heir*
* heri *yesterday*
  heus! *hey!*
  hī *these*
* hic *this*
  hiemō, hiemāre, hiemāvī *spend the*
    *winter*
* hiems, hiemis, f. *winter*
  hippopotamus, hippopotamī, m.
    *hippopotamus*
  hoc *this*
  hōc *this*

*hodiē *today*
*homō, hominis, m. *person, man*
homunculus, homunculī, m. *little man, pip-squeak*
*honōrō, honōrāre, honōrāvī *honor*
hōra, hōrae, f. *hour*
*horreum, horreī, n. *barn, granary*
*hortus, hortī, m. *garden*
hōs *these*
*hospes, hospitis, m. *guest, host*
*hūc *here, to this place*
humilis *low-born, of low class*
hunc *this*

# i

*iaceō, iacēre, iacuī *lie, rest*
iaciō, iacere, iēcī *throw*
iactō, iactāre, iactāvī *throw*
*iam *now, already*
*iānua, iānuae, f. *door*
ībam *see* eō
*ibi *there*
id *it*
iēcī *see* iaciō
*igitur *therefore, and so*
*ignāvus, ignāva, ignāvum *cowardly, lazy*
ignōrō, ignōrāre, ignōrāvī *not know about*
iī *see* eō
illa *that, she*
illā *that*
illam *that*
illās *those*
*ille *that, he*
illī *they, those, that*
illinc *from there*
illīs *those*
illōs *those*
*illūc *there, to that place*
illum *that*
immemor, *gen.* immemoris *forgetful*
immortālis *immortal*
immōtus, immōta, immōtum *still, motionless*
impavidus, impavida, impavidum *fearless*
*impediō, impedīre, impedīvī *delay, hinder*
impellō, impellere, impulī *carry, push, force*

*imperātor, imperātōris, m. *emperor*
*imperium, imperiī, n. *empire*
*impetus, impetūs, m. *attack*
impetum facere *charge, make an attack*
impiger, impigra, impigrum *lively, energetic*
impleō, implēre, implēvī *fill*
importō, importāre, importāvī *import*
*in *in, on; into, onto*
incēdō, incēdere, incessī *march, stride*
incendēns, *gen.* incendentis *burning, setting fire to*
incendō, incendere, incendī *burn, set fire to*
*incidō, incidere, incidī *fall*
incipiō, incipere, incēpī *begin*
*incitō, incitāre, incitāvī *urge on, encourage*
incolumis *safe*
incurrō, incurrere, incurrī *run onto, collide*
inēlegāns, *gen.* inēlegantis *unattractive*
*īnfāns, īnfantis, m. *baby, child*
īnfēlīx, *gen.* īnfēlīcis *unlucky*
īnfēnsus, īnfēnsa, īnfēnsum *hostile, enraged*
*īnferō, īnferre, intulī *bring in, bring on*
iniūriam īnferre *do an injustice to, bring injury to*
mortem īnferre *bring death upon*
vim īnferre *use force, violence*
īnfestus, īnfesta, īnfestum *hostile, dangerous*
īnfirmus, īnfirma, īnfirmum *weak*
īnflō, īnflāre, īnflāvī *blow*
ingenium, ingeniī, n. *character*
*ingēns, *gen.* ingentis *huge*
ingravēscō, ingravēscere *grow worse*
iniciō, inicere, iniēcī *throw in*
*inimīcus, inimīcī, m. *enemy*
iniūria, iniūriae, f. *injustice, injury*
iniūstē *unfairly*
innocēns, *gen.* innocentis *innocent*
*inquit *says, said*
īnsānus, īnsāna, īnsānum *insane, crazy*
īnsidiae, īnsidiārum, f.pl. *trap, ambush*
īnsiliō, īnsilīre, īnsiluī *jump onto, jump into*
īnsolēns, *gen.* īnsolentis *rude, insolent*
*īnspiciō, īnspicere, īnspexī *look at, inspect, examine*

---

īnstrūctus, īnstrūcta, īnstrūctum
*drawn up*
īnstruō, īnstruere, īnstrūxī *draw up*
sē īnstruere *draw oneself up*
* īnsula, īnsulae, f. *island*
* intellegō, intellegere, intellēxī
*understand*
* intentē *intently*
intentus, intenta, intentum *intent*
* inter *among, between*
inter sē *among themselves, with each other*
intereā *meanwhile*
* interficiō, interficere, interfēcī *kill*
interpellō, interpellāre, interpellāvī
*interrupt*
interrogō, interrogāre, interrogāvī
*question*
* intrō, intrāre, intrāvī *enter*
intulī *see* īnferō
inūtilis *useless*
invādō, invādere, invāsī *invade*
* inveniō, invenīre, invēnī *find*
invicem *in turn*
* invītō, invītāre, invītāvī *invite*
* invītus, invīta, invītum *unwilling,*
*reluctant*
iocus, iocī, m. *joke*
ipsa *herself*
* ipse *himself*
* īrātus, īrāta, īrātum *angry*
īre *see* eō
* irrumpō, irrumpere, irrūpī *burst in*
Īsiacī, Īsiacōrum, m.pl. *followers of Isis*
ista *that*
istam *that*
* iste *that*
istī *that*
istum *that*
* ita *in this way*
* ita vērō *yes*
Ītalia, Ītaliae, f. *Italy*
Ītalicus, Ītalica, Ītalicum *Italian*
* itaque *and so*
* iter, itineris, n. *journey, trip, progress*
* iterum *again*
iubeō, iubēre, iussī *order*
Iūdaeī, Iūdaeōrum, m.pl. *Jews*
* iūdex, iūdicis, m. *judge*
* iuvenis, iuvenis, m. *young man*

# 1

* labōrō, labōrāre, labōrāvī *work*
lacrima, lacrimae, f. *tear*
lacrimīs sē trādere *burst into tears*
lacrimāns, *gen.* lacrimantis *crying,*
*weeping*
* lacrimō, lacrimāre, lacrimāvī *cry, weep*
laedō, laedere, laesī *harm*
* laetus, laeta, laetum *happy*
languidus, languida, languidum
*weak, feeble*
lapis, lapidis, m. *stone*
lateō, latēre, latuī *lie hidden*
lātrō, lātrāre, lātrāvī *bark*
* latrō, latrōnis, m. *robber*
* lātus, lāta, lātum *wide*
* laudō, laudāre, laudāvī *praise*
* lavō, lavāre, lāvī *wash*
* lectus, lectī, m. *couch, bed*
legiō, legiōnis, f. *legion*
lēgō, lēgāre, lēgāvī *bequeath*
* legō, legere, lēgī *read*
lēniō, lēnīre, lēnīvī *soothe, calm down*
lēniter *gently*
* lentē *slowly*
* leō, leōnis, m. *lion*
levis *changeable, inconsistent*
libellus, libellī, m. *little book*
* libenter *gladly*
* liber, librī, m. *book*
* līberālis *generous*
līberī, līberōrum, m.pl. *children*
* līberō, līberāre, līberāvī *free, set free*
lībertās, lībertātis, f. *freedom*
* lībertus, lībertī, m. *freedman, ex-slave*
lībō, lībāre, lībāvī *pour an offering*
līmōsus, līmōsa, līmōsum *muddy*
liquō, liquāre, liquāvī *melt*
* lītus, lītoris, n. *seashore, shore*
* locus, locī, m. *place*
Londinium, Londiniī, n. *London*
longē *far, a long way*
* longus, longa, longum *long*
loquāx, *gen.* loquācis *talkative*
lucrum, lucrī, n. *profit*
lūdus, lūdī, m. *game*
lūdī fūnebrēs *funeral games*
* lūna, lūnae, f. *moon*

# m

madidus, madida, madidum  *soaked through, drenched*

magicus, magica, magicum  *magic*

magis  *more*
   multō magis  *much more*

magister, magistrī, m.  *foreman*

magnificus, magnifica, magnificum  *splendid, magnificent*

* magnus, magna, magnum  *big, large, great*

maior, *gen.* maiōris  *bigger, larger, greater*

mālus, mālī, m.  *mast*

mandō, mandāre, mandāvī  *order, entrust*

* māne  *in the morning*

* maneō, manēre, mānsī  *remain, stay*

mānsuētus, mānsuēta, mānsuētum  *tame*

* manus, manūs, f.  *hand*

* mare, maris, n.  *sea*

* marītus, marītī, m.  *husband*

marmoreus, marmorea, marmoreum  *made of marble*

* māter, mātris, f.  *mother*

mātrōna, mātrōnae, f.  *lady*

maximē  *most of all, very much*

* maximus, maxima, maximum  *very big, very large, very great*

mē  *see* ego

medicāmentum, medicāmentī, n.  **ointment, salve**

medicīna, medicīnae, f. *medicine*

* medicus, medicī, m.  *doctor*

* medius, media, medium  *middle*

mel, mellis, n.  *honey*

* melior  *better*
   melius est  *it would be better*

* mendāx, mendācis, m.  *liar*

* mēnsa, mēnsae, f.  *table*

mēnsis, mēnsis, m.  *month*

* mercātor, mercātōris, m.  *merchant*

merx, mercis, f.  *goods, merchandise*

mēta, mētae, f.  *turning point*

metallum, metallī, n.  *a mine*

* meus, mea, meum  *my, mine*
   mī dulcissime!  *my good man!*
   mī Salvī!  *my dear Salvius!*
   mihi  *see* ego

* mīles, mīlitis, m.  *soldier*

mīlitō, mīlitāre, mīlitāvī  *be a soldier*

* minimē!  *no!*

* mīrābilis  *marvelous, strange, wonderful*

mīrāculum, mīrāculī, n.  *miracle*

* miser, misera, miserum  *miserable, wretched, sad*
   o mē miserum!  *oh wretched me!*

miserrimus, miserrima, miserrimum  *very sad*

* mittō, mittere, mīsī  *send*

modicus, modica, modicum  *ordinary, little*

molestus, molesta, molestum  *troublesome*

moneō, monēre, monuī  *warn, advise*

* mōns, montis, m.  *mountain*

mōnstrum, mōnstrī, n.  *monster*

monumentum, monumentī, n.  *monument*

moritūrus, moritūra, moritūrum  *going to die*

* mors, mortis, f.  *death*

* mortuus, mortua, mortuum  *dead*

moveō, movēre, mōvī  *move*

* mox  *soon*

mulceō, mulcēre, mulsī  *stroke*

* multitūdō, multitūdinis, f.  *crowd*

* multus, multa, multum  *much*

*  multī  *many*
   multō magis  *much more*

* mūrus, mūrī, m.  *wall*

mūs, mūris, m.f.  *mouse*

mystēria, mystēriōrum, n.pl.  *mysteries, secret worship*

# n

* nam  *for*

* nārrō, nārrāre, nārrāvī  *tell, relate*

natō, natāre, natāvī  *swim*

nātūra, nātūrae, f.  *nature*

naufragium, naufragiī, n.  *shipwreck*

naufragus, naufragī, m.  *shipwrecked sailor*

* nauta, nautae, m.  *sailor*

* nāvigō, nāvigāre, nāvigāvī  *sail*

* nāvis, nāvis, f.  *ship*

Neāpolis, Neāpolis, f.  *Naples*

* necesse  *necessary*

* necō, necāre, necāvī  *kill*

nefāstus, nefāsta, nefāstum  *terrible*

* neglegēns, *gen.* neglegentis  *careless*

* negōtium, negōtiī, n.  *business*

* nēmō  *no one, nobody*

neque . . . neque  *neither . . . nor*

nīdus, nīdī, m. *nest*
niger, nigra, nigrum *black*
* nihil *nothing*
  nihil cūrō *I don't care*
Nīlus, Nīlī, m. *the river Nile*
nitidus, nitida, nitidum *gleaming,*
  *brilliant*
niveus, nivea, niveum *snow-white*
* nōbilis *noble, of noble birth*
nōbīs *see* nōs
nocēns, *gen.* nocentis *guilty*
noceō, nocēre, nocuī *hurt*
noctū *by night*
* nōlō, nōlle, nōluī *not want*
  nōlī *do not, don't*
nōmen, nōminis, n. *name*
* nōn *not*
* nōnne? *surely?*
nōnnūllī, nōnnūllae *some, several*
* nōs *we, us*
  nōbīscum *with us*
* noster, nostra, nostrum *our*
* nōtus, nōta, nōtum *well-known, famous*
* novem *nine*
* nōvī *I know*
* novus, nova, novum *new*
* nox, noctis, f. *night*
* nūbēs, nūbis, f. *cloud*
* nūllus, nūlla, nūllum *not any, no*
* num? *surely . . . not?*
* numerō, numerāre, numerāvī *count*
numerus, numerī, m. *number*
* numquam *never*
* nunc *now*
* nūntiō, nūntiāre, nūntiāvī *announce*
* nūntius, nūntiī, m. *messenger, message*
nūper *recently*
nūptiae, nūptiārum, f.pl. *wedding*


## o

obdormiō, obdormīre, obdormīvī
  *fall asleep*
obeō, obīre, obiī *meet*
obruō, obruere, obruī *overwhelm*
obstinātus, obstināta, obstinātum
  *stubborn*
* obstō, obstāre, obstitī *obstruct, block the*
  *way*
obtulī *see* offerō
occāsiō, occāsiōnis, f. *opportunity*
occupātus, occupāta, occupātum *busy*

* octō *eight*
* oculus, oculī, m. *eye*
offendō, offendere, offendī *displease*
* offerō, offerre, obtulī *offer*
officīna, officīnae, f. *workshop*
* ōlim *once, some time ago*
ōlla, ōllae, f. *vase*
omittō, omittere, omīsī *drop*
* omnis *all*
operae, operārum, pl. *hired thugs*
opportūnē *just at the right time*
oppugnō, oppugnāre, oppugnāvī *attack*
* optimē *very well*
* optimus, optima, optimum *very good,*
  *excellent, best*
* ōrdō, ōrdinis, m. *row, line*
ōrnāmentum, ōrnāmentī, n. *ornament*
ōrnātrīx, ōrnātrīcis, f. *hairdresser*
ōrnātus, ōrnāta, ōrnātum *decorated,*
  *elaborately furnished*
ōrnō, ōrnāre, ōrnāvī *decorate*
ōsculum, ōsculī, n. *kiss*
* ostendō, ostendere, ostendī *show*
ostrea, ostreae, f. *oyster*
ōtiōsus, ōtiōsa, ōtiōsum *at leisure,*
  *with time off, idle, on vacation*
ōvum, ōvī, n. *egg*


## p

* paene *nearly, almost*
palaestra, palaestrae, f. *palaestra,*
  *exercise ground*
palūs, palūdis, f. *marsh, swamp*
* parātus, parāta, parātum *ready, prepared*
* parēns, parentis, m.f. *parent*
pāreō, pārēre, pāruī *obey*
* parō, parāre, parāvī *prepare*
* pars, partis, f. *part*
  in prīmā parte *in the forefront*
* parvus, parva, parvum *small*
* pater, patris, m. *father*
patera, paterae, f. *bowl*
* paucae, paucārum, f.pl. *few, a few*
* paucī, paucōrum, m. pl. *few, a few*
paulātim *gradually*
* paulīsper *for a short time*
paulum, paulī, n. *little, a little*
pavīmentum, pavīmentī, n. *floor*
* pāx, pācis, f. *peace*
* pecūnia, pecūniae, f. *money*
pendeō, pendēre, pependī *hang*

* per *through, along*
percutiō, percutere, percussī *strike*
* pereō, perīre, periī *die, perish*
* perīculōsus, perīculōsa, perīculōsum
*dangerous*
* perīculum, perīculī, n. *danger*
perītē *skillfully*
perītia, perītiae, f. *skill*
perītus, perīta, perītum *skillful*
* persuādeō, persuādēre, persuāsī
*persuade*
perterritus, perterrita, perterritum
*terrified*
* perveniō, pervenīre, pervēnī *reach,*
*arrive at*
* pēs, pedis, m. *foot, paw*
* pessimus, pessima, pessimum *very bad,*
*worst*
* pestis, pestis, f. *pest, rascal*
* petō, petere, petīvī *head for, attack;*
*seek, beg for, ask for*
pharus, pharī, m. *lighthouse*
philosophus, philosophī, m. *philosopher*
pīca, pīcae, f. *magpie*
pictor, pictōris, m. *painter, artist*
pictūra, pictūrae, f. *painting, picture*
pīla, pīlae, f. *ball*
pingō, pingere, pīnxī *paint*
pius, pia, pium *respectful to the gods*
* placeō, placēre, placuī *please, suit*
placidus, placida, placidum *calm,*
*peaceful*
plānē *clearly*
* plaudō, plaudere, plausī *applaud, clap*
* plaustrum, plaustrī, n. *wagon, cart*
plēnus, plēna, plēnum *full*
pluit, pluere, pluit *rain*
* plūrimus, plūrima, plūrimum *very*
*much, most*
* plūrimī, plūrimae *very many*
plūs, *gen.* plūris *more*
* pōculum, pōculī, n. *cup (often for wine)*
poena, poenae, f. *punishment*
poenās dare *pay the penalty, be punished*
* poēta, poētae, m. *poet*
* pompa, pompae, f. *procession*
Pompēiānus, Pompēiāna,
Pompēiānum *Pompeian*
* pōnō, pōnere, posuī *put, place, put up*
pontifex, pontificis, m. *high priest*
* porta, portae, f. *gate*
portāns, *gen.* portantis *carrying*

* portō, portāre, portāvī *carry*
* portus, portūs, m. *harbor*
* poscō, poscere, poposcī *demand, ask for*
possideō, possidēre, possēdī *possess*
* possum, posse, potuī *can, be able*
* post *after, behind*
* posteā *afterwards*
* postquam *after, when*
* postrēmō *finally, lastly*
* postrīdiē *(on) the next day*
* postulō, postulāre, postulāvī *demand*
posuī *see* pōnō
potuī *see* possum
praeceps, *gen.* praecipitis *headlong*
praecursor, praecursōris, m. *forerunner*
praedium, praediī, n. *estate*
praemium, praemiī, n. *profit, prize, reward*
praeruptus, praerupta, praeruptum *steep*
* praesidium, praesidiī, n. *protection*
* praesum, praeesse, praefuī *be in charge of*
praetereō, praeterīre, praeteriī *go past*
prāvus, prāva, prāvum *evil*
* precēs, precum, f.pl. *prayers*
premō, premere, pressī *push*
* pretiōsus, pretiōsa, pretiōsum
*expensive, precious*
pretium, pretiī, n. *price*
prīmō *first*
* prīmus, prīma, prīmum *first*
in prīmā parte *in the forefront*
* prīnceps, prīncipis, m. *chief, chieftain*
* prior *first, in front*
* prō *in front of*
prō dī immortālēs! *heavens above!*
probus, proba, probum *honest*
* prōcēdō, prōcēdere, prōcessī *advance,*
*proceed*
procul *far off*
* prōcumbō, prōcumbere, prōcubuī
*fall down*
* prōmittō, prōmittere, prōmīsī *promise*
* prope *near*
prōsiliō, prōsilīre, prōsiluī *leap forward*
prōvideō, prōvidēre, prōvīdī *foresee*
proximus, proxima, proximum *nearest*
psittacus, psittacī, m. *parrot*
* puella, puellae, f. *girl*
* puer, puerī, m. *boy*
pugil, pugilis, m. *boxer*
pugiō, pugiōnis, m. *dagger*
* pugna, pugnae, f. *fight*
pugnāns, *gen.* pugnantis *fighting*

\* pugnō, pugnāre, pugnāvī *fight*
\* pulcher, pulchra, pulchrum *beautiful*
\* pulsō, pulsāre, pulsāvī *hit, knock on, whack, punch*
pūmiliō, pūmiliōnis, m.f. *dwarf*
\* pūniō, pūnīre, pūnīvī *punish*
puppis, puppis, f. *stern*
pūrus, pūra, pūrum *clean, spotless*
puto, putāre, putāvī *think, consider*

## q

quā *from whom*
\* quadrāgintā *forty*
quae *who, which*
quaerēns, *gen.* quaerentis *searching for, looking for*
\* quaerō, quaerere, quaesīvī *search for, look for, inquire*
\* quam (1) *how*
\* quam (2) *than*
  quam celerrimē *as quickly as possible*
  quam (3) *whom, which*
\* quamquam *although*
quārtus, quārta, quārtum *fourth*
quās *whom, which*
\* quattuor *four*
\* -que *and*
quem *whom, which*
\* quī *who, which*
quid? *what?*
  quid agis? *how are you?*
  quid vīs? *what do you want?*
quīdam *one, a certain*
quidquam *anything*
quiēscō, quiēscere, quiēvī *rest*
quiētus, quiēta, quiētum *quiet*
quīndecim *fifteen*
quīngentī, quīngentae *five hundred*
\* quīnquāgintā *fifty*
\* quīnque *five*
\* quis? *who?*
\* quō? *where? where to?*
quō (2) *from whom*
quō modō? *how?*
\* quod (1) *because*
quod (2) *which*
\* quondam *one day, once*
\* quoque *also, too*
quōs *whom, which*
quot? *how many?*
quotannīs *every year*

## r

rādō, rādere, rāsī *scratch, scrape*
\* rapiō, rapere, rapuī *seize, grab*
rārō *rarely*
raucus, rauca, raucum *harsh*
recidō, recidere, reccidī *fall back*
\* recipiō, recipere, recēpī *recover, take back*
  sē recipere *recover*
recitāns, *gen.* recitantis *reciting*
recitō, recitāre, recitāvī *recite*
rēctā *directly, straight*
rēctus, rēcta, rēctum *straight*
recumbēns, *gen.* recumbentis *lying down, reclining*
\* recumbō, recumbere, recubuī *lie down, recline*
\* recūsō, recūsāre, recūsāvī *refuse*
\* reddō, reddere, reddidī *give back*
\* redeō, redīre, rediī *return, go back, come back*
referō, referre, rettulī *carry, deliver*
reficiō, reficere, refēcī *repair*
rēgīna, rēgīnae, f. *queen*
regiō, regiōnis, f. *region*
\* relinquō, relinquere, relīquī *leave*
\* remedium, remediī, n. *cure*
rēmus, rēmī, m. *oar*
renovō, renovāre, renovāvī *restore*
reportō, reportāre, reportāvī *carry back*
\* rēs, reī, f. *thing, affair*
  rem cōnficere *finish the job*
  rem intellegere *understand the truth*
  rem nārrāre *tell the story*
  rēs rūstica *the farming*
\* resistō, resistere, restitī *resist*
\* respondeō, respondēre, respondī *reply*
respōnsum, respōnsī, n. *answer*
\* retineō, retinēre, retinuī *keep, hold back*
retrahō, retrahere, retrāxī *drag back*
\* reveniō, revenīre, revēnī *come back, return*
\* rēx, rēgis, m. *king*
rhētor, rhētoris, m. *teacher*
\* rīdeō, rīdēre, rīsī *laugh, smile*
rīpa, rīpae, f. *river bank*
rōbustus, rōbusta, rōbustum *strong*
\* rogō, rogāre, rogāvī *ask*
rogus, rogī, m. *pyre*
Rōmānus, Rōmāna, Rōmānum *Roman*
rosa, rosae, f. *rose*

rota, rotae, f. *wheel*
rudēns, rudentis, m. *cable, rope*
* ruō, ruere, ruī *rush*
rūsticus, rūstica, rūsticum *country, in the country*
   rēs rūstica *the farming*

# S

saccus, saccī, m. *bag, purse*
* sacer, sacra, sacrum *sacred*
* sacerdōs, sacerdōtis, m. *priest*
sacrificium, sacrificiī, n. *offering, sacrifice*
sacrificō, sacrificāre, sacrificāvī *sacrifice*
* saepe *often*
* saeviō, saevīre, saeviī *be in a rage*
saevus, saeva, saevum *savage*
saltātrīx, saltātrīcis, f. *dancing-girl*
* saltō, saltāre, saltāvī *dance*
* salūtō, salūtāre, salūtāvī *greet*
* salvē! *hello!*
sānē *obviously*
* sanguis, sanguinis, m. *blood*
sānō, sānāre, sānāvī *heal, cure*
sapiēns, *gen.* sapientis *wise*
* satis *enough*
* saxum, saxī, n. *rock*
scapha, scaphae, f. *small boat*
scelestus, scelesta, scelestum *wicked*
scēptrum, scēptrī, n. *scepter*
scindō, scindere, scidī *tear, tear up*
scio, scīre, scīvī *know*
scōpae, scōpārum, f.pl. *broom*
scopulus, scopulī, m. *reef*
* scrībō, scrībere, scrīpsī *write*
scrīptor, scrīptōris, m. *writer, sign-writer*
scurrīlis *obscene, dirty*
* sē *himself, herself, themselves*
   sēcum *with him, with her, with them*
secō, secāre, secuī *cut*
* secundus, secunda, secundum *second*
   ventus secundus *favorable wind, following wind*
sēcūrus, sēcūra, sēcūrum *without a care*
* sed *but*
sedēns, *gen.* sedentis *sitting*
* sedeō, sedēre, sēdī *sit*
seges, segetis, f. *crop, harvest*
* sella, sellae, f. *chair*

sēmirutus, sēmiruta, sēmirutum *half-collapsed*
* semper *always*
* senātor, senātōris, m. *senator*
* senex, senis, m. *old man*
* sententia, sententiae, f. *opinion*
* sentiō, sentīre, sēnsī *feel, notice*
* septem *seven*
sēricus, sērica, sēricum *silk*
* sermō, sermōnis, m. *conversation*
serviō, servīre, servīvī *serve (as a slave)*
* servō, servāre, servāvī *save, protect*
* servus, servī, m. *slave*
* sex *six*
sī *if*
sibi *to him (self), to her (self), to them (selves)*
* sīcut *like*
signātor, signātōris, m. *witness*
signō, signāre, signāvī *sign, seal*
* signum, signī, n. *sign, seal, signal*
silentium, silentiī, n. *silence*
* silva, silvae, f. *woods, forest*
* simulac, simulatque *as soon as*
* sine *without*
situs, sita, situm *situated*
situs, sitūs, m. *position, site*
sōl, sōlis, m. *sun*
* soleō, solēre *be accustomed*
sollemniter *solemnly*
sollicitūdō, sollicitūdinis, f. *anxiety*
* sollicitus, sollicita, sollicitum *worried, anxious*
sōlum *only*
* sōlus, sōla, sōlum *alone, lonely, only, on one's own*
solūtus, solūta, solūtum *untied, cast off*
solvō, solvere, solvī *untie, cast off*
somnium, somniī, n. *dream*
* sonitus, sonitūs, m. *sound*
sonō, sonāre, sonuī *sound*
sonus, sonī, m. *sound*
* sordidus, sordida, sordidum *dirty*
spargō, spargere, sparsī *scatter*
sparsus, sparsa, sparsum *scattered*
* spectāculum, spectāculī, n. *show, spectacle*
spectātor, spectātōris, m. *spectator*
* spectō, spectāre, spectāvī *look at, watch*
splendidus, splendida, splendidum *splendid*
spongia, spongiae, f. *sponge*
stāns, *gen.* stantis *standing*

*statim *at once*
statua, statuae, f. *statue*
stilus, stilī, m. *pen, stick*
*stō, stāre, stetī *stand, lie at anchor*
*stola, stolae, f. *(long) dress*
studeō, studēre, studuī *study*
stultē *stupidly, foolishly*
*stultus, stulta, stultum *stupid, foolish*
suāvis *sweet*
*suāviter *sweetly*
sub *under*
*subitō *suddenly*
sūdō, sūdāre, sūdāvī *sweat*
sufficiō, sufficere, suffēcī *be enough*
*sum, esse, fuī *be*
summergō, summergere, summersī
  *sink, dip*
summersus, summersa, summersum
  *sunk*
*summus, summa, summum *highest,
  greatest, top*
superbus, superba, superbum *arrogant,
  proud*
*superō, superāre, superāvī *overcome,
  overpower, overtake*
*supersum, superesse, superfuī *survive*
supplicium, suppliciī, n. *death penalty*
surdus, surda, surdum *deaf*
*surgō, surgere, surrēxī *get up, stand up,
  rise*
suscipiō, suscipere, suscēpī *undertake,
  take on*
sustulī *see* tollō
susurrāns, *gen.* susurrantis *whispering,
  mumbling*
susurrō, susurrāre, susurrāvī *whisper,
  mumble*
*suus, sua, suum *his, her, their, his own*
Syrī, Syrōrum, m.pl. *Syrians*
Syrius, Syria, Syrium *Syrian*


# t

*taberna, tabernae, f. *store, shop, inn*
tabernārius, tabernāriī, m. *store-owner,
  storekeeper, shopkeeper*
tablīnum, tablīnī, n. *study*
*taceō, tacēre, tacuī *be silent, be quiet*
tacē! *shut up! be quiet!*
*tacitē *quietly, silently*
tacitus, tacita, tacitum *quiet, silent,
  in silence*

*tam *so*
*tamen *however*
*tandem *at last*
tangō, tangere, tetigī *touch*
tantus, tanta, tantum *so great, such a
  great*
tardus, tarda, tardum *late*
taurus, taurī, m. *bull*
tē *see* tū
tempestās, tempestātis, f. *storm*
*templum, templī, n. *temple*
*temptō, temptāre, temptāvī *try*
tenēns, *gen.* tenentis *holding, owning*
*teneō, tenēre, tenuī *hold, own*
tergeō, tergēre, tersī *wipe*
*tergum, tergī, n. *back*
  ā tergō *behind, in the rear*
*terra, terrae, f. *ground, land*
*terreō, terrēre, terruī *frighten*
terribilis *terrible*
*tertius, tertia, tertium *third*
testāmentum, testāmentī, n. *will*
theātrum, theātrī, n. *theater*
tibi *see* tū
tībīcen, tībīcinis, m. *pipe player*
*timeō, timēre, timuī *be afraid, fear*
timidus, timida, timidum *fearful,
  frightened*
toga, togae, f. *toga*
*tollō, tollere, sustulī *raise, lift up, hold up*
*tot *so many*
*tōtus, tōta, tōtum *whole*
tractō, tractāre, tractāvī *handle*
*trādō, trādere, trādidī *hand over*
  lacrimīs sē trādere *burst into tears*
tragoedia, tragoediae, f. *tragedy*
*trahō, trahere, trāxī *drag*
tranquillitās, tranquillitātis, f.
  *calmness, serenity*
trānseō, trānsīre, trānsiī *cross*
trānsfīgō, trānsfīgere, trānsfīxī *pierce*
*trēs *three*
triclīnium, triclīniī, n. *dining-room*
*trīgintā *thirty*
tripodes, tripodum, m.pl. *tripods*
trīstis *sad*
trivium, triviī, n. *crossroads*
trūdō, trūdere, trūsī *push, shove*
*tū, tuī *you (singular)*
  tēcum *with you (singular)*
*tuba, tubae, f. *trumpet*
tubicen, tubicinis, m. *trumpeter*

tulī *see* ferō

* tum *then*

tumultus, tumultūs, m. *riot*

tunica, tunicae, f. *tunic*

* turba, turbae, f. *crowd*

turbulentus, turbulenta, turbulentum
*rowdy, disorderly*

tūtus, tūta, tūtum *safe*
tūtius est *it would be safer*

* tuus, tua, tuum *your, yours*

# u

* ubi *where, when*

ultor, ultōris, m. *avenger*

* umbra, umbrae, f. *ghost, shadow*

* umerus, umerī, m. *shoulder*

* unda, undae, f. *wave*

unde *from where*

unguentum, unguentī, n. *perfume*

unguis, unguis, m. *claw*

unguō, unguere, ūnxī *anoint, smear*

* ūnus, ūna, ūnum *one*

urbānus, urbāna, urbānum *fashionable,
sophisticated*

* urbs, urbis, f. *city*

urna, urnae, f. *bucket, jar, jug*

ursa, ursae, f. *bear*

ut *as*

* ūtilis *useful*

* uxor, uxōris, f. *wife*

# v

* valdē *very much, very*

* valē *good-by*

valvae, valvārum, f.pl. *doors*

varius, varia, varium *different*

* vehementer *violently, loudly*

vehō, vehere, vēxī *carry*

* vēnātiō, vēnātiōnis, f. *hunt*

* vēndō, vēndere, vēndidī *sell*

venia, veniae, f. *mercy, forgiveness*

* veniō, venīre, vēnī *come*

ventus, ventī, m. *wind*

vēr, vēris, n. *spring*

* verberō, verberāre, verberāvī *strike,
beat*

verrō, verrere *sweep*

versus, versūs, m. *verse, line of poetry*
versus magicus *magic spell*

* vertō, vertere, vertī *turn*
sē vertere *turn around*

vērus, vēra, vērum *true, real*

vestiō, vestīre, vestīvī *dress*

* vexō, vexāre, vexāvī *annoy*

* via, viae, f. *street*

vibrō, vibrāre, vibrāvī *wave, brandish*

vīcīnus, vīcīna, vīcīnum *neighboring,
nearby*

victima, victimae, f. *victim*

* victor, victōris, m. *victor, winner*

vīcus, vīcī, m. *village*

* videō, vidēre, vīdī *see*

* vīgintī *twenty*

vīlicus, vīlicī, m. *overseer, manager*

vīlis *cheap*

* vīlla, vīllae, f. *villa, (large) house*

* vincō, vincere, vīcī *win, be victorious*

vindex, vindicis, m. *champion,
defender*

vindicō, vindicāre, vindicāvī *avenge*

* vīnum, vīnī, n. *wine*

* vir, virī, m. *man*

virga, virgae, f. *rod, stick*

vīs, f. *force, violence*

vīs *see* volō

vīsitō, vīsitāre, vīsitāvī *visit*

* vīta, vītae, f. *life*

vītō, vītāre, vītāvī *avoid*

vitreārius, vitreāriī, m. *glassmaker*

vitreus, vitrea, vitreum *glass, made of
glass*

vitrum, vitrī, n. *glass*

* vituperō, vituperāre, vituperāvī *find
fault with, tell off, curse*

* vīvō, vīvere, vīxī *live, be alive*

* vix *hardly, scarcely, with difficulty*

vōbīs *see* vōs

* vocō, vocāre, vocāvī *call*

* volō, velle, voluī *want*
quid vīs? *what do you want?*

* vōs *you (plural)*
vōbīscum *with you (plural)*

* vōx, vōcis, f. *voice*

vulnerātus, vulnerāta, vulnerātum
*wounded*

* vulnerō, vulnerāre, vulnerāvī *wound,
injure*

* vulnus, vulneris, n. *wound*

vult *see* volō

# z

zōna, zōnae, f. *belt*

# Guide to Characters and Places

(The numeral in parentheses identifies the Stage in which the person or place is first featured.)

Aegyptius (adj.) (16): Egyptian, or resident of Egypt.

Aegyptus (16): Egypt.

Aethiopes (19): Ethiopians, people whose native land Ethiopia was located southeast of Egypt.

Alātor (13): son of the sick miner executed by Salvius; attempted to murder Salvius in revenge.

Alexandrīa (16): Alexandria, port-city in Egypt on the Mediterranean coast; founded in 331 B.C. by Alexander the Great.

Alexandrīnus (adj.) (18): Alexandrian, or resident of Alexandria.

Anna (20): hairdresser of Plotina.

Anti-Loquāx (13): young slave of Salvius, dancer, twin brother of Loquax.

Arabia (17): Arabia, a peninsula of southwestern Asia, lying between the Red Sea and the Persian Gulf.

Arabs (adj.) (17): Arabian, or resident of Arabia.

Ariēs (19): Aries (the "Ram"), sign of the zodiac.

Aristō (19): Greek poet and tragedian, friend of Barbillus.

Athēnae (16): Athens, major city in Greece.

Athēniēnsis (adj.) (20): Athenian, or resident of Athens.

Atlās (18): mythological giant, who supports the sky on his shoulders.

AUGUSTUS Caesar (17): Roman emperor (27 B.C. – A.D. 14), worshiped as a god after his death.

Tiberius Claudius BARBILLUS (17): rich merchant of Alexandria; business associate of Caecilius; friend of Quintus.

Belimicus (15): British chieftain, governor of the Cantiaci, rival of Dumnorix.

Bregāns (13): native (British) slave of Salvius, unskilled laborer.

Britannī (13): Britons.

Britannia (13): Britain, once a province of the Roman empire.

Britannicus (adj.) (13): British.

Campānia (14): area in Italy around Pompeii.

Cantiacī (13): British tribe, inhabitants of area now called Kent.

Cervīx (13): native (British) slave, plowman on Salvius' farm.

Chaldaeī (19): Chaldeans, a near-eastern people who were famous as astrologers and magicians; once ruled Babylon.

Claudius (15): Roman emperor (A.D. 41–54), who made Cogidubnus king of the Regnenses; had sent into Britain the Second Legion under the command of Vespasian (A.D. 43).

Quīntus Caecilius CLĒMĒNS (17): freedman of Quintus; now owner of a glass-store in Alexandria.

Tiberius Claudius COGIDUBNUS (13): elderly ruler of the Regnenses; had been appointed "client king" under the Emperor Claudius; friend to Salvius.

Diogenēs (17): Greek craftsman of Alexandria; gave shelter, during a riot, to Quintus and his Egyptian slave-boy guide.

Domitilla (14): Rufilla's slave-girl, probably brought from Rome.

Dumnorix (15): a chieftain of the Regnenses, rival of Belimicus.

Durotrigēs (16): British tribe, inhabitants of area now called Dorset, west of the Regnenses' territory.

Eupor (20): Greek friend of Rufus; medical student at Alexandria, later doctor in Athens.

Eutychus (18): owner of glass-blowers' workshop in Alexandria; operated protection racket for glassmakers and glass-store owners.

Galatēa (19): complaining wife of Aristo.

Graecia (16): Greece.

Graecus (adj.) (16): Greek, or resident of Greece.

Helena (19): beautiful daughter of Aristo and Galatea.

Īsis (18): Egyptian goddess of fertility; wife of the god Osiris or Serapis.

Ītalia (13): Italy.

Ītalicus (adj.) (13): Italian.

Iūdaeus (adj.) (17): Jewish, or Jew.

Londinium (14): London, city in Britain.

Loquāx (13): young slave of Salvius, singer, twin brother of Anti-Loquax.

Marcia (14): elderly slave-woman in Salvius' house.

Marcus (20): slave of Barbillus.

Narcissus (20): poet; half-Egyptian suitor of Helena.

Neāpolis (16): Naples, city in Italy near Pompeii.

Nīlus (19): Nile, river of Egypt.

Petrō (20): Barbillus' Greek doctor.

Philadelphus (20): slave of Barbillus.

Philus (13): skilled (Greek) slave of Salvius, bookkeeper.

Phormiō (19): overseer of Barbillus' household.

Plancus (17): an educated bore in Alexandria.

Plōtīna (20): deceased wife of Barbillus.

Pompēius Optātus (13): kindly overseer of iron mine in area now called Kent.

QUĪNTUS Caecilius Iūcundus (14): Rufilla's relative, who lost his parents and home in Pompeii (see Unit 1, Stage 12) during the eruption of Mt. Vesuvius; narrator of Stages 17–20; son of Caecilius.

Rēgnēnsēs (15): British tribe (named Atrebates before the Roman conquest), inhabitants of area now called Sussex and Hampshire.

Rōmānus (adj.) (17): Roman, or resident of Roman empire.

Rūfilla (13): noble-born wife of Salvius.

Tiberius Claudius RŪFUS (20): son of Barbillus and Plotina; escaped, during a voyage, from the storm that drowned his mother.

Gāius SALVIUS Līberālis (13): self-made wealthy man, Italian senator, appointed by the emperor to be circuit judge in southern Britain.

Scorpiō (20): Scorpio (the "Scorpion"), sign of the zodiac.

Semprōnia (14): Rufilla's friend in London whose husband was very wealthy and, unlike Salvius, indulgent.

Serāpis (17): god of fertility and of the underworld; sometimes worshiped with Isis.

Syrī (17): Syrians, residents of Syria.

Syrius (adj.) (20): Syrian.

Vārica (13): manager of Salvius' farm.

Vespasiānus, or Vespasian (16): Roman emperor (A.D. 69–79), whom Cogidubnus may have helped when Vespasian was only commander of the Second Legion against the Durotriges.

Volūbilis (13): skilled (Egyptian) slave of Salvius; cook.

# Index of Cultural Topics

The page references are all to the background sections at the ends of the Stages. You will also find cultural information in the Latin stories.

# Index of Grammatical Topics

Key: AL = About the Language  RvG = Review Grammar  RfG = Reference Grammar

Page references are given first, with paragraph references (i.e. references to numbered sections in the language notes and the Review Grammar) following in boldface; Roman numerals following page numbers denote sections in the Reference Grammar, which are sometimes followed by paragraph references.

In general, AL references are only to the *first* language note in this Unit on the grammatical topic in question: in a few cases, additional pages are cited.

# Time Chart

| B.C. | EGYPT & BRITAIN | ROME | THE WORLD | B.C. |
|---|---|---|---|---|
| c. 3100–1166 | Egypt ruled by Pharaohs | | | c. 3100–1166 |
| c. 2100 | | | Indo-European migrations | c. 2100 |
| c. 1500 | | | Minoan civilization at its height | c. 1500 |
| c. 1450 | | | Development of Hinduism | c. 1450 |
| c. 1200 | Exodus of Jews from Egypt | | | c. 1200 |
| 753 | | Foundation of Rome (traditional date) & rule of kings | | 753 |
| c. 563 | | | Buddha born in India | c. 563 |
| c. 551 | | | Confucius born in China | c. 551 |
| 525–401 | Egypt under Persian rule | | | 525–401 |
| 509 | | Expulsion of kings & founding of Roman Republic | | 509 |
| 500–400 | | | { Persia invades Greece / Golden Age of Athens | 500–400 |
| 390 | | Rome briefly captured by Gauls | | 390 |
| 336 | | | Alexander becomes ruler of Greece | 336 |
| 332 | Alexander enters Egypt | | | 332 |
| 331 | Alexander founds Alexandria | | | 331 |
| 323 | | | Alexander dies in Babylon | 323 |
| 311 | Ptolemy I Soter, first Greek ruler of Egypt | | | 311 |
| 300–200 | | { Rome gains control of Italy / Wars with Carthage | Building of Great Wall of China | 300–200 |
| c. 295 | Ptolemy I founds Museum/Library | | | c. 295 |
| c. 280 | Ptolemy II builds Pharos lighthouse | | | c. 280 |
| 218 | | Hannibal crosses the Alps | | 218 |
| 200–100 | | Rome extends rule outside Italy | | 200–100 |
| 58–49 | | Caesar conquers Gaul | | 58–49 |
| 55–54 | Caesar's expeditions to Britain | | | 55–54 |
| 51 | Cleopatra VII Queen of Egypt | | | 51 |
| 49 | | Caesar is made "Dictator" | | 49 |
| 44 | | Caesar is murdered | | 44 |
| 44–31 | | Civil War between Octavian (Augustus) & Antony | | 44–31 |
| 30 | { Antony and Cleopatra commit suicide / Rome annexes Egypt | | | 30 |
| 27 | | Augustus becomes Emperor | | 27 |

| A.D. | British events | Roman events | Religious events |
|---|---|---|---|
| 13 | Two obelisks re-erected before Caesareum in Alexandria | | |
| c. 4 | | | Birth of Jesus |
| 14 | | Tiberius becomes Emperor | |
| c. 29 | | | Crucifixion of Jesus |
| 37 | | Caligula becomes Emperor | |
| 41 | | Claudius becomes Emperor | |
| 42 | | St. Peter brings Christianity to Rome | |
| 43 | Invasion of Britain under Aulus Plautius / Britain becomes province of Rome / Vespasian leads second Legion against Durotriges | | |
| 45–57 | | | Missionary journeys of St. Paul |
| 54 | | Nero becomes Emperor | |
| 61 | Revolt of Iceni under Boudica | | |
| 64 | | Great Fire at Rome / Persecution of Christians by Nero | |
| 69 | | Year of Four Emperors / Vespasian becomes Emperor | |
| 70 | | | Romans sack Jerusalem and Temple |
| 75 | Roman palace at Fishbourne begun | | |
| 78–84 | Agricola is Governor of Britain | | |
| 79 | | Titus becomes Emperor / August 24 : Vesuvius erupts | |
| 81 | | Domitian becomes Emperor | |
| 83–84 | ?Salvius arrives in Britain / Agricola's campaigns in Scotland | | |
| 96 | | Nerva becomes Emperor | |
| 98 | | Trajan becomes Emperor | |
| 117 | | Hadrian becomes Emperor | |
| 208–11 | Emperor Severus campaigns in Britain and dies in York | | |
| 296 | | Emperor Diocletian lays eight-month siege to Alexandria | |
| 313 | | | Emperor Constantine officially supports Christianity in Roman Empire |
| 330 | | | Capital of Roman Empire moved to Constantinople |

| Date | | |
|------|---|---|
| 400–500 | | Anglo-Saxons settle in Britain |
| 410 | Visigoths sack Rome | Rome formally renounces Britain |
| 476 | Last Emperor of Rome deposed | |
| 570 | Birth of Mohammed | |
| c. 643 | | Arabs conquer Egypt |
| 800 | Charlemagne crowned Emperor of Holy Roman Empire | |
| 800–1100 | Period of turmoil in Italy | |
| 1066 | | Normans conquer England |
| 1143 | Rome becomes an independent city-state | |
| c. 1400 | The Renaissance begins in Italy | |
| 1453 | Turks capture Constantinople | |
| 1492 | Columbus arrives in America | |
| 1497 | Cabot explores Canada | |
| 1517 | | Turks occupy Alexandria and Egypt becomes part of Ottoman Empire |
| 1521 | Reformation begins | |
| 1620 | Pilgrims land at Plymouth, Mass. | |
| 1776 | United States declare their Independence | |
| 1798 | | Napoleon captures Alexandria |
| 1806 | End of Holy Roman Empire | |
| 1815 | Napoleon finally defeated at Waterloo | |
| 1861 | | Victor Emmanuel II becomes King of a united Italy |
| 1863 | Lincoln emancipates American slaves | |
| 1867 | Canada becomes a Dominion | |
| 1869 | | Suez Canal opened |
| 1879 | | Obelisk from before Caesareum given to New York City |
| 1914 | | Egypt becomes British Protectorate |
| 1914–1918 | First World War | |
| 1922 | | Egypt becomes independent |
| 1931 | Canada becomes a Commonwealth nation | |
| 1939–1945 | Second World War | |
| 1946 | | Italy becomes a Republic |

**Quick Reference to Grammatical Information**

# Time Chart

| B.C. | THE WORLD | ROME | EGYPT & BRITAIN |
|---|---|---|---|
| c. 3100–1166 | | | Egypt ruled by Pharaohs |
| c. 2100 | Indo-European migrations | | |
| c. 1500 | Minoan civilization at its height | | |
| c. 1450 | | | |
| c. 1200 | Development of Hinduism | | Exodus of Jews from Egypt |
| 753 | | Foundation of Rome (traditional date) & rule of kings | |
| c. 563 | Buddha born in India | | |
| c. 551 | Confucius born in China | | |
| 525–401 | | | Egypt under Persian rule |
| 509 | | Expulsion of kings & founding of Roman Republic | |
| 500–400 | { Persia invades Greece / Golden Age of Athens } | | |
| 390 | | Rome briefly captured by Gauls | |
| 336 | Alexander becomes ruler of Greece | | |
| 332 | | | Alexander enters Egypt |
| 331 | | | Alexander founds Alexandria |
| 323 | Alexander dies in Babylon | | |
| 311 | | | Ptolemy I Soter, first Greek ruler of Egypt |
| 300–200 | Building of Great Wall of China | { Rome gains control of Italy / Wars with Carthage } | |
| c. 295 | | | Ptolemy I founds Museum/Library |
| c. 280 | | | Ptolemy II builds Pharos lighthouse |
| 218 | | Hannibal crosses the Alps | |
| 200–100 | | Rome extends rule outside Italy | |
| 58–49 | | Caesar conquers Gaul | |
| 55–54 | | | Caesar's expeditions to Britain |
| 51 | | | Cleopatra VII Queen of Egypt |
| 49 | | Caesar is made "Dictator" | |
| 44 | | Caesar is murdered | |
| 44–31 | | Civil War between Octavian (Augustus) & Antony | |
| 30 | | | { Antony and Cleopatra commit suicide / Rome annexes Egypt } |
| 27 | | Augustus becomes Emperor | |

| Date | British & Egyptian events | Roman Emperors | Religious events |
|---|---|---|---|
| 13 | Two obelisks re-erected before Caesareum in Alexandria | | |
| c. 4 A.D. | | | Birth of Jesus |
| A.D. | | | |
| 14 | | Tiberius becomes Emperor | |
| c. 29 | | | Crucifixion of Jesus |
| 37 | | Caligula becomes Emperor | |
| 41 | | Claudius becomes Emperor | |
| 42 | | St. Peter brings Christianity to Rome | |
| 43 | Invasion of Britain under Aulus Plautius; Britain becomes province of Rome; Vespasian leads second Legion against Durotriges | | |
| 45–57 | | | Missionary journeys of St. Paul |
| 54 | | Nero becomes Emperor | |
| 61 | Revolt of Iceni under Boudica | | |
| 64 | | Great Fire at Rome; Persecution of Christians by Nero | |
| 69 | | Year of Four Emperors; Vespasian becomes Emperor | |
| 70 | | | Romans sack Jerusalem and Temple |
| 75 | Roman palace at Fishbourne begun | | |
| 78–84 | Agricola is Governor of Britain | | |
| 79 | | Titus becomes Emperor; August 24 : Vesuvius erupts | |
| 81 | ?Salvius arrives in Britain | Domitian becomes Emperor | |
| 83–84 | Agricola's campaigns in Scotland | | |
| 96 | | Nerva becomes Emperor | |
| 98 | | Trajan becomes Emperor | |
| 117 | | Hadrian becomes Emperor | |
| 208–11 | Emperor Severus campaigns in Britain and dies in York | | |
| 296 | Emperor Diocletian lays eight-month siege to Alexandria | | |
| 313 | | | Emperor Constantine officially supports Christianity in Roman Empire |
| 330 | | | Capital of Roman Empire moved to Constantinople |

| Date | | |
|---|---|---|
| 400–500 | | Anglo-Saxon settle in Britain |
| 410 | Visigoths sack Rome | Rome formally renounces Britain |
| 476 | Last Emperor of Rome deposed | |
| 570 | Birth of Mohammed | |
| c. 643 | | Arabs conquer Egypt |
| 800 | Charlemagne crowned Emperor of Holy Roman Empire | |
| 800–1100 | Period of turmoil in Italy | |
| 1066 | | Normans conquer England |
| 1143 | Rome becomes an independent city-state | |
| c. 1400 | The Renaissance begins in Italy | |
| 1453 | Turks capture Constantinople | |
| 1492 | Columbus arrives in America | |
| 1497 | Cabot explores Canada | |
| 1517 | | Turks occupy Alexandria and Egypt becomes part of Ottoman Empire |
| 1521 | Reformation begins | |
| 1620 | Pilgrims land at Plymouth, Mass. | |
| 1776 | United States declare their Independence | |
| 1798 | | Napoleon captures Alexandria |
| 1806 | End of Holy Roman Empire | |
| 1815 | Napoleon finally defeated at Waterloo | |
| 1861 | | Victor Emmanuel II becomes King of a united Italy |
| 1863 | Lincoln emancipates American slaves | |
| 1867 | Canada becomes a Dominion | |
| 1869 | | Suez Canal opened |
| 1879 | | Obelisk from before Caesareum given to New York City |
| 1914 | | Egypt becomes British Protectorate |
| 1914–1918 | First World War | |
| 1922 | | Egypt becomes independent |
| 1931 | Canada becomes a Commonwealth nation | |
| 1939–1945 | Second World War | |
| 1946 | | Italy becomes a Republic |